The
Autobiography
of
JAMES T. SHOTWELL

BOOKS by JAMES T. SHOTWELL

James Thomson Shotwell at his desk in the Carnegie Endowment for
International Peace Building, New York, 1960

The
Autobiography
of
JAMES T. SHOTWELL

THE **BOBBS-MERRILL** COMPANY, INC.
A SUBSIDIARY OF HOWARD W. SAMS & CO., INC.
Publishers • INDIANAPOLIS • NEW YORK

To

MARGARET

The past is more than prologue to the drama of human fate,
The ice-age minds are with us still, with their iron claws of
   hate, . . .
But, rising through sorrow and suffering, the central theme
   grows clear,
Welding peace and justice, freedom from want and fear.
Not by wishful thinking can the task be carried through,
Nations have still to learn their part that never freedom knew;
Not by a code of rigid law, enforced by a world police,
With nations surrendering freedom in the search for lasting
   peace . . .
The mind that has ranged the universe must now itself control,
For the force in the mighty atom is less than the human
   soul . . .

from *The Way*
by James T. Shotwell

Contents

Illustrations

Preface

EVEN before I reached the age of eighty my friends kept telling me that I should write my memoirs. I had had a varied and, in some ways, an unusual life. But I have never cared much for the kind of autobiography which is a sort of monastic chronicle of things that happened and how the writer felt about them. So my first efforts to meet this generous interest in the record of a long life seemed too personal. Then, after I had been writing a few chapters in the accepted way of autobiographies, it occurred to me that what was missing was the central theme, which was the record of a series of exploits, in both the mind of the pioneer and the changing world in which he lived.

Of course the pioneer is not always pioneering. He has a life of routine, in which the days and years repeat themselves in the tradition of his fathers. While the horizon changes and his world is being transformed by ax and machine, by the revolutionary forces of war and peace, the new must be fitted into the pattern of the old. For pioneering is not merely exploration; it is—it must be—creative work as well.

Looking back, I find the clue to my life in this world of the pioneer, first in history and then in world affairs. Fortunately in both fields I touched the major theme of history, exploring the past with such penetrating minds as that of my old professor James Harvey Robinson, and serving my apprenticeship in politics under the inspiration of the Wilsonian regime. To me this life has been absorbingly interesting; but the important thing is not the story of personal experiences but of the new world which opened up in the exploration of the mind and the task of statesmanship in this revolutionary era.

Because of the varied fields which it covers, this volume has not been an easy one to write, and the author owes much to the editorial experience and judgment of his friend Mr. Nicholas G. Balint, who read the whole manuscript, and to Miss Antoinette Booth for her skill in discovering forgotten episodes and her textual suggestions as she prepared the volume for the press. I am also deeply indebted to Mr. Monroe Stearns, the Editor-in-Chief of Bobbs-Merrill for his valuable suggestions and co-operation in the final completion of the text.

JAMES T. SHOTWELL

The
Autobiography
of
JAMES T. SHOTWELL

CHAPTER 1

Against a Pioneer Background

As I look back to the world of my boyhood across more than eighty years of remembered life, it seems as though centuries had passed between then and now. The quiet, pleasant country town of Strathroy in Western Ontario, on the outskirts of which I was born on August 6, 1874, was, like most places in the Middle West, still in touch with America's heroic age, that of the pioneers. Both my grandfathers cleared their farms from the wilderness with the ax. My mother's girlhood home was built from logs on the farm, and, although by my time a frame kitchen had been added, the great fireplace was still used on occasion for cooking. There were stumps of the primeval forest in the pasture lot by the creek, and across it on a hill a dark, uncut hemlock wood, by which Indians from the reservation ten miles away used to camp when the stream was filled with fish in the spring freshet, using the bark for roofing their little huts. Beavers built their dams on the smaller creeks, and if one crept quietly down the hillside one could see them chewing down the willow trees. Apparently the Indians did not hunt them, and we liked to have the creatures there.

By my time the clearing of land was fast becoming only a dimly remembered legend, treasured by the few remaining pioneers. But the pine-stump fences were witness to the size of those primeval trees, for their roots spread out in a tangled circle as much as ten feet in width. So complete had been the work of the pioneers with no bulldozers, but only axes, levers and oxen, that there were no pine forests left, only maple, elm or oak in the wood lots at the back of the farms.

By my own time only one winding pioneer road still remained, running alongside the streams to the nearest market town. The whole country had been cut through by the straight "concession lines" and "side roads" of government engineers, blocking out square or oblong farms. There, as elsewhere all over the continent, the surveyor mapped the country for the settler. Orchards, gardens and fields were set primly side by side for miles on end, with houses and farm buildings spaced a little back from the road. The layout was symmetrical, with all the farms alike, but here, as elsewhere on the continent, it made prose instead of poetry of the countryside.

Strathroy itself began, like all other country towns on the continent, as a trading post for farmers who brought their wheat to the grist mill on the little river and sold or bartered their farm produce at the weekly market. Stores soon lined the village street, and in course of time the storekeepers became the aristocracy of the growing town, with larger houses and spreading lawns on the low hills crowning the valley. The weekly market held its own, however, for the "market price" set in this miniature version of an Oriental bazaar, was generally a few cents less than the price of "store goods," on which the merchants had to make their margin of profit. Butter was twelve cents a pound; eggs, nine cents a dozen; strawberries, from two to five cents a quart (berrypickers were allowed to fill pails to the brim with blackberries for nothing); chickens were twenty cents or two for thirty-five; and in winter beef by the quarter sold for four or five cents a pound. Tomatoes were so plentiful that they were often given away. This price list I found on a yellowing page of the local paper, without date.

The market was more important for the farmers, however, than for the townspeople, for selling their produce there was almost the only way they had of getting a little spending money for current expenses. And it was almost the only chance the farmers and their wives had to compare their produce with that of the more distant sections of the neighborhood. For the men it also meant political talk; for the women, more intimate gossip. At intervals there would be a sale of livestock or grain or garden produce in larger bulk; but,

16

as the average farm was only one hundred acres, including farmyard and pasture lots, the total cash revenue was seldom more than a few hundred dollars a year. The rest of the livelihood was home-grown.

The coming of the railroad ended the isolated economy of both town and country. The towns began to bid against one another for new factories to give more work to more people, as in the case of the railroads, and offered bonuses to attract the capitalists of the new industrial age. Like other small towns, Strathroy could not afford such costly financing for more than a foundry, a textile mill and furniture factory, and, like other such market towns trying to stretch themselves into the new capitalist era, it never grew to be a city, but remained at about three thousand inhabitants.

The coming of the railroad was the great event which lay behind this change in the way of life, not only in Strathroy, but everywhere. Railroading in Ontario suffered from the disadvantage that the province has no coal mines, and therefore the coal had to be imported from the mines of Pennsylvania. The result was that the earliest locomotives burned wood. I recall distinctly the wood-burning locomotives of the Great Western Railroad (later the Grand Trunk, and now the Canadian National) with their funnel-shaped chimneys throwing showers of sparks high in the air when the firemen threw the logs into the firebox. There was constant danger of fire catching in dried grass by the railway and in the wooden roofs at the stations. One of the worst fires in Strathroy was that of a grain warehouse, said to have been set by a locomotive. But to my boyhood eyes something was lost when the romantic cascading of engine sparks gave way to the black smoke of the coal-fed engines.

The coming and going of trains broke the monotony of village life to an extent hard to realize now. Journeys by train were so infrequent that the comings and goings of townspeople were matters of gossip. The station platform was a common meeting place when the evening train came in from the east. The stationmaster, with his blue uniform set off by a heavy gold watch chain, was a dignitary. The telegraph operator watching from the bay window had an added responsibility because it was a single-track railroad, and he transmitted the authority for the movement of trains. It was all an open door to the far-off world of Toronto or Niagara Falls in the East, or

Chicago in the West. The isolation of the horse-and-buggy days was following that of the pioneers into a world of which even the memories were growing dim.

The great yearly event was a civic holiday excursion by rail to Sarnia and by boat down the St. Clair River to an Indian Reservation and picnic grounds on Walpole Island, or to Detroit. It was always a moving experience to see the lake boats with their cargoes of ore for Cleveland or Pittsburgh, but more impressive were the great passenger boats, like floating hotels, pushing strongly upstream against the swiftly running current of the river. For a Canadian boy there was a disquieting sense of the contrast between the two riverbanks; for, before the days of the automobile, rich Americans built elaborate summer houses or lived in large expensive hotels. These dotted the Michigan shore line, while on the Canadian side there were only farm houses. This glimpse of another, and richer, world than ours was looked forward to for weeks before and talked about for weeks afterward.

As far as travel to the Old World was concerned, anyone who ventured overseas was a known and marked figure in town and country. Only one person in Strathroy had ever been to Paris—the wife of the leading physician—and when she appeared on Front Street or came to church on Sundays, I recall seeing people nudge one another, or whisper envious or admiring comment. Two exceptions to this story of isolation from Europe must be noted, however. In the first place, one of the Geddes brothers, who kept a dry goods store, went back yearly to their native Scotland to buy wholesale at prices so much lower than anywhere in America that it paid them for their journey. The other exception was that cattle buyers took a few young farmers each year over in a cattleship to tend the cattle on the voyage. When I recall what the stuffy, ill-ventilated lower deck of a good Cunarder was like twenty years later, I can imagine what it must have been like when it was a stable to be kept clean for a fortnight at sea. The reward was a week or so of sight-seeing in Britain, and a free voyage home. There were some hardy lads who went more than once.

In drawing the contrast between this quiet, isolated life and the cosmopolitan world of today, one might easily give a totally wrong

18

impression. It was not a trivial world. Indeed, I am inclined to think that age was much less trivial than this. If the interests were local, they were real. I cannot imagine the old pioneering farmers and storekeepers and professional men whom I knew over half a century ago ever listening with any complacency to the flood of vaudeville vulgarity which now inundates our homes, day in, day out. The weekly newspapers made at least a conscious effort at choosing only the most important things to write about. The great American magazines, *Century, Scribners, Harpers* and the *Atlantic* were available in the libraries and in the homes of the well-to-do, offering rich reservoirs of stimulating thought from masters of literature. There was nothing cheap or blatant in the stories, descriptive articles and poems which appeared in their pages. It was before the day of the literary trickster, arranging his shoddy goods in the shop windows of the illustrated weeklies.

This relative isolation of nineteenth-century life in the little town of Strathroy and the surrounding country had its compensations, not the least of which was that time moved slowly. There was time to read such masterpieces of English literature as the King James version of the Bible, Shakespeare, Milton and a galaxy of classic English poets. The poetry was not of the kind that takes its place with higher journalism today. It was something to be memorized and become a part of one's spiritual life. Those who took this training to heart learned with certainty to know the difference between pure gold and dross in the reading of later years.

Long before the day of the Carnegie public libraries, English labor leaders had founded lending libraries in what were called Mechanics Institutes. The name seems to imply other activities, but I do not remember that the one in Strathroy was more than a library. That, however, meant everything to me. There were complete editions of the English classics, prose as well as poetry. But my earliest and clearest memories are of taking home bound copies of magazines, especially of the *Century Magazine,* which had the pictorial history of the Civil War written by generals from both sides. One series was of the war as seen by a private, and it was much more graphic and exciting than the discussion of strategy by the generals. The books were too heavy for a boy to hold, so I read them lying on

19

the floor, propped up by my elbows. Later these articles were published as *Battles and Leaders of the Civil War*. But I doubt if the boys of today can get the thrill from them that I did, for my father remembered how the Quakers helped the fugitive slaves, one of whom was still alive in our town.

After all, was this isolation—with books and periodicals as constant companions? The scene was circumscribed and remote from the bustling activity of the great commercial centers, but the doors were open to the great essentials of human experience.

One of the most interesting things, as I look back to it, although it seemed perfectly natural at the time, was that there was almost no movement away from the farms to the cities. Although all the farmland was already occupied, leaving neither enough work nor enough opportunity for the younger sons of the farmers, instead of going to the factories, they followed the example of their forefathers and moved on to pioneering life either in the woods of northern Michigan or in the Western states, or, more frequently, in the Canadian northwest. This was in the early 1880's, before there was a web of railways across northern Canada. Later on they were drawn by the higher wages in Detroit and Chicago, but I do not recall anyone's having moved to these cities from Strathroy in my early boyhood. On the other hand, I recall dozens of young farmers who joined in what was the last chapter in the great westward movement for the conquest of the continent.

The business section of Strathroy with its main street had one building—a hotel—three stories high. The rest were mainly false-fronted two-story stores, giving what seemed to me an air of dignity without overdoing it. There was a stretch of cedar-block pavement between the wooden sidewalks. The creek, which could become a muddy torrent in floodtime, ran through the flats just back of the main street which were pasture lands in the summertime. Across the flats on low hills lived the wealthier merchants and bankers. For even in a town of that size and in that simple economy, there were social distinctions. There was, however, no foreign element in the population. It remained altogether British in origin: Scotch, English and Irish. It was a sober world; there was little drinking. There

20

were, of course, some hotel bars, but they played no such part in the life of the town as did the English pub or the American saloon.

Respectability meant churchgoing and, for the most part, church membership. Generally, church membership also meant more than attending church services; it meant family worship as well. In both my grandfather's home and our own, not only was "grace" said at every meal, but there were scripture reading and prayer after breakfast. Perhaps because of his Quaker upbringing my father hardly changed from ordinary manner of speech, but my grandfather, though the strictest of Presbyterians, used to intone both reading and prayer almost as in a liturgy. The echo of this religious service in the home still rings in my memory. Something was lost when the day's work ceased to begin by a dedication.

Although my contact with Quakerism was limited, it made a strong impression on me. Once or twice in the year, Father drove to the monthly or quarterly meeting at the hamlet of Coldstream ten miles away, and I was keen to go along. It was the occasion when the Quakers came from near and far—sometimes from as far as the United States—both to renew acquaintances and to govern the community. "Govern" is the word, for the meeting was held not only for worship and the discussion of religious affairs, but was also a deliberative assembly on social questions and could pass in review matters which had been up before each monthly meeting. To be a member in good standing one must not do anything injuring the good name of the community. Even the farmer who let thistles grow so that the wind could carry them to neighboring farms was admonished for his lack of social conscience. Not only was violence banned in daily intercourse, but tempers were not allowed to rise above the even tenor of self-control. This may be a little idealized; but it was a life so glaringly in contrast with that of the unrestrained temper of vigorous men elsewhere that even the silences were forceful.

Quakerism is the acme of Puritanism, rejecting the whole sacramental system of ceremonial cults, on the ground that all life is sacred at all times. It was the complete renunciation of religious formalism. All days were as sacred as Sunday, so meetings were held weekly on Wednesdays, the "Fourth Day," as well as on the "First Day" (the days and months of the year were numbered to avoid the use of names of pagan deities). I used to wonder how the Quakers discovered the power of silence. They used it differently from that of monks or mystics. In Meeting its use was almost like a ritual, with an emotional effect beyond the pealing of organs or vested choirs. The "inner light" and the "still small voice" were all that were needed for this religion without ceremony or creed. Only those broke the silence who had experienced its power.

Although farming and gardening dominated the world of my boyhood, and although we lived in it, yet we were always a little apart from it. For my father's profession as a schoolteacher gave us a distinct place in the community. His salary was only $400 a year, yet his was a profession to which America owes a debt it can never repay, for with all due regard to the other professions, only that of the teacher made its impress day by day, year in, year out, on the minds of the young, shaping them for life. The little red schoolhouse has its well-known place in the American-Canadian epic; but it was the teacher that made it a national institution. His scholarship was necessarily limited; but it took character to deal with exuberant youths, and, as the English have long shown in their great public schools, character is more important than learning in the early shaping of a way of life. Many tributes to my father's influence upon his students came in later years; but I took them for granted, because our family life never ceased to be touched by his selfless gentleness of spirit.

The daughters of pioneers seldom had a fair chance in life. They never had more than the merest elementary education, and while they were still young children they were broken into their life work of housekeeping. (I use the term advisedly, for everything was done, even by good people, to break the will of an ambitious girl.) High school education was legally open to them, but there was no high school in Strathroy in my mother's girlhood, and I doubt that she would have been allowed to go anyway, for her parents needed her at home. She was small and not strong, but she knew how to work to advantage, and so an end was put to her schooling.

She suffered for this all her life long, for those denied education feel that they live behind barred doors and that the educated are inherently superior. It is a natural mistake, but a very real one. Some of the most foolish people I have known had every advantage in education, and some of the wisest had never learned their wisdom in the schoolroom. My mother's sense of loss, while real and constant, never embittered her toward her parents, for she knew that they had come through even greater hardships. But she was determined not to repeat the mistake with her own children; and as our education moved on to the upper grades, she shared in the wider outlook. I did not fully realize at the time how much this had meant to her, but I have before me her last letter to me, written about a year before her death in 1923, and it is as clear about the work I was then doing in Europe and as well written and beautifully expressed as any I ever received from anyone. There is no other heritage that can compare with that of the love and understanding which I received from my parents.

Our home was almost half a mile from the town schools, but there were others who had farther to go and we thought nothing of it, except in winter storms. Our ambitions were stimulated even in these hard times by Father's courage and nobility of character and Mother's unfailing confidence that her boys would not only go through high school but college as well. To us, in that time and place, a college degree was something like a patent of nobility.

Ambition is contagious, and from early life my brother and I hitched our wagons to the stars. But the stars have no power to pull the wagon through examinations which block the path unless they are forced open by hard work. We worked hard, but not all the time. The memories of my boyhood are mostly those of happy hours at play.

Then there was poetry, and the hours spent in that realm of gold were the richest of all. I reveled in the collection of volumes of poetry in our small library at home, which was increased yearly by school prizes won by my brother or me. It was inevitable that from an early age I should try my hand at verse, and I learned, even then, that creation in art, however inadequate it may be, carries one into another realm from that of the enjoyment of the works of others. There were fugitive poems published in the local and Toronto pa-

23

pers, one of which won a prize in a high school poetry competition in English. Once the habit is formed it lasts on; and poetry became an inner life, not always finding expression, but always able to

"bring back the hour
Of splendor in the grass, of glory in the flower."

While Scott furnished the model for an unfinished epic (age twelve), I have no explanation for the choice of other long poems on Egypt and Japan, unless it be that I felt freer in writing about countries of which I knew next to nothing. Somehow Byron never appealed to me, but I read nearly all of Shelley and all of Keats. Wordsworth, however, was my special favorite, for at his best he gave incomparable expression to that life of the imagination which doubled the world of reality. To share in that other world of reality by writing my own poems was the richest of all experiences, but they were for the most part experiences too personal to be shared outside my family and an intimate circle of friends. Finally, however, in my eightieth year I published a volume of lyrics and sonnets, some of which I quote in the course of this narrative.*

Among those who came to play tennis on our lawn was Margaret Harvey, the daughter of a physician of outstanding reputation in the neighboring town of Wyoming, a leader in his profession, whose unerring diagnoses and treatment of his patients' illnesses was matched only by his generosity and devotion to their welfare. She had come to attend the Strathroy High School, or Collegiate Institute, as it was then called. With her cousin, Jessie Murdock, Margaret Harvey came sometimes after school to play on our tennis court, the only one then available. I had seen her on summer visits to her cousin from early childhood, and on my seventieth birthday recalled that fact in the following verse, with which I finish this chapter.

I raise my glass to memory,
    Magician beyond compare,
And to the little girl on a galloping horse,
Cheeks aflame, eyes straight on the course,
    As I stood in the dust-filled air.

* *Poems.* New York: Simon and Schuster, 1953.

That was the way I saw her first,
    And the way I would have it be,
For through the whole wide country-side
Nobody else was known to ride
    So well and daringly.

I knew her only distantly
    For she lived in another town
And she didn't deign to look at me,
Or in any case seemed not to see,
    For she never once looked down.

But in her eyes lay laughter
    And a gleam of pure delight,
I had only a glimpse of her passing by
Her head was bare, she held it high,
    And her hair was braided tight.

Only a little wisp of a girl
    She rode with idle rein
Up the road and over the hill
And I turned to watch her, standing still
    And guessed I should see her again.

But a happier fate was mine
    For we travel together through life,
Yet over the years I still look back
To that summer day by the dusty track
    When first I met my wife.

CHAPTER 2

School and College Days

I still have vivid memories of my school days. Our elementary school system in Ontario was modeled largely on that of the adjacent United States. While the inevitable lessons in arithmetic spilled over in the higher grades into algebra and geometry, and writing and spelling remained basic subjects, the whole educational process centered in the "Reader." Each grade from the second to the fifth had its own Reader, a series adapted from those great classics of American education, the McGuffey Readers,* from which anthologies of literature and folklore were taken, many of them literally.

They were well chosen, for they made such impressions on my mind that I can remember them from even the Second Reader, studied at the age of six. There were tales of heroism, like that of "brave John Maynard," a Lake Michigan pilot who beached his burning ship at the cost of his own life; or of the pioneer lost in the woods who kept off the wolves by building a circle of brush fires around him; or of pleasanter themes like "sugaring-off" in the thaws of March (an essay by Charles Dudley Warner), and fishing with Izaak Walton. These selections were interspersed by gems of poetry, both English and American. Of the former, Tennyson was in the lead; of the latter, Longfellow. There were also poems from less

---

* Throughout most of the nineteenth century these textbooks with their homely moralizing dominated American literary taste to an astonishing degree. The total sales reached over one hundred and twenty million copies.

familiar authors, snatches of which still hold their charm in memory.

Another subject that was well taught was geography. We learned in the best way, by map making. The outlines of coasts or the boundaries of countries were fitted into squares of latitude and longitude, like those in the atlas, and then redrawn freehand, either at the blackboard or in "exercise books," a training which stood up well in later years. Along with the memorizing of important places, we were given useless lists of the relative sizes of cities, at a time when Brooklyn was a separate city, larger than Chicago. But all in all, the instruction in geography was far better than that in history.

There was no history of the United States taught in the public schools, the high schools, or even the university as late as the closing years of the nineteenth century. What seems incredible now was that there was no history of Canada either in the elementary schools until about 1887, when I entered high school. About that time a publishing firm in Toronto brought out a little paper-bound pamphlet of thirty or forty pages, as an appendix to the manual on English history, which contained all the Canadian history offered in the schools. There was a short account of the founding of Canada, quickly getting to the conquest by the British; but most of the text was about the War of 1812. My first lesson in international outlook was in fighting over again the battle of Queenston Heights. We boys at school used to divide and fight that battle out between ourselves, that is, whenever we could persuade or force any unfortunate victims to take the American side. The school yard was as flat as a table, but one could charge up the woodpile with gallant General Brock.

There was a special reason for the relative lack of interest in Canadian history, for the early age had been French, and to us in Western Ontario that meant almost a foreign past. We had no contact with the French, who at that time had hardly spread beyond the confines of Quebec. I never saw a French Canadian until the Premier, Sir Wilfred Laurier, came to address a political meeting in our town, and he used—with consummate skill and eloquence—the language of Shakespeare and Milton.

In spite of all educational theory, the character of the education which any child receives is largely dependent upon the character of the teacher and especially of the headmaster of the school. The headmaster of the Strathroy High School was a classically trained teacher of literature and poetry named Wetherell. He taught us the difference between false rhetoric and genuine literature by forcing us to learn by heart many of the great poems which are classics in the English language. That was a training for which I am still profoundly grateful, for I can now recall many a shining verse to give expression to the changing moods of life and the beauty and mystery of the world.

Along with this training in aesthetics there was discipline in English grammar when taught by a classical master and studied side by side with Harkness' *Latin Grammar* and Arnold's *Latin Prose*. We have lost something of the discipline these studies demanded, for then Latin was a compulsory study in the university, and therefore ranked high in the curriculum of the high school which prepared for it. There was, however, no subject more abhorrent to the casual student than Latin prose, a fact which proved of great advantage to me because I was able to pay my way through the university by tutoring for Latin prose examinations.

In those days the Strathroy High School was one of the two or three leading high schools in the province. Therefore, it is all the more disappointing to have to report that history was poorly taught by a superbly good teacher of mathematics, who taught history on the side. Green's *Short History of the English People*, however, needed no teacher's commentary; for it opened, even to the thirteen-year-old student, not the dull chronicle of kings and dates but the story of the people themselves, and a story that was a prose poem crowded with facts but shining with romance. The facts interested my mathematics teacher, but I reveled in the romance—"the bright human sympathy" of Chaucer or the "deep understanding sadness" of Piers Plowman, whose "gaunt rimer stalks silently along the Strand" in a world that is out of joint, and above all the contrast between the great days of Elizabethan and Puritan England when "life became hard, rigid, colorless, as it became intense."

I am tempted to quote whole sections of the book that influenced my school life more than any other. Still it left me unsatisfied, for it stopped at the opening of the nineteenth century; and, as I have

28

noted above, Gladstone meant more to me than his most eloquent predecessor the Elder Pitt, though Pitt had created the world empire which Gladstone was ready to renounce, holding justice and freedom above self-interest and power. It was under Gladstonian liberalism that I had been brought up; a lasting heritage.

I never had much time for sport, though I used to stay sometimes after school for a game of football—the soccer kind still most popular in England. The other game, in which the ball, oval instead of round, is carried by the player and signals are checked in huddles was the invention of the English school, Rugby, under the headmastership of Thomas Arnold, father of Matthew Arnold. It was this same Rugby headmaster who was largely responsible for our curriculum, when in the 1840's he carried through a reform at Rugby which added mathematics, modern history and modern languages to the customary Greek and Latin. This revolutionary departure from the "humanities" of classical education, which had dated from the Renaissance, stopped short of the sciences.

There was no science taught in the Strathroy High School when I first entered it in 1887, though a little chemistry laboratory was set up for simple experiments shortly after, and an elementary course opened in botany. I avoided contamination by these intruders into the world of literature, however—to my regret in later years—but it would be wholly wrong to think that there was any lack of stiff discipline in the humanities. Harkness' *Latin Grammar* set a standard for English, French and German grammars which made languages not only difficult but artificial—as I found out when I first visited France.

The one organization of the high school students was the Literary Society, or "the Lit" for short. Although its program included readings, recitations and songs by the glee club, its chief interest was in debates, modeled on those of the Toronto University "Lit" which in turn reflected the glories of the Oxford Union. There was no frivolity here. The subjects were mostly political, and the debates generally followed party lines. I remember distinctly one such debate on "Reciprocity with the United States," in which I upheld the Liberal position along with another Liberal, Arthur Currie. I doubt if I should have remembered that incident in my years of friendship

29

with the boy who became Canada's greatest soldier,* if it had not been for an incident which happened on the way home from school that afternoon. We were held up at the railroad crossing by a long freight train from Chicago to the East, and Currie, turning to the group, pointed with an eloquent gesture to the loaded cars as the final argument for freer trade. That is my last distinct memory of Arthur Currie until we met again on the fields of France in March, 1919, some forty years later, although we must have been school-mates for a year or two longer, and I visited his home occasionally. It was a farm of his widowed mother, some three miles from the school—a long walk when there must have been some chores to do as well.

As I look back to the school system of Ontario at the close of the nineteenth century and contrast it with the schools of today, the thing which stands out most strongly is that the narrower field of knowledge which it covered gave a greater chance for mental—and moral—discipline than in the immensely widened field. The student could not then escape from what it irked him to do on the tricky excuse that by following his own bent he would give fuller play to his capacities. This theory of what is called progressive education runs the danger of mistaking whims for capacities and fails to develop character. For character develops by facing up to situations or problems we want to avoid. The steeling of the will is more important than cleverness.

Crowning the closely knit system of schools and high schools or collegiate institutes was the provincial University of Toronto. The other universities in Toronto were sectarian, maintaining good standards, and some of them were already federated with the University of Toronto. I do not need to describe them here, for they do not enter into my story. It was "Varsity," as it was affectionately called by the students and graduates, which was the goal of my dreams. Life at it seemed something apart, a strange interlude before the serious business of living. Once there was a dollar excursion to Toronto, and I can still remember how I looked at University College with feelings akin to awe. It is a noble pile, one of the noblest on the continent, and even the imposing new wing, with its taller, graceful tower, cannot match—for me at least—the charm of that

* Sir Arthur Currie, Commander of the Canadian army in World War I.

great Norman doorway with which some inspired architect adorned the old building in the mid-nineteenth century.

I was in the class graduating from the high school in 1893, but held back a year to earn the money to go on to the University. By tutoring and other work and by a loan from my brother who had been teaching at Kinkardin, I was able to enter the University as a freshman in 1894. My brother had saved enough by teaching to enter the year before, and we roomed together in a house on Huron Street, northwest of the University. Happily the spell continued; life at college was all that I had dreamed of and more.

I chose the honor course in Modern Languages, as my brother had done. Most of our classes were small, held in recitation rooms where we had regular lessons in reading or grammar as in the high schools, although the professor in his academic gown seemed more remote from his students than the high school teacher. This was much more the case in a few general lecture courses in which a hundred or more met in the great hall of the college. We were repeatedly warned that, as there were no tests until the end of the college year in May, it was up to us to keep up with the work as it went along, or face failure at the end. The warnings were only partially listened to, however, and when lectures stopped before examinations began, the heaviest work of the year was concentrated in these days and weeks, "cramming up for the exams."

This was the way of Oxford and Cambridge. Only a few Canadians could afford a tutor to coach them, and to be thrown on one's own was not so bad as it may seem. The whole year's work would be wasted if one didn't make good, and we couldn't afford that. When I came to Columbia University, both as student and professor, I had to get used to the other way of working, under constant supervision throughout the year, and I must confess that I never got wholly used to keeping track of the daily recitations of students. It seemed to me the wrong way to treat growing and grown young men. They ought to have more of a sense of responsibility of their own. But the American schools had not prepared them for anything but constant checking up. Fortunately, when one worked for a doctorate the gates were open for opportunity—which is another word for responsibility.

I paid most of my way through college by tutoring. This employ-

31

ment I owed to the registrar of the university, James Brebner.* But for his interest in my college career I could not have finished it, at least with my class of 1898. I tutored sometimes as much as ten hours a day, while keeping full time with my classes. The tutoring was mostly in Latin prose, the bane of the ill-prepared, but a blessing to me.

In the spring of 1898, Mr. Brebner sent for me to tell me that I should drop some of my other pupils to take on Alec Mackenzie, son of William Mackenzie, president of the Canadian Northern Railway—which he was then building in the Northwest—and head of other great concerns, including the Toronto Street Railway. He was director of others outside as well as inside Canada, such as the Cuban Railway and the public utilities of São Paulo, Brazil. I found that Alec, although naturally a ready student, had been so badly prepared that it was impossible for him to be brought up to the grade required to pass his exams. But by hard work and long hours, he almost succeeded. Just before the examinations, however, he was very depressed over the outlook and asked me if I would be willing to work with him during the summer in case he had to take the supplemental examinations in the fall. We agreed that after the examinations were over I should have a talk with his father. The family would be going away to their summer home in Muskoka, and Mr. Mackenzie would be living alone most of the time with Alec, so the arrangement was that I should come to the house and live there with them during the summer.

I formed a very real attachment for Alec, who was one of the most lovable young men I had ever known. Many evenings, however, were spent with Mr. Mackenzie, who apparently liked the quiet and silence of the front porch and lawn of his hilltop home where, with a good cigar, he used to watch the evening lights come out over the city. He talked to me about all kinds of things—his own early life, his adventures into finance, and his plans for Canada. I have met other "empire builders" in succeeding years, but have never known anyone who had quite the characteristic outlook of the pioneer which gave the high purpose to Mackenzie's planning.

* Father of the distinguished historian of Canada, Professor J. B. Brebner, late Professor of History at Columbia University.

32

I remember one evening when he had come back from a day spent in presiding over boards of corporations such as the Toronto Street Railway, and other utilities, and he went over with me the number of decisions he had had to make on the spur of the moment —decisions involving vast sums of money and the interests of many people. I ventured to remark that he could not possibly be sure that he was right in some of these decisions; and he said that he likely had been wrong in some of them, but a decision had to be made and he had to make it. Then it would be left to others to make a go of it.

This was my introduction into big business, and I at least had the satisfaction before the summer was over of having him ask me if I would take an office in one of his enterprises and see what I could do in the field of business. The one he chose was the public utilities of the City of São Paulo, Brazil, in which a Canadian syndicate had got control of streetcars, gas works, electric lighting, and, perhaps, even waterworks. I believe that it still remains the largest foreign enterprise of Canadians. He said he would send me down there to give me a try-out if I would turn from university work to the kind of life he was living. I was to be personally in touch with him. It was a rare business opportunity. I thought seriously of it for a while, and have often wondered since what might have happened if I had gone to South America under his watchful direction. I imagine that I would not have lasted very long as a business executive!

Mr. Mackenzie had no use for the man who yielded to "the salary curse." He said that the desire for security undermined courage and lessened a man's capacity for creative work. The salaried man was bound to be inferior to the one who took the risks of relying upon his own capacity to meet any situation at any given time. In this regard he used to say that it would really make no difference to him personally if he lost his fortune because he had been just as happy as a young man when he started out with a pick and shovel in a railroad gang. He said, however, that he owed it to his family, of course, not to let that happen if he could avoid it. Personally, he had no false pride, and his sense of realities kept him from imagining that a rich man is happier than a poor one who has health and strength and a chance to rise in the world. He had the courage of the pioneer and also the stubborn persistence which refused to accept defeat.

Meanwhile I had won a scholarship at Columbia University from my senior year in Toronto, but the money I earned during the summer had to go to pay some college debts. So when September came I had nothing left, not even the price of a railroad ticket to New York. When Mr. Mackenzie found out this state of affairs, by abruptly asking me, he offered to lend me the money for my first year at Columbia. I accepted $200, came to New York, and lived on that $200 from the first of October until Easter, with enough left over so that when Easter came I could pay my railroad fare back to Toronto. Columbia gave me a full year's record of attendance and a fellowship for the following year.

When Easter came I had an offer from the Harboard Street Collegiate Institute in Toronto offering me a substitute place in the department of Modern Languages there for the remainder of the year at what seemed a princely salary of $1500 a year. I at once wrote to Mr. Mackenzie and asked him how Alec was getting on, and said that I would be willing to choose Harboard Collegiate, although it was not in the field of history—my chosen subject—if he wished me to tutor Alec again during the spring of 1899. I told him that if I could tutor Alec I should perhaps be able to clear off my indebtedness of $200 that way, by working evenings while teaching during the days. He at once invited me to come to Toronto and live during April and May with the family in their home on the hill so that I could be at hand to work with Alec at odd times. Alec had again fallen so far behind his class that he did not make the grade, although his standing was high enough to allow him to continue with his class, provided he could pass the supplemental examinations in September.

The family were all going to Europe for the summer and everyone wanted Alec to go along. It would have been a little more than human nature could stand for him to stay behind and grind in Toronto while his family went for a vacation abroad. So Mr. Mackenzie asked me if I could go along, especially as Mrs. Mackenzie was anxious that I should take the younger son, Joe, in hand.

I doubt if any voyager across the Atlantic, since the days of

Columbus, had a more vivid sense of adventure than I as I watched the shore line of America fade out behind the Cunarder *Etruria* as it nosed out into the ocean beyond the Ambrose Channel light. The Old World—a term not often used now—had been the dream world of my youth, both because in the Canada of those days it offered the only great literature we had and because it was the seat of the empire of which we were part. Continental Europe had meant less to us than England, but the sense of distance gave a touch of romance to its history. These impressions of childhood had begun to be cut into by the new intellectual life at Columbia University and the impact of the power and the problems of the United States; but my field remained the history of Europe, and now I was to see this world of dreams and history.

The *Etruria* was reckoned a first class ship, although its eight thousand tons and its crowded, stuffy cabins would place it far down in the shipping lists of today. Its firemen and engineers worked in poorly ventilated, terribly overheated stoke holes, but day after day I took my place on the prow as it cut through the waves with what seemed like race-horse speed until, after a little over a week, the Scilly Islands emerged from the blue haze of the horizon, and before the day was over England was in sight.

London, of course, was overpowering. I thought, and still think, that the much abused Gothic architecture of the nineteenth century rose to imperial majesty in the houses of Parliament, and that Big Ben chimes the hours with all the pomp and circumstance of empire. But it was an incident in the lobby of the House of Commons which outshone all other memories. The House was in session, and gathering together all the courage I could muster I sent in my card, inscribed as "a student of history," to the Right Honorable James Bryce, former ambassador to the United States, whose brilliant essay *The Holy Roman Empire* had been published ten years before I was born, and whose *American Commonwealth,* with its penetrating analysis of United States politics, we were using in my class. He came out to see me, and instead of dismissing me with formal courtesy sat down to ask me all about history at Columbia—a half hour worth to me all the cycles of Cathay.

I shall refrain from descriptions of travel in Europe, although my capacity for realizing dreams was tested to the full by the journey to London and to Paris by way of the Rhine and Switzerland! From mid-summer on, Alec Mackenzie and I lived in a quiet boarding house in Paris, the Villa des Dames, which like so many other residences of the aristocracy of the old regime, hid from the street a large stretch of shaded lawn. It seemed hardly the place for a summer of Latin prose, but Alec was a good sport and kept steadily at work. At the end of the summer he went back to Toronto and passed his examination. I stayed on, for Paris was re-enacting history before my eyes. First there was the bitterness against Britain over the Fashoda incident. Although years had passed since Kitchener in his war against the Mahdi had ordered the French tricolor to be hauled down, which Major Marchand had planted at Khartoum, after a forced march across the desert from western Africa, the anger of the French against the British was still at the hottest point just short of war. We had English-made tweeds, and were ready marks for the street rabble, throwing stones or anything else at hand, whenever there was a chance. It was a common thing to be refused places in restaurants, and commoner still to be booed in the street. I have never seen a nation at such war-fever pitch except in the Ruhr when Poincaré attempted to occupy it after World War I.

These incidents seem hardly worth recalling in themselves, but they are full of meaning to the·historian. At one point war was so near that it was prevented only by delicate diplomacy and the fact that France was not ready. If that war had happened, historians could have shown how "inevitable" it was. Since the Hundred Years' War, France and England had been traditional enemies, and the Fashoda incident, on the far rim of their rival empires, was but a repetition of Fort Duquesne or Plassey. But the "inevitable" war never happened. Instead, in 1904, came the *Entente Cordiale* and, in London then, I watched the first armed French troops march past Nelson's column in Trafalgar square, bayonets glistening on rifles, bands playing the Marseillaise and Londoners cheering this spectacle, unparalleled in English history. With even better sense of drama, Paris greeted Edward VII in 1905 almost like an adopted king. This I also saw, and learned the unforgettable lesson that

36

statesmanship can mold the destinies of nations, almost without their knowing how it is being done.

More thrilling to me in 1899, however, than British-French antagonism, was the Dreyfus case, then at the retrial in a military court in Rennes, and the rioting in Paris over it by a band of anti-Dreyfusards, or rather anti-Semites, surreptitiously supplied by their friends, apparently with some connivance of the police, who, however, had the help of the army in preventing actual fighting. Naturally, this was too much like the outbreaks of Paris revolutions to leave untested by study on the spot. It was the first and only time I have been charged by cavalry, as the Chasseurs, with glittering helmets and breastplates and still more glittering swords, came in solid ranks down the boulevard to disperse the crowd, which had already begun to dig up the pavement stones for barricades. Escape into a little tobacconist shop gave me a safe but firsthand view of the affair. The soldiers acted with assurance and *sang-froid,* but the "flics," the street police, knocked people down, and kicked them when down—the acts of bullies when frightened. The one most notable incident was the Paris Prefet de Police who walked down the middle of the street—alone, for the police—and the crowd melted away in front of him. He had only a little riding whip in his hand and acted as though he had forgotten it. His fearless personality, and its effect on the crowd was unbelievable. Around me I heard, half whispered, *"C'est Lepine, c'est Lepine."*

CHAPTER 3

Columbia University at the Turn of the Century

I must go back and pick up the story of my senior year at Toronto, when I decided to make history my life work, instead of teaching French or German to high school students who had no interest in them. History seemed to me both literature and life itself.

Green's *History of England,* which had thrilled me in my boyhood days in high school with "old, unhappy, far-off things and battles long ago," made way for the rich tapestry which Macaulay hung on the walls of Parliament and along the streets of London town for the triumph of Whig rule, and the sense of Empire in his essay on the trial of Warren Hastings for misrule in India.

But it was Thomas Carlyle who carried history over into poetry and drama for me by the happy blending of imagination and hero worship. At least it seemed a happy blending to my uncritical mind. Who could forget the "Night of Spurs" when the sun rose over the forests on the road to Varennes as the net was closing on the fugitive Louis XVI, or the word painting of the battles of Frederick the Great? I fully agreed with the heart-warming attack on dry-as-dust historians which opens the volumes of Cromwell's "Letters and Speeches." My hero worship of Carlyle was expressed in the highly colored rhetoric of an article by me in the university paper, *Varsity.* Then, suddenly, came the great yawning doubt that perhaps he was not the last word on the French Revolution. This disturbing thought was due to lectures given in the autumn of 1897 at Toronto University by Professor Morse Stephens, then of Cornell. He had begun the publication of his own history of the French Revolution based on recent researches, and the chief theme of his lectures was a devastating criticism of the inadequacy of Carlyle's *History*. I had mixed feelings. It was a sad blow to learn that Carlyle's *French Revolution* was found lacking; but surely that meant that the subject was still open and a challenge to any future historian.

I spent the next four days sketching out an opening chapter headed toward a new outlook, but written—or rather clothed—in Carlyle's rhetoric. The trouble with this was that I did not know what the new outlook really was; so I stopped writing and went over to the university library to find out what Morse Stephens had had in mind. There were no courses on modern history, and I found that the new volumes of source material had not yet been catalogued but lay on the floor of an unused upper room.

To my intense surprise the first volumes I opened were the edition by the French historian Aulard of the Minutes of Committees of the Convention during the Reign of Terror; and among them were the minutes of the terrible "Committee of Public Safety," the very center of the tyranny of the Terror. It seemed incredible to me that here I could follow the proceedings, not only of this committee but of others paralleling it, hour by hour, debate by debate, telling not only their conclusions but why they had reached them. Before long it became clear that here was something more than a source for the history of those tragic yet epochal days: government by committee is necessary when the sovereign power resides in a large legislative body; the structure of government under the Convention was setting a model for the later government of France.

I settled down to the hard work of digging out the plan as well as the content of the committees, and wrote a seventy-five-page study on this technique. All this was headed toward an analysis of the Terror. But I didn't get that far, for the preliminary committees had to be worked out and I had no guide to go by—so I stayed at work through most of the Christmas holidays. I had begun pioneering in scholarship.

The reason for this intensive work was that, since there were no postgraduate courses in history in any Canadian university, I decided to try for a fellowship in one of the American universities. In the notices they sent out they put all emphasis on original writing submitted with the application. This documentation had to be finished before February, so for the first time in my life I concentrated on research. The only university that showed any interest in my study was Columbia University, which awarded me a scholarship covering remission of fees. At last the door was open and, having paid back some of the money my brother had lent me during my senior year by tutoring the son of William Mackenzie as described in the last chapter, and then accepting his loan of $200 for a year in New York, I set out on my great adventure.

A great adventure it was, in every sense of the word. Of the millions of immigrants who were then pouring into the United States from the Old World, I doubt if there were any who had a greater thrill than I; for in spite of the fact that Canada and the United States were neighbors, they were still foreign to each other. The United States was rapidly leaving the nineteenth century behind in a fabulous new era of wealth and power which made a strange new world for Canadians as well as for Europeans. New York was a dreamland for me, as the link between this new world and the old.

I had to get my bearings in the university. First of all, of course, there was a formal visit to pay to the head of the History Department, Professor William Milligan Sloane. He asked me what interested me in history and why I had taken it up. With naïve innocence, I told him the truth: I wanted to find out in history more about myself and the world around. I was not interested in political events as much as in social and intellectual developments.

He looked puzzled and then said: "Well, you're in the wrong department; you should go to sociology and work under Professor Giddings."

In haste I explained that I didn't want to be a sociologist. I had no desire to take the comparative point of view or study statistics or get involved in sociological methods. I wanted to trace national attitudes through history.

He was still puzzled and frankly gave me up, but said I could take his course, as I happened to hold the position of Scholar in European History.

Then I went to the first lecture of a course on the French Revolution, in which I had written the study that got me the scholarship. The professor was unknown to me; he was James Harvey Robinson. He struck me as a rather shy personality, wearing at that time the insignia of foreign scholarship in the shape of a beard. His first lecture on the French Revolution was merely an opening of the general background. At the close he asked those present to hand him a slip of paper bearing their names and their status as students. When he saw my name he called me back and said he wanted to speak to me. When we were alone, he turned with a rather puzzled look and asked me what courses I had had in the French Revolution. When I told him that there were no courses even on modern history in Toronto University and that my study was simply written from the sources, he merely commented that I would find the same kind of analysis in his lectures.

That ended the interview as far as he was concerned, but it meant more to me than I can ever express. Here was a professor who, in the month of February, had read my little study, and in the month of October remembered what it was. Because of his interest in that study he had nominated me for a scholarship and so opened the doors of Columbia to me. From that time on, I always felt that one of the most important duties of any professor in a graduate faculty was to study carefully the applications for fellowships, especially those that came in from other colleges, and try to find if there was someone there who was eating his heart out for the chance to go on in academic life and who would be worthy of the honor bestowed in the shape of a scholarship or fellowship. I have always felt that the examination of the credentials of such applicants was one of the most important things in the graduate work at Columbia. In this case, of course, it had been vital for me.

To Professor Robinson I owed not only the scholarship in Columbia but the chance to pioneer in history; to study and later to teach whatever seemed most important to me in that long process of which he wrote a classic analysis in his *The Mind in the Making*.

In addition to the lecture course on the French Revolution attended by only a few students—a dozen or so—he had already begun the lecture course on the history of the intellectual class which ultimately became so famous that the largest lecture hall in the uni-

41

versity was crowded to the doors. In these early days, however, he was only explaining the historical background of that freedom of thought which he later applied, like a modern Abelard, to ridicule the pretentious self-satisfaction of uncritical minds. The author of *The New History* was still finding his way in the remaking of historical perspective by comparing the accepted record with the source material. The Middle Ages took on new meaning in the analysis of feudal anarchy and the institutions of Capetian royalty on the one hand, and the medieval church on the other. Renaissance and Reformation also took on new meaning when studied in the contemporary sources; and the real emancipation of the intellect came with the dawn of science.

At the close of his life Robinson followed this road where it seemed to lead him. He turned from the scholarly study of historical texts to the scientist's instrument, the microscope. But in 1898 his chief interest was still research and his seminars. His *The Mind in the Making* is a classic, because from the standpoint of a scientist he stood back and looked over his life as a scholar. It is really a synopsis of his lectures, the mimeographed outlines of which were never published, for at the close of his life he had lost interest in them.

It was not in his lectures but in his research courses—seminars, as they were called in the German universities—that Robinson left his deepest impress upon his students. The first of these which I took was a study of Martin Luther. The text we studied was Luther's *Briefwechsel,* a collection of his correspondence partly in crabbed Latin and partly in crabbed German. We had to dig out of the original text some understanding of the character of the man and the trend of his thinking. There must be no carelessness in translation; the exact meaning had to be brought out. There was no one in the academic world who had a stricter sense of the obligations of scholarship than James Harvey Robinson. While we had to read secondary works to get the general bearing of the details we worked on, they never were to be cited in class—only the original sources. The same stern discipline was maintained in the study of the Middle Ages, the complicated structure of feudalism, the rise of the national state, and above all the Medieval Church.

42

Next to Robinson, my closest friend in Columbia was Charles Beard. He was a year behind me in his academic work, having spent a year at Oxford, not as a regular undergraduate but as a student in Ruskin College, the creation of the intellectual socialists. Our offices were close together—Robinson's, Beard's and mine. At the end of the day we generally got together and talked over the state of the world and of our own souls, and were very frank about both.

Beard was a lovely spirit—one of the most likeable men I have ever known. He was a man of absolute integrity, a scholar of the first order. He had been a student at DePauw University before going to Oxford, and I doubt if his socialism dated as far back as that. But his wife, Mary Beard, was much more of an orthodox and confirmed socialist. I always felt that she carried him along to make sure he would say the startling things he loved to utter and would herself make sure people understood that his view of history was socialistic.

His first great contribution, though he did some work in the Industrial Revolution previously, was the book called *Economic Interpretation of the Constitution*. The title was intended to imply a Marxian interpretation of the Constitution. But Beard put solid research and genuine scholarship into the book, and brought into the perspective of American history things that had been unexplored before, such as the way in which the debts of the Revolution were taken over and the poorer veterans of the Revolution lost out on their scrips. His theory that the speculators were those who had a sinister interest in putting the Constitution through is not carried to an extreme in the text. It was carried to an extreme by his followers afterward and has been criticized by recent historians.

Beard and I later differed very much in outlook. He became an isolationist and I went into the field of international relations. Our differences were never minimized in our talks with each other. I am happy to say, though, that they never created a moment's difference in our personal feeling toward each other. When I sent him my book on the Paris Peace Conference, although by that time we were miles apart in our world outlook, he wrote me a warm letter saying: "It is a rare thing to have a historic document from one who knows historic documents. I have found your book delightful reading and illuminating at the same time." I keep that letter in my personal file, for I cherish loyal friendship above almost anything else—and so, I'm sure, did he. On his death I wrote to Mary Beard, referring to that fact. In her letter back to me she said that Charles had always felt the same.

Both Beard and I naturally looked to Robinson as the pioneer in what he termed "The New History." The academic freedom in the study of history was supported by even those members of the Faculty of Political Science who held to the traditional conceptions of the fields to be covered by it. The founder of this faculty (in 1880) and its Dean, John William Burgess, was thoroughly imbued with the doctrines of national sovereignty held by his German professors—doctrines strongly driven home by the Civil War in which, in a divided Tennessee family, he took service in the northern armies. Fortunately, over against absolute sovereignty he put an even greater emphasis on the "sphere of liberty," of which the Supreme Court was the guardian. Although his interpretation of history and public law was too legalistic, and his classroom lectures were merely readings from the proof sheets of a new edition of his *Constitutional Law,* his influence as a personality was felt even by students who used the lecture period to read other books. I was especially critical of his method, because he had no appreciation of the safeguards of freedom in a parliamentary system like that of England. Bryce brings out this point in his *American Commonwealth,* stating that a federal system is necessarily held together by legal contracts, which are less adjustable than acts of parliament.

Fortunately for Columbia, Dean Burgess brought from Germany not only a system of public law, but also the spirit of academic freedom, the *"Lehrfreiheit"* which was as much a heritage of its intellectual life as contributions of its nineteenth-century thought. Burgess gave free rein to his colleagues, for most of them had the same training. The distinguished economist, John Bates Clark, studied at Heidelberg; the jurist Monroe Smith and Robinson the historian came from Freiburg; Goodnow, professor of public law, later president of Johns Hopkins, and Nicholas Murray Butler of the Philosophy Department studied at Berlin. The head of the History Department, William Milligan Sloane, had had especial advantages in

44

Germany as Secretary to the American Ambassador in Berlin, George Bancroft, the most famous American historian of that time. This was followed up by studies under the German historian Droysen, but Sloane's most important work was an elaborate life of Napoleon, which led President Seth Low to found a history professorship for him to induce him to leave his Chair at Princeton.

It was not only in Columbia but in other leading universities as well that graduate faculties were almost like colonial offshoots of those in Germany where they had been trained. There was nothing derogatory in such a relationship. The age of Goethe was giving way to that of textual criticism—from Wolf's analysis of the Homeric poems, proving that there had been more than one Homer, to the higher criticism of the Bible and the reconstruction of ancient and medieval history based on new studies of the sources. It was a great achievement, that of German scholarship, paralleling the discoveries of the physical scientists. There were, however, as great—or even greater—figures in the intellectual life of other countries; as, for instance, Faraday, Darwin, Rutherford and the Curies in science; Champollion, Rawlinson or Evans in archeology; Michelet, Fustel de Coulanges, Acton or Maitland in history and law. These names are listed only as reminders of the fact, too often ignored, that the apparent leadership of Germany in scholarship and science was more in mass production than in the discoveries made by individual intellectual power of genius. Neither Germany nor any other country had a monopoly of pioneering thinkers. But nowhere else in the nineteenth century was there so general a movement to apply the new knowledge in education.

The German-trained professors maintained a formality in their relations with students which was probably an academic inheritance of the medieval classroom. I came upon an instance of extreme professional aloofness at the end of my second year. In the course on Roman Law there had been only two of us, myself and W. K. Boyd, later professor at Trinity College, North Carolina. I dropped out at Easter to prepare for my examination in other subjects. At the last lecture, Professor Monroe Smith, one of the greatest scholars in his field, leaned over the desk and asked Boyd to give him his name so that Boyd might get credit for the course! We two had been reading the Latin texts together under Monroe Smith's critical scholarship all term.

The only other course in law which I had was a semester on the history of international law, by the distinguished jurist John Basset Moore, later a judge on the World Court. It is worth noting that this was the only course that had any bearing on international relations in the Faculty of Political Science, a subject which now tends to crowd history to second place in the curriculum and one on which most of my later life was spent.

At the end of my second year at Columbia, in the spring of 1900, I took my examination for the degree of Ph.D. in the work done in courses. It was tough going, for I had no undergraduate preparation, and the graduate courses were mostly research studies on special subjects in which the general background was taken for granted. My ignorance of United States history was colossal. But somehow I survived the ordeal and was accepted as an assistant in the Department of History. I was to teach a course in world history, required of freshmen or sophomores—the famous History A—three times a week for both terms. My class was to be in Barnard College, but that year Barnard had a great influx of students, and over a hundred of them enrolled for the course. This meant dividing them into three classes, thus giving me nine hours of teaching per week—for four hundred dollars for the year.

Professor Robinson went to President Low about it. He sent for me, telling me that there had been a miscalculation and, if I didn't mind having it all straightened out at once, he would give me a check for eight hundred dollars. I thanked him, took the check, and it was only when I was out on the street that I saw it was his personal check. It was so simply done and so friendly. Columbia was fortunate in having for its president a millionaire, but doubly fortunate in the quality of the man, who a few years later left Columbia to become Mayor of New York City. He had charm and a quiet dignity which probably came from shyness, especially among scholars. Perhaps that was one reason why he often sought out the table at the Faculty Club where the young men lunched together. He was easily at home with them and they repaid his friendliness with loyalty.

46

At the first university commencement I attended, President Low showed his mettle in what would have been an embarrassing incident but for his quickness of mind. The degrees until then had been given in Latin, along with a Latin citation carefully prepared for each by Professor Peck, the distinguished Latinist professor. These President Low had memorized, but while bestowing an honorary degree on a great engineer his memory failed him, and for a moment or so he groped unsuccessfully for the missing Ciceronian periods. There was a dead silence in the audience as well as on the platform. Then President Low turned to the expectant recipient of the degree and with a courteous gesture said that it was only fitting that one whose work was for the future should be addressed in the language of the present. He then continued the citation in English. There was applause from all over the hall; and from that moment on, Columbia degrees have been granted only in a language that everyone can understand.

The next president, Nicholas Murray Butler, was a striking contrast to President Low. President Butler lacked Low's warmth of personality, avoiding anything like intimacy with all but a half dozen of the older professors. He is, however, too large a figure and too self-contradictory a character to fit into this limited canvas. While he held himself aloof from professors as well as students, he was both immensely proud of the university and jealous of its academic freedom. Once a woman prominent in New York society reproached him for having on his faculty a professor who taught atheism. He expressed surprise and interest; but when she told him it was Professor Giddings, the sociologist, for whom he had high regard, his reply was that he was glad to hear it "for we aim to teach everything in the university." Both the President and Giddings told me this, with almost equal glee.

On another occasion, both Beard and I had been invited by the Rand School, a Socialist institution, to give history lectures there. In order to make sure that there would be no objection, we went to Butler about it. He said to go ahead by all means—that the only thing that counted was that our courses should be sound in scholarship and not propagandist for anything. It was the scholar that counted, not the auspices under which he lectured. This would have been heresy twenty years later, but no one could ever accuse Nicholas Murray Butler of being a Red! On the contrary, he was even too reactionary for most of the Republican party, as was shown, not only by his failure to win more than the votes of Utah and Vermont when he ran for the Vice-Presidency with Taft in 1912, but also by his failure to be nominated by the Republican Convention in 1920. His conservatism was that of the nineteenth-century liberal, who reacted violently against federal social legislation as in the Square Deal of Theodore Roosevelt or the New Freedom of Woodrow Wilson. It was this same liberalism which made Butler an outstanding leader in the movement to repeal the Eighteenth Amendment on Prohibition and also led him to give support to woman suffrage.

Columbia was fortunate to have so eloquent and courageous a president, for the qualities which blocked his political career were greatly needed in the university. There his conservatism meant holding the line for the liberal arts against the drive for vocational and purely technical education; while his nineteenth-century liberalism, which made him a reactionary in politics, showed itself in support of such a radical as John Dewey, in Butler's own field of philosophy. No wonder Columbia University grew great under his presidency.

CHAPTER 4

Discovering the Middle Ages

History had always been to me like a voyage of discovery, but it was never so charged with romance or so richly rewarding as in those first years at Columbia University. I reveled in the huge quartos and folios of the collections of sources which opened up a world so different from my own: lives of the saints, laws of the Franks or Angles and Saxons, "customaries" of feudal life and times, chronicles from monasteries and documents of church and state. In the library alcoves, where the many hundreds of these volumes of records of the past were kept, I worked happily day and night, centuries away from the busy world of the great city. The voice of its streets never reached the silent library room of the university, which was then not so crowded as it is now. Most of the time I was alone with the books, trying, in imagination, to recreate the Middle Ages out of their crabbed texts. Like Keats on first reading Chapman's Homer, though much had I traveled in the realms of gold, yet here there was discovery, and there were times when I, too, felt "like some watcher of the skies when a new planet swims into his ken,"* as the centuries of the Middle Ages opened up before me.

If this seems extravagant, test it by adventuring as I did in the world of historical research, beyond the well-worn pathways of textbook history. To be sure, all of it had been explored and mapped

---

* The rest of this sonnet always intrigued me. It made no difference to Keats that it was not "stout Cortez" but Balboa who discovered the Pacific. From Homer's *Iliad* to Tennyson's *Idylls of the King,* poetry has always won out over history.

out by the European scholars who had edited the vast collections of sources, and most of them had furnished guides to the ground they covered. But none of these useful manuals were to be taken for granted; everything had to be checked against the original documents, and in their light I began to see that the work of the historian is not the storing of a tired memory with textbook data but the training of the imagination to reconstruct the past from records written for the most part without any thought that they would some day be used for the light they might throw on the long processes of history.

It was fascinating work. It was also a revelation, as the Middle Ages came to life in documents dealing with the day-to-day business of church and state, or the varied arrangements of lord, vassal and villein in the feudal system. It was a rich experience to follow Robinson's exploration of this world of which I had known so little. The Middle Ages and the Dark Age had been almost synonymous terms to me, a thousand years between the fall of Rome and the Renaissance, a dreary stretch of history devoid of almost everything we care for or seek after today. There were even exact dates for its opening and closing—476 for the setting aside of the last Roman Emperor in the West, to 1453, the conquest of Constantinople by the Turks. But Robinson made an end of this periodizing, showing that the dismemberment of the Roman Empire had been a process lasting throughout the whole of the fifth century, and that the Greek scholars from Byzantium had begun to influence Western thought before the conquest of Constantinople.

These were only two of many reconstructions of medieval history in Robinson's "new history." He especially enjoyed destroying the "myth of the year one thousand" which still was repeated in textbooks—that as the year 1000 approached mankind prepared for the Last Judgment, that the earth "covered itself with the white mantle of churches" and like a penitent watched in terror and in prayer for the fatal dawn. This legend, however, is not to be found in the contemporary sources. The reckoning of years from the birth of Christ was not yet universal, even in the chancelleries of governments; and one wonders how that most enduring type of architecture, the

50

Romanesque, could reach its maturity among men who thought that the earth itself was so soon to "shrivel like a parched scroll." The legend of the year 1000 served a useful purpose, however, as a reminder that the Dark Age of invasions and tribal wars was drawing to a close, and that the century which it ushered in became, before it ended, the springtime of Europe—that springtime which produced the splendor of Gothic cathedrals, the revival of Roman law on the continent and the development of the common law in England, the rise of the universities and the growth of cities as centers of a new web of commerce, while feudal courts listened to a new literature in the common speech.

This was the wide and varied subject of our history courses. We had not only to study it, but to live it, so far as the fragmentary records permitted. Strangely enough, some of the most revealing came from the heart of the Dark Age—not only the native pagan legends and poems, like Beowulf and the Nibelungenlied, but the naïf monastic writings like *The History of the Franks** by Gregory of Tours, whose narrative of murders is vouched for in his preface by a recital of the Nicene Creed. This was a different Middle Ages from that of the textbooks. Feudalism, studied in detail "on the spot," proved to be very different from the commonly accepted idea of it as a "system" of society. It was more like anarchy held together or held down by force. Just as the young Teutonic civilization was being held to law and order by the Church and by such rulers as Alfred of England, a second wave of invasion came dashing over it. The Vikings, whom Charlemagne's aged eyes may have seen stealing past the hills of Calais, not only swept the northern seas, but harried Frankland from the Rhine to the Rhone until progress was at a standstill and the one thought of the ninth century was that of defense. The Magyars came raiding down the Danube-Tisza valley, and along the coasts of the Mediterranean the Moorish corsairs were stifling the weak commerce of Italian towns, and even sacked a part of Rome. The nascent civilization of the Teutons was forced

* The only English translation is that by Ernest Brehaut, published by the Columbia University Press in 1916, in *Records of Civilization,* a series begun under my editorship.

51

to meet a danger such as would call for all the legions of Augustus.

In such a situation self-defense became a system. The palisade upon some central hill, the hedge and thicket in the plain, or the ditch in the morass became the center and shelter of life for every neighborhood. The owner of the fortress led in battle his tenants who owed military service. The palisades became stone walls and the little camps *(castella)* became castles. Those grim battlemented towers were the signs of hope. Society was saved, but it was transformed. The protection of times of danger became oppression in times of safety, until the feudal structure of society had to yield to that of nationalism under kings—a process which interested Robinson less than the Middle Ages which it left behind.

Far more important, however, than the recasting of the social and political life of the Middle Ages was the history of its great institution, the Church. This was the new planet that swam into my ken. It was not only the religious monitor and guardian of morals as we know it today; it helped to preserve the best things of antiquity, for as Rashdall, the historian of the universities, put it, when the barbarians were led to destroy what was of no use to them it was the Church which widened the sphere of utility. It, more than the sword of Charlemagne, tamed the barbarian Germans, and through its codes of penance—with punishments almost as severe as the laws of Draco—it curbed the instincts of savagery and taught our ancestors the ethics of Moses while promising them the salvation of Christ. Its monks were not only the pioneer farmers in the fastnesses of the wilderness, but their entertainment of travelers made commerce possible. Its parish church furnished a nursery for democracy in the gatherings at the church door for counsel and deliberation. It opened to the sons of peasants a career that promised equality with the haughtiest seigneur, or even dictation over kings.

I have quoted here from an article "A Survey of the History of the Middle Ages" which I contributed in 1902 as the introduction to the seventh volume of the *Historians' History of the World*. I must quote some more from it, for it not only mirrors my main interests at that time, but was destined to change my whole life. My glorification of the medieval mind continued in the following enthusiastic terms:

In depicting this wonderful system which so dominated Europe in the early Middle Ages, we must be careful not to give too much of an air of religiosity to the whole Middle Ages. The men of the Middle Ages did not all live in a cowl. Symonds in his brilliant history of the Renaissance in Italy likens the whole medieval attitude to that of St. Bernard, the greatest of its ascetics. St. Bernard would walk by the blue waters of Lake Geneva intent only upon his rosary and prayer. Across the lake gleam the snows of Mont Blanc—a sight no traveler forgets once he has seen it—but the saint, with his cowl drawn over his eyes, sees only his own sin and the vision of the Last Judgment. So, says Symonds, humanity walked along its way, a careful pilgrim unheeding the beauty or delight of the world around. Now this is very striking, but is it true? First of all, the Middle Ages, as ordinarily reckoned, include a stretch of ten centuries, which differed from each other as much as any centuries before or since. The nineteenth is hardly more different from the eighteenth than the twelfth was different from the eleventh. This became clearer the more we studied the sources for the history of those centuries. Some gave us the *Chansons des Gestes,* the *Song of Roland,* the legends of Charlemagne and his paladins. Others gave us the lyrics of the minnesingers and troubadours, of Walter von der Vogelweide and Bertran de Born. And as for their variety, we must again recall that the same century which gave us St. Francis of Assisi, that jongleur of God, also gave us Magna Carta and representative government.

We learned under Robinson to be distrustful of generalizations. The monks were not all alike; some were worldly, some were religious, some were scholars, and some were ambitious and some merely indolent. The monastery was a home for the scholar, a refuge for the disconsolate, and an asylum for the disgraced. A monk might often be a man whose sensibilities, instead of being dull, were sharply awake, his faith kindling an imagination that brought the next world down into his daily life. And one who is in communion with eternity is an unconscious poet as well as a devotee. Dante's great poem is just the essence of a thousand years of such visions.

One of the happiest memories of those years were the meetings of a little group of medievalists which I had been invited to join. There were in addition to Professor Robinson and myself, Henry Osborn Taylor, author of the magisterial work *The Medieval Mind,* formerly a lawyer, who commented with light-hearted banter on the unconscious, homely humor in the lives of the saints; Professor McGiffert, of Union Theological Seminary, author of *The Apostolic Age;* Professor Knox, also of Union Seminary, a specialist in Oriental religions; and the artist John La Farge, also an accomplished medieval scholar. We met monthly through three or four winters in the Century Club, with its library at hand containing so many of the original sources. Except that there was nothing formal about it, it was a miniature academy. To me, as the youngest of the group, it was a joy and an inspiration.

As the Church was the outstanding institution of the Middle Ages, I made it the center of my studies for most of my two years of student life at Columbia. This meant exploring a field of which I was almost entirely ignorant, the theology and structure of Catholicism—on the one hand, the writings of the early Fathers and their medieval successors and, on the other hand, the canon law. I found it a thrilling experience to explore the great edifice of Christian faith and morals under the guidance of such masters as Hinschius, whose *Kirchenrecht,* by its orderly massing of detail, made even a German text as luminous as the *Droit Canonique* of Viollet. There was no work in English to match those of the Continental scholars.

More important was the lack of any comprehensive series of texts on the rise of the papacy. So Professor Louise R. Loomis of Barnard College and I prepared a volume, *The See of Peter,** containing in translation all the texts bearing on the history of the papacy until it had become a virtual monarchy, under Pope Leo I—the pope who in 452 persuaded Attila to turn back from the invasion of Italy. Dr. Loomis and I worked separately. I took all the early texts and she translated those from the third century on. As both translators were Protestants, I was anxious to avoid controversy and sent a copy to Cardinal Gasquet, whom I had known in London, and one bound in white silk for His Holiness. The Cardinal was then at Rome, in charge of the revision of the text of the Bible, a monument of Catholic scholarship. He made the presentation and wrote me a cordial note, adding, however, that there were other sources which we should have translated. However that may be, it still remains

* The volume was published by the Columbia University Press (1927), in the *Records of Civilization* series.

the only book of its kind and is used in Catholic as well as Protestant seminaries.

The central doctrine of the medieval church, on which the whole structure of Catholicism rests, is that of the sacraments, and the central sacrament is that of the altar—the Eucharist, or the Lord's Supper as it is called in Protestant churches. To understand the history of the church I had, therefore, to concentrate on the history of the sacraments, and I finally wrote my doctoral dissertation on the early history of the Eucharist—probably the only one on that subject ever submitted to a Faculty of Political Science. But I made my defense for it in the opening paragraphs, in which I pointed out that it was a study in history and not in theology, that it attempted to explain the rise of "an institution which has had an influence upon the history of Europe hardly less vast than that of such products of the antique world as Greek philosophy and Roman law. . . . In the political world it was the control of the sacraments which enabled the church to take over so largely the task of Rome. Its enactments against sin and evil would have remained mere moral censures, if it had not been able to attach a penalty to them. That penalty was exclusion from the sacraments, graded into a penitential system. As the framework of the political world loosened, it was this system which substituted for the primitive German sense of right and wrong the ethics of Moses and of Christ, and it was by the great miracle of the Mass that the German mind was subdued to accept such an authority."

I am tempted to quote more from this defense of my excursion into a field so far outside the range of political history—in which historians were supposed to stay. The historical seminar room of Johns Hopkins University bore this motto from Freeman on its wall: "History is past politics and politics present history." There was at least safety in limiting the field to purely secular data. The only thing wrong about it was that it left out of account a vastly important part of human experience.

But what was—or is—a sacrament? One thing was clear; it was the very opposite of Quakerism, which has neither priest nor ceremonial. I could also look at it in the long perspective of history and in the wider reaches of anthropology, both of which I did.

55

First, the history. For over a thousand years, the church of the sacraments never undertook to describe them in an adequate definition. It was only in the Paris of Abelard, when everything human and divine was being questioned by the Scholastics, that Hugh, Abbot of the Monastery of St. Victor close by the university, added to St. Augustine's inadequate statement that "a sacrament is the sign of a sacred thing" the meaningful phrase "not only the sign of a sacred thing, but the visible form of an invisible grace which confers that of which it is the sign or meaning." But this is explaining one mystery by another: what is "grace"?

The starting point, the key to the understanding of sacramental religion, evidently lay in an understanding of grace. The word *gratia,* used in its theological context, was not the ordinary Latin word used to mean merely a favor shown for service rendered. It was a potency, a miraculous power conveyed from the Divinity to the worshiper. Puzzling over the way in which this Christian mystery slowly took shape in the sacramental system of seven sacraments, I turned from history to anthropology and found that the primal thing in all primitive religions was just this sense of mysterious potency—in short, that sacrament, older than myth, was the first reaction of man to the data of religion.

The pioneers in this interpretation of the origin of religion were two sociologists of the University of Paris, Mauss and Hubert, whose study entitled *Outline of a Theory of Magic (Esquisse d'une Théorie Générale de la Magie)* marked a new stage in the history of comparative religion. They pointed out that behind both magic and religion there is a mysterious something which all primitive peoples feel, and which was best described by Bishop Codrington in Melanesia as *mana,* a supernatural power or influence outside the ordinary processes of nature. To get this *mana* for one's self, religious practices develop—prayers and sacrifices. Cult is the first expression of religion; creeds come later.

I was discovering far more than the Middle Ages! As I worked in this borderland of history and anthropology, my colleagues in the Faculty of Philosophy, especially Dean Woodbridge, became interested in our discussions and finally invited me to sum up my theories of the origin of religion in a course of three public lectures at the university. To my astonishment, the largest hall in the Schermerhorn building was filled to overcrowding. The text was never published, but I repeated some of the same material in a series of lectures at Amherst College in 1910, which was published under the title *The Religious Revolution of Today.*

It may seem strange, in the light of my later life, that throughout those early years at Columbia University I lived more in the other side of the thirteenth than in the twentieth century. But the discipline of historical research is not limited to any special problems; it has general application. In my last chapter I mentioned that Boyd of North Carolina took work with me in the seminar on Roman law. He wrote his dissertation on the Theodosian Code; yet when he went back to teach in his old college, Trinity, all his courses were in American history. When I asked him about it, he said that he had taken his doctorate in subjects in which he could not take sides, so that he, a Southerner, could free himself from prejudices in dealing with the Civil War.

I have an idea that my Canadian background served somewhat the same purpose. But then I didn't have to test it, for never, during all the years from student to professor, did anyone at Columbia ever raise the question of my Canadian origin. There was never a trace of nationalism in the attitude toward my work—not until August, 1914, that is, and then not in criticism. I was astonished, however, when at a luncheon at the Faculty Club in that year some of my colleagues turned to me to get the British point of view, of which they knew as much as I.

This reminds me of another episode. After the sinking of the *Lusitania,* the professors of the Faculty of Political Science were invited by the Dean to an informal meeting, a sort of caucus, to get an expression of opinion on whether we should go to war with Germany. Feeling ran very high. Quite a number were for immediate action leading to war. I won their rather violent dissent when I said that the case was not clear because the *Lusitania* was carrying munitions. I remained opposed to the entry of the United States into the war until December, 1916, when the disasters on the Western Front threatened an Allied defeat; in which case our country would be drawn in, under conditions which would involve a far greater loss of life to us as well as to the Allies. Having reached this conclusion, I entered into the campaign for our participation without hesitation or reserve.

Meanwhile, I had been carrying the usual teaching load of a young instructor. For the general course in World History—History A—my opposite number in Columbia College, William R. Shepherd, prepared with me a syllabus of readings based on Fisher's *Universal History,* a textbook now happily extinct. As we surmounted this obstacle, we were given the next optional course in modern European history. Then he and I divided the world between us—he taking the history of the United States and Latin America and I that of Europe, in both Barnard and Columbia College.

As everything seemed to be going well, I was married in 1902 to Margaret Harvey, the "little girl on the galloping horse" of my poem. We had exchanged vows in high school days in Strathroy. Then she, too, went through Toronto University, and as I had nothing for us to get married on, she spent the next three years after her graduation studying modern languages in Germany, Italy and Geneva. Then in 1901 she taught in the Paterson, New Jersey, high school, making a great success by her quick understanding of the adolescent mind. Finally in 1902 we were married in her father's home in Wyoming, Ontario. It was a romance that lasted untouched by time, although time seemed to move too slowly through the years. Now it moves too fast.

In 1904 I was told that I could not expect any advancement into the glorified circle of professorship unless I spent some time studying in Europe. But how? My salary was about two thousand dollars, to which I added only a little by lecturing for ten dollars a night on medieval history to sleepy audiences in the New York public schools and at Cooper Union in an effort at adult education planned by a benefactor of university instructors, Dr. Leipziger of the New York public school administration. In those days before motion pictures, the lectures were illustrated by photographic slides of feudal castles and cathedrals—about which I wove as much fantasy as I dared, to enliven the theme.

More important than the pictures was the fact that my wife had the moral endurance to go with me to the lecture halls and act as

58

my tutor in public speaking. She would sit at the back of the room and make signs to me when I was too professorial, or dropped my voice at the ends of sentences, or lowered my head so that only those in the front rows could hear. None of these matters had seemed important in the small classrooms, and I was completely surprised at how often she signaled to me that something was wrong. She was as persistent, however, as she was long-suffering; and if I ever learned the art of public speaking, the credit should go to her.

There were a few lectures to teachers in cities as distant as Pittsburgh. I also wrote articles for newspapers at ten dollars an article.

Finally, there was a gorgeous chance to help edit the many-volumed *Historians' History of the World,* to which I have referred above, made up of extracts chosen from the works of the great historians of an earlier day, whose works, incidentally, were no longer in copyright. The editing of the texts of the old masters in the light of recent scholarship fitted in with the course I was giving on the history of history. I mention this because it bears directly on my life work. The profession of the historian is not like that of a "teller of tales." The difference between Homer—or even Herodotus—and Gibbon is that criticism cuts in on the narrative with tests for accuracy or truth, and the study of the Middle Ages, with its uncritical monkish chronicles to be checked against other contemporary evidence, is a discipline which is an education in itself. The sifting of evidence breeds—or should breed—that caution of temper which is the mark of the judicious mind. There could be no better place to acquire it than in a study of the far-off, slowly moving Middle Ages, dealing with issues that were settled centuries ago.

CHAPTER 5

Adventure in Europe

The Arabs have a saying that Allah looks after those who don't look after themselves. In any event, as I look back over our journey to Europe in 1904, we needed looking after.

We had almost no resources, for what could one save on a two-thousand-dollar salary—although that was double its present value? Besides, Margaret Grace had just come to bring the joy of babyhood into our home. How could our blessed family spend a year in Europe on almost nothing? With the boldness of youth neither my wife nor I faltered. Professor Sloane, the head of the History Department, endorsed a note of mine at the University branch of the Colonial Bank (now the Chemical Bank New York Trust Company) for two thousand dollars, and we sailed for Europe. Margaret Grace was just six weeks old!

When we reached London our funds were already getting low, and we took rooms in a boardinghouse on Bloomsbury Square, near the British Museum, a section of London that had once been fashionable but was now mostly filled with cheap, respectable boardinghouses. In the one we stayed at the landlady presided at the dinner table to cut the "joint" with microscopic thinness, and the most voluble boarder was a retired funeral director whose mind was still on his former profession.

Then, at once, I tried my luck. The publishers of the *Historians'* *History* on which I had worked, Messrs. Hooper and Jackson, had bought the *Encyclopaedia Britannica* and had made a fortune bringing out a tenth edition by adding supplementary volumes to the famous ninth edition, one of the proudest monuments of Victorian scholarship and still regarded almost as an institution of the British Empire. The sale of this tenth edition of the Britannica has no parallel in the annals of publishing. Both in Great Britain and in the colonies a great spread of advertisements announced that the sales would end at five o'clock on a fateful day a few weeks later. Then in the last week the Hooper and Jackson firm sent out over a hundred thousand telegrams to the prospective British buyers warning them that the sands were running out. Nothing like this had ever happened in England before. Of course the music halls took it on— "Have you bought your Britannica?"—which was good advertising. One of their quips was that out in Australia ranchers came galloping in to be in time only to find to their disgust that the Britannica was merely a row of books. All in all, the sales ran up to enough millions of dollars to enable Hooper and Jackson to bring out an entirely new edition, the famous eleventh on which they were then planning to begin.

I had written to Mr. Hooper from the office of the *Historians' History,* expressing the hope that I might do some articles on the *Britannica,* and this was the slender hope on which I had counted in what otherwise would have meant a very short stay in Europe. And so, the first day I arrived in London I went to see Mr. Hooper, and to my amazement, instead of offering me a few articles, he asked me how I would like to be the general editor of the whole encyclopaedia! I have had a number of major surprises in my life but nothing to compare with this incredible incident of 1904. Soon, by inquiry, I found that Mr. Hooper had quarreled with the editor, Hugh Chisholm, had dismissed him, and was awaiting my arrival to offer me the vacant post. It seemed that in his eyes my extensive revamping of the *Historians' History* had saved it from failure. But of this I was ignorant, and the situation seemed incredible. Almost at the end of my resources, I was suddenly offered a position worth something like $15,000 a year—as long as the job lasted or I lasted in it.

As soon as I found out what the situation was, however, I refused the offer, for I had never lived in that commercial world where such ruthless things are done. I saw Chisholm and liked him. He came to terms with Hooper, who, however, insisted that I was to be a managing editor with the same salary as if I were editor in chief.

My first task was to prepare a memorandum outlining the kind of revision which was needed to bring the *Britannica* up to the level of recent scholarship. I spent a week in the library of the British Museum examining the leading articles in history. Most of them had become almost classics. The article on English history was a brilliant essay by Freeman, who was still regarded as an Olympian of the Victorian era. I showed, however, how his glorification of Anglo-Saxon origins had been challenged and its medieval sections rendered practically obsolete by later historians. I did the same for the histories of France and Germany. When Mr. Hooper studied these criticisms, he said that it meant that he would have to junk property which he had thought worth about a million dollars, but that he would make three million by recasting the whole encyclopaedia for the twentieth century. His judgment was justified, for he was a great salesman, and he had seen from his sale of the tenth edition how the British public would respond to a brand-new *Britannica*.

Hooper had made a partnership arrangement with the *Times* to act as publisher of the tenth edition, and shortly after I joined the editorial staff we were moved to the third floor of the *Times* building, a rambling red brick reminder of Victorian England, and of the years when "The Thunderer" was a power in British politics only less than Parliament itself. The family of its eighteenth-century founder, John Walter, still owned it, but the head of that house seldom wandered in—and almost only of a late evening when the paper was being made up—for everything was left to George E. Buckle, the editor in chief, and C. Moberly Bell, the manager, a veteran newspaperman, who had once been *Times* correspondent in Egypt.

Here was a new world for me, even more absorbing than the making of an encyclopaedia. But it was also something new for the staff of the *Times,* for we developed a card index of men and events to keep the encyclopaedia articles up to date. I persuaded Mr. Bell to use it in the paper to fill in the telegraphic news items of foreign correspondents, often only a line or two which were meaningless unless one knew the background. We supplied the rest of the story, separated from the telegram by a leaded line. The card index was also the origin of the "Times Index." Up to that time there had only been a thin volume called "Palmer's Index of the Times," prepared by a man who was simply doing it on his own. The card index was much fuller and was organized with sectional headings; and this was taken over by the *Times* in 1905 and has continued ever since. The *New York Times* Index followed the same model. Both of them are indispensable guides to current history. So happy was Mr. Bell over these developments that he asked me to go on the *Times,* after the encyclopaedia was finished, instead of going back to Columbia. It was a great temptation, but again, as in the case of Mr. Mackenzie's offer to try to make a businessman out of me, I chose medieval history instead of a career on the *Times.*

There was more to it than this editing of the news. I discovered that the reference library was sadly out of date. Political editors like Sir Valentine Chirol, the dean of British newspaper correspondents, knew the political scene at first hand and had their own private libraries. But the leader-writers were often at sea for lack of reference books. Mr. Buckle, the editor in chief, somehow never seemed to need them. He was intimately acquainted with all political leaders. The only books he kept on the shelf behind his swivel chair, for ready consultation, were the Greek classics! Mr. Bell knew how handicapped the leader-writers felt and, under his direction, I undertook revamping the library in a major way. Had I stayed on at the *Times,* my position was to be that of a reference editor to help both in the news and on the editorial page. I have on the desk before me a collection of the handwritten letters of Mr. Bell, in which all of these projects were discussed. In the grand old English manner, he wrote letters by hand, making the points clear and precise, instead of leaving everything for the imprecision of a conversation. These letters are among my most cherished possessions.

From the boardinghouse on Bloomsbury Square we moved to a furnished house. Furnished houses in summertime in London are a regular institution, as the owners leave the city for the country or for travel. Among the established real estate agents engaged in this business we found the firm of Chesterton—of the family of G. K.

Chesterton—provided with a long list of middle class houses, and began our first experience with cook, maid and chambermaid, a small but to us oppressive hierarchy with strictly defined duties and a polite but definite feeling that we needed their guidance in our daily life—as we did, in England.

Work on the encyclopaedia was still mostly in the planning stage, and that meant consultation with prospective contributors. The great reputation of the ninth edition of the *Britannica* still lasted on, and to be listed as the author of a major article in a new edition under the sponsorship of the *Times* was an accolade of distinction. This meant that much of my time was spent in Cambridge and Oxford, and finally we took a house in Oxford from which I commuted regularly. Just opposite Magdalen College we found a little cottage in Rose Lane, apparently as old as the college itself, with diamond-paned windows in its thick walls, along which roses climbed. I visited the spot a couple of years ago, and nothing of house or garden remains, not even a name. But then, although the towns and quads of Oxford remain, the world of scholars in which it was my incredible good fortune to live has also completely changed. There were, among others, Professor Vinogradoff for all things Russian; Professor Cheyne at Oriel College for Biblical scholarship; Ernest Barker, then a rising young historian at New College; Sidney Ball, the academic socialist, at St. John's, with its high church traditions—the college of Archbishop Laud. Above all, there was Professor Gilbert Murray, whose poetic rendering of Greek verse was already a classic in itself. I met him in his home on Boar's Hill overlooking Oxford from the south, and I was to cherish his friendship throughout the years.

At Cambridge, which I visited from time to time, there was an equally long list of contributors. I discussed the whole editorial problem with Professor Ward, the editor of the *Cambridge Modern History;* but the outstanding experience was to get to know and to work with Professor R. W. Maitland of Downing College, historian of English law, one of the greatest of English historians, and Professor (later Sir James) Frazer of Trinity College, author of the twelve-volume survey of primitive magic and religion, *The Golden Bough,* which I had used in Columbia University in my class on comparative religion. I had pleasant visits with him in his study and he gave me a letter of introduction to his Oxford friend and colleague, Frederick Conybeare, whose *Myth, Magic and Morals* applied Frazer's work to the history of religion. Conybeare, unlike Frazer, was of a combative temperament, a Huxley in anthropology. There was a saying in Oxford, which no one verified, that his family crest bore the inscription, "God made the world and the Conybeares."

There were, of course, many scholars in London, among them Professor A. F. Pollard of the University of London, the historian of the Tudor and Stuart periods of English history; and Dr. Hubert Hall, the head of the Record Office, as modest as he was capable. I also got to know Catholic scholars like Baron Hegel; Abbot, later Cardinal, Gasquet; and Robert Wilberforce of the Foreign Office, grandson of the Liberator.

My colleagues at Columbia were generous in their recognition of my work on the *Britannica,* but after all it was not original research. So the next year, 1905, was spent at Paris, Rome and Heidelberg. At Paris I listened to lectures by that galaxy of historians who were the glory of the Third Republic: Gabriel Monod, the pioneer in historical criticism, then giving his lectures on Michelet at the Collège de France; Seignobos recasting the perspectives of modern history at the Sorbonne, along with Aulard, the historian of the French Revolution, whose collection of texts on the Reign of Terror had first set my feet on the pathway of research. He was then carrying on a polemic against Taine, whose conservative views were based on inadequate scholarship, as Aulard showed by finding Taine's reading slips for the books he had used in the Bibliothèque Nationale.

It was like a detective story. The French Revolution was still a battleground in the years after the Dreyfus case, in which, it must not be forgotten, the professors of the University of Paris had taken a courageous and important part. From the polemic of modern history, it was always a relief to sink back into the Middle Ages, reading a chronicle of the Albigensian Crusade of the thirteenth century with the greatest historian of that period, Achille Luchaire, or the sources of English history in France under the Plantagenets with Professor Bemont, or canon law with Viollet, or medieval paleography with Prou—the latter in that sanctuary of the Middle Ages, the École des Chartes. Alongside these courses I still went on editing the *Britannica,* securing French and other continental scholars, and writing articles myself—some sixty or more—among them the article "History" drawn from my own course in Columbia.

It was, therefore, a welcome change to go to Rome, where I practically lived in the French school for medieval and church history, in a palazzo on the Piazza di Campo dei Fiori facing the statue of Giordano Bruno, who had been burned on that spot for heresy in 1600.

The month in Rome also called for studies in the Vatican library and archives, at that time under Monsignor, later Cardinal, Ehrle. He questioned me only about my work, never once referring to the fact that I was a non-Catholic. But I found the library catalogue confusing. It had never been modernized: American documents were still filed away under "The Indies." Years later I had some hand in securing a vote of Carnegie funds to re-catalogue the library on new, modern iron shelving.

From Rome I turned north for a semester in Heidelberg. It was March, and the peach orchards were in bloom in the valleys by the hill towns of Tuscany and Umbria. I had come to Europe to recover the more intimate sense of the Middle Ages, but everywhere, even in Umbria, the new world was crowding the old world out. I had glimpsed this on my first arrival at Glasgow in 1899. Dumbarton Castle still stood picturesquely on guard over the Clyde, but in the channel where now the ocean liners docked, the water had not been too deep to wade across when Watt was playing by its side. The castles at Oxford and Canterbury had been turned into warehouses. London and Paris had long ago become as modern as New York. The horizons opened to me by the *Britannica* and the *Times* were expanding into the twentieth century instead of the thirteenth. The semester in Heidelberg was to carry me further toward the new perspective; for there was no medieval history there that seemed worthwhile, and I therefore concentrated on the lectures in politics under the political philosopher Jellinek. Even they were not so stimulating as those I had attended as a student in Columbia.

From Heidelberg I went to Brittany to rejoin my wife and young daughter at Saint Briac, where Margaret had joined a painting class under Edwin Scott, a pupil and friend of Whistler and Carrière. She continued painting under him in later years, catching the subtle beauty of light and color with such mastery that one of her canvases in the Paris Salon was judged to be the best painting of the year by a woman artist. We have it still, along with others—a little street gamin with a roguish smile. A few years later, Mr. Scott bought Millet's birthplace in Normandy, and the next time we came to Europe, in 1911, we spent the summer at Cherbourg, of which many delicately interpretative paintings were made.

CHAPTER 6

The World of Today

Although I continued to give the research courses in Columbia University on the Church and State in the Middle Ages, the European adventure of 1904-1905 proved to be a turning point in my interest in history. From then on I was drawn more and more into the world of today. The Middle Ages still held its charm as I concentrated on researches in the thirteenth century, but in contrast with the world in which I lived at the *Britannica* and the *Times* I found a clue to the understanding of history itself which determined my whole outlook on life and society from that time on. I had had some glimpse of it in the courses which I had been giving in Columbia, but now it became clear as a law of nature.

Stated in simplest terms it was this: Life in the pre-modern world —primitive, ancient and medieval—was dominated by repetition, held down to the limited capacity of human strength to deal with nature by tools or weapons which were only the projection of brawn and muscle. All this was changed by the invention of machines, which took over the processes of work, for in the machine the mind begins to be in command. Invention puts thought into the method of work, and thought continues to find new and better ways of doing things; so the result is an escape from a static to a dynamic society, one in which change is the law of life, each new discovery and invention creating new conditions of living, a process increasing in geometric ratio as each new way of life calls for new adjustments

—and so on forever. In short, civilization has just begun to show the capacity of thought.

All this is commonplace now, but in 1905 there was no history department in any American university which gave a course on the Industrial Revolution. That was left for the economists, who dealt with it mainly in connection with the philosophy of *laissez faire* or in an attack on the theories of Karl Marx.

When I came back to Columbia in the autumn of 1905, along with my graduate courses on medieval history I gave an undergraduate course on what I called Social (instead of Economic) History, to avoid seeming to trespass on the territory of the Department of Economics. It was, so far as I could find out, the first college history course in which models of a steam engine and a locomotive were studied to understand the nature of invention. My excuse to my colleagues was that I used pictures of cathedrals and feudal castles in my courses on the Middle Ages, and this was simply applying the old technique to the fundamentals of the industrial world of today. I'm not sure that this excuse carried conviction to the faculty, but the principle of academic freedom prevailed and I went my pioneering way with no impediments.

As a matter of fact, it was pioneering on farther frontiers of history than the economist had ever thought to explore. Alongside my little models of engines and machines I laid two stone hatchets of pre-historic man. Both were designed to be used by the hand or with a thong at the end of a stick, but one was crudely chipped and the other ground smooth by other stones. Between these two techniques lay thousands of years, probably a longer interval than all the subsequent history of mankind. Through all those almost countless centuries power was man-power and the chief characteristic in the life of man was repetition—season after season, generation after generation, doing the same things over and over again. I made this point more telling by bringing to class a small round stone with a hole in the middle. It was a spindle whorl, twisted by the stick running through it, to spin wool into yarn. It came from a cave near Mentone on the Riviera, where the women still sit out on the sunny shore of the Mediterranean, whirling spindles as they did a thousand years before Rome was founded. All through the centuries those fingers have been at work doing the same task the same way. Such power of repetition, of which the calendar is only a visible, if not outstanding symbol, extended over all the recurring needs of life.

Against this prodigious background I placed the industrial revolution and the impact of science, showing that the greatest achievement of science is that it has changed the very nature of society, for as the law of the pre-scientific era was repetition, that of the scientific era is change. The rhythm still repeats, but in ever varied tones. The past and future were once alike, they are now eternally different, for every invention, every discovery, causes a displacement in society that calls for new discoveries and inventions.

My lectures were cast in the general philosophy of history so familiar in German universities. It was the same philosophy that I had developed in my courses in Columbia, of the history of the Industrial Revolution. Its central point was that the new world of science was a different one from that in our geographies and histories, while the philosophical framework for it remained the same; land, water, river, the relations of people were no longer indicated by the map. New inventions changed the centers of industries from one land to another as was the case of that English invention which became the basis of the iron and steel works of the Ruhr. These shifting activities are not chartered by the old-time calculations of seasons; but in sheets recording the prices of the money market, that mysterious index of the dynamic forces let loose in the world by the Industrial Revolution. Commerce is no longer a mere exchange of the margin of production but an interchange of necessities as well. This means that a world community is emerging. It is not yet realized, but we can already see the dominant historical characteristic which marked it off from the pre-scientific age. One thing at least is clear: its future will not merely repeat its past.

For some time I still gave research courses in medieval history. The one I myself got most out of was the textual analysis of the manual of a thirteenth-century inquisitor, Bernard Guy. The procedures used for uncovering heretics, particularly the non-confrontation of witnesses, were fresh in my mind a half-century later when I gave support to the clause on Human Rights in the Charter of the United Nations, and the criticism of inquisitional processes in Washington, especially those advocated by the late Senator McCarthy.

Those years of free exploration in history, working out my own philosophy, were the happiest of my academic life. I still kept my interest in comparative religion, steadily shifting away from the world of *Mont Saint Michel and Chartres*. Unlike Henry Adams I found intellectual peace in the dynamic world of today, with its never-ceasing challenge to intelligence. It was a challenge which had just been thrown at the conscience of America by that band of brilliant and fearless critics of the evils of unrestrained capitalism whom Theodore Roosevelt, their hero, dubbed "The Muckrakers." Although I sympathized with this crusade, I took no part in it, keeping to my academic tasks. But when women's suffrage became an issue, I supported it, joining in the famous Suffragette parade down Fifth Avenue, alongside Professor John Dewey—the only parade I ever marched in!

The crusading "muckrakers" used their pens as swords against entrenched corruption in local governments and exploitation by high finance. History has not yet paid full tribute to this movement which struck such a powerful blow at that complacent yet fundamentally false philosophy of life which regarded mere wealth or power, however attained, as the measure of success and the model for the young.

The drama of history in the world outside reached within the academic precincts as well, and there were heated arguments in the Faculty Club. Few of the faculty were as conservative as President Butler, but the nineteenth-century liberalism which he cherished left us all free to take sides in politics, so long as we kept it out of the classroom. I was strongly for the "Square Deal" of Theodore Roosevelt, for whom I cast my first vote as a citizen, but, as my field was European history, I could treat the era of reform as a whole, not merely as an American episode. The long struggle for social legislation in Great Britain reached a climax in Lloyd George's battle cry that the one enemy was poverty, and in the sudden emergence of a powerful Labor Party. Even reactionary Bismarck had brought social legislation to Germany a generation earlier, and France in its slow, traditional but steady pace moved into the new era. Humanity, I insisted, was on the march, not merely because of its leaders, but because the Industrial Revolution

71

forced it out of its old grooves, which had worn deep with ancient wrongs and would lead to the dead end of revolution if reforms were not at hand.

It was into this world which was concentrating upon the problems of peace that World War I came with a devastating force unparalleled since the fall of Rome. No wonder that those whose lives had been spent in social reform, and statesmen like Senator La Follette and President Wilson himself, led in a movement for neutrality. There was an echo of Washington's Farewell Address in Wilson's call for neutrality in thought as well as in action—an echo repeated through the entire history of the United States until it had become the unquestioned voice of the nation.

As long as it was a purely European war the policy of non-involvement held, but for those who like me were convinced—and historical research now bears me out—that Germany and Austria were guilty of having forced the issue on the battlefield, neutrality in thought was utterly immoral. Yet, as the mass murder of the trenches continued month after month, the conscience of the nation seemed deadened. By the autumn of 1916 it was clear that unless we joined the embattled forces of freedom, we should find ourselves alone, without allies, faced with a ruthless German military power, dominant not only in Europe but on the high seas and throughout the world. In short, the European war was already becoming a world war before we joined in it. I had no idea then, however, that I would have any part to play in the mobilization of the country for war or in the shaping of the peace, still less that the quiet sequestered life of a history professor was ended. But that is what happened.

Almost immediately after the United States declared war in April, 1917, I went to Washington to see what historians could do by way of national service. A group of us from all the larger universities gathered together in the offices of the American Historical Association, with Dr. John F. Jameson, the executive head of that body, and Waldo G. Leland, his secretary, cooperating to the full, and I found myself chairman of a National Board for

Historical Service. Although a voluntary body, it was a branch of the wartime Committee on Public Information, which consisted of the Secretaries of War, Navy and State, with a forthright journalist, George Creel, as its director.

George Creel was a very impulsive and outspoken Colorado product. He was a journalist who used American slang to the full. However, he was not a self-seeker, and his loyalty to Wilson was a complete and absolute loyalty for the rest of his life. He was loyal also to Newton Baker, and the only thing that could be brought against him was that Wilson himself, who liked Creel and liked his outspoken, frank and open methods of dealing with people, kept him there when there was a great deal of opposition to him. He was a roughneck through and through but an honest man.

The Committee on Public Information became the propaganda organ of the Government for the war.

There were other such semi-official bodies in Washington. It is the way a democracy, unprovided with a great bureaucracy, mobilizes its non-military resources. Both Great Britain and the United States met the demands of war without militarizing themselves. As for our National Board for Historical Service, we began work by sending a circular to historians insisting that wartime writings should not reflect wartime emotions—nothing that one would be ashamed of ten years after the war was over—an admonition not easy to carry out in the strain and stress of war. The main document we published was *The President's War Message and the Facts Behind It*. This was distributed very widely throughout the country. Some five million copies or so were printed by the Committee on Public Information. It may have had some influence on American public opinion, but from my experience in connection with it I am rather doubtful. I think the country swung in support of Wilson under his leadership rather than from arguments of an academic and historical nature.

I say this because of an experience that I had myself. In the very early days of the war there was doubt in the minds of men like Secretary of War Baker and his associates as to whether the country would respond to the call to arms. This was especially felt in territories like Wisconsin, and perhaps Minnesota and Iowa, very largely populated by settlers of Germanic origin. It was also felt that the country was utterly unprepared for it, and on that I can bear definite witness. The isolation of the United States in 1916 can best be illustrated by the fact that while the Battle of Verdun was at its height—a murderous and desperate battle in which over two million Frenchmen either perished or were forced out of the fighting as wounded or prisoners—I recall going down to Times Square and seeing half a dozen people watching the war bulletins on one side of the *Times* building, and a mob of a thousand people watching the baseball score on the street opposite. That is a good example of the way in which the war had deadened the horrors of the conflict, and how the continued, apparently ineffective action of either side had led to a dead, dull feeling of apathy concerning the issue itself on the part of a great many Americans.

That was the situation which Baker and the Cabinet felt might prove serious when the draft began, and that was one reason why George Creel, as a lively journalist, was put at the head of the Committee on Public Information, and we, as historians, were invited to co-operate. The evidence was clear, however, in the office of the Committee. Its main floor front room—formerly the parlor of a private house—was filled nearly a foot high with unsorted letters of inquiry from families in the United States asking why their boys were going to be forced into a world war. It was a puzzlement, a bewilderment, a symbol of uncertainty in our national purpose.

We thought we were doing something that might counter that movement. The reason I think that our efforts were unnecessary from one point of view, at least with reference to the major reaction of the country, was this: the part of the United States that first passed its quota in the draft was not New York City, where the people were calling upon the Middle West not to fail in its duty in the hour of crisis—it was Indiana that led! When I saw that that was the case, and that after Indiana came Iowa and the other Midwestern states, all of them ahead of New England and the Eastern states in filling the draft, I came to the conclusion that our academic conception of American patriotism was wrong. I learned from the people who came in from the Middle West that there was just one battle cry for the Americans at that time—a simple one: "Uncle Sam wants us. He needs us, and we're coming."

I remember speaking at that time of the need of conceiving of Uncle Sam as an American sovereign—some kind of individualizing of the national purpose, such as the English have in the Crown.

The National Board for Historical Service developed other pamphlets similar to the one on the President's war message in a series called "The Red, White and Blue Pamphlets." These were marked across the corners with the colors of red, white and blue. Among them were a war dictionary, an encyclopedia of events that were taking place in Europe and their background, and historical discussions of the great questions that were being raised by the war itself and regarding our future relations with European powers. The whole series became quite important, and was carried on by my successor, at that time the Dean of the Graduate Faculty of the University of Illinois, Evarts B. Greene.

Another aspect, however, of the Board's work was our connection with historians, libraries, and archives throughout the country, especially the state archives and state libraries, to make sure that there was a record kept of American history during the war. This was not to be merely military history, which would be looked after by the Department of War and other official organs, but would describe the impact of the war upon American thought, literature and social life.

Another of the problems, of course, was to make sure that some of the records in Washington would be kept and made more available for future historians. We didn't get very far with that, however, because the records piled up so fast and the activities of the war grew so tremendous in Washington that it was impossible to keep a current record. That became a subject of my later investigations when I took over the *Economic and Social History of the World War* for the Carnegie Endowment for International Peace.

CHAPTER 7

The Paris Peace Conference

The Inquiry, Colonel House and President Wilson

One day in September, 1917, there was a telephone message from Mr. Herbert Croly, editor of the *New Republic,* that Colonel House wanted to see me. I had spent the late spring and most of the summer in Washington, from the first weeks of America's entry into the World War, as chairman of the National Board of Historical Service, the wartime organization of the historians of the country, and then had fallen ill, a victim to heart and germs, and spent most of August and September in the country. I had, therefore, no knowledge of any antecedent action which led to the telephone call, but gathered from Mr. Croly's few cautious words that "the Colonel" wanted to see me in connection with preparations for the Peace Conference which would sooner or later have to be called at the end of the World War.*

Mr. Croly had no further information or directions for me, except one personal caution, that I must be at my appointment next morning with Colonel House at the exact time set for it, for not only did he insist on punctuality, but this was too important an appointment to be delayed a moment.

I met Colonel House for the first time in his own apartment where he introduced me to his brother-in-law, Dr. Sidney E. Mezes, president of the College of the City of New York. I learned that Dr.

* Much of this chapter is drawn from my book, *At the Paris Peace Conference* (New York: Macmillan, 1937), now out of print.

Mezes was to have charge of the organization of a group of students of international affairs drawn chiefly from the faculties of the universities, whose duty it would be to study the political, economic, legal, and historical elements of the problems which would have to be faced in the treaty of peace. Technically it was connected with the State Department, but really it was to be the President's personal staff under Colonel House's direction. Our only other colleague as yet was David Hunter Miller, whom I then came to know as a lawyer in whose judgment Colonel House had learned to place great confidence and whose great services at the Peace Conference are known to the few who have studied the documents of its history which he had printed for researchers. Mr. Miller became at Paris one of President Wilson's most trusted advisers. At the opposite pole from this quiet but sure jurist was the sensitive and imaginative genius of his associate, Walter Lippmann, who during the early months of the work of the organization (he left to become a captain in Military Intelligence in the following summer) acted as secretary under Dr. Mezes, and so became the chief liaison between it and Colonel House, as well as being directly in touch with the President. My first task was to help procure the acceptance of a group of associates in the fields of history, geography, and economics who would be able to concentrate upon specific questions and have the results of their research ready when these issues came up for decision at the Peace Conference.

Those who joined the group in the autumn of 1917 under the direction of Dr. Mezes found in him a quiet-mannered gentleman of the old school, devoted to his task with patriotic ardor and modestly aware of the fact that not only was the task an unfamiliar one—for never before had universities been mobilized for such a service—but that it called for specialists whose interests lay in a different academic world from that of undergraduate instruction, in which he had been chiefly engaged. The distinction between research and education consists almost as much in an attitude of mind as in a difference of occupation. The problems of education call for different administrative methods from those of research. Researchers in proportion to their competence must be granted freedom in methods and conclusions. The researchers in this instance were to be drawn from the highest academic capacity in the country and it was not long before they began to form a democracy of their own. Dr. Mezes clearly felt that he was not one of them, but now and again made the mistake of attempting to control when he could not direct.

One of the first to join us was Professor Archibald Coolidge, of Harvard, recognized as the outstanding authority in the American academic world on the history of Eastern Europe and a master of the literature of European diplomatic history. Coolidge and I were in agreement that in preparation for the coming Peace Conference, geography would play a large part, and this led to the suggestion that we should at once secure the co-operation of Dr. Isaiah Bowman,* Director of the American Geographical Society, the one scientific body for geographical research in America. So secret was the organization as yet, however, that Dr. Bowman could not lay the matter before the whole body of his trustees, and it was only toward the close of the year that a conservative statement was made to the Council of the American Geographical Society. It is impossible to estimate Dr. Bowman's services both before the Peace Conference and during it, for there was more than one critical period in the history of the research organization in which his steadfastness and directness of purpose, as well as the confidence of his colleagues in his high scientific competence, saved the organization not only from disintegration but almost from complete collapse.

Very different from his associates, both in temperament and in method of work, was George Louis Beer, to whom was assigned the important section of Anglo-American relations and the question of colonial policy as well as certain economic problems. Mr. Beer was looked upon by many as having a pro-British bias, but his ancestry was Continental and German, and the judgments which he had reached concerning British colonial policy had been based solely upon historical investigation. Carefully discriminating between prejudice and fact, he had written in outspoken protest against false conceptions of British history which had so largely colored popular American opinion. He was to justify his appointment by earning the confidence of every person at the Peace Con-

* Later President of Johns Hopkins University.

ference. His death a year after the Peace Conference was over was a greater loss to his country and the organization of world affairs than can ever be measured.*

Our first quarters were in the New York Public Library, where our work was to be carried on in absolute secrecy. There were no names or labels attached to any of our material which would give an outsider the least idea of what we were doing.

It was necessary to find some name for the organization which would be perfectly blind to the general public, but which, nevertheless, would serve to identify it among the initiated. I suggested "The Inquiry," and although none of us was quite satisfied that this was a good name for it, it was adopted by the paradox that its very inadequacy was its best recommendation.

My work slipped back into that of history, diplomatic and social, dealing with problems that on the side were germane to those of international law—as for instance in the study of the question of the Straits and Constantinople—and on the other hand were both political and economic. At this juncture, I transferred my office to the Library of Columbia University, partly because the Geographical Building became rather crowded and partly because Columbia had a more nearly complete collection of source material in my field.†

My division contributed miscellaneous studies on all kinds of subjects—ready reference guides to European diplomatic history, studies on German, British and French foreign policy, the alignment of European political parties on questions like those which might come up at the Peace Conference, analysis of public opinion in Trade Unions, Chambers of Commerce, speeches, and periodicals.

Some of this work was academic and unusable in the rapid hours of the Peace Conference, and the career diplomats in Paris ridiculed the mass of reference books and documents of which I had charge,

---

* I have written an account of Mr. Beer's services at the Peace Conference in a memorial volume, *George Louis Beer,* published after his death by The Macmillan Company (New York, 1924). (He was the originator of the plan for mandates to deal with colonial problems.)

† I had been on leave of absence from Columbia University from the time the United States entered the war.

but they soon found that even some of the more obscure studies were of real importance in the making of a treaty which was recasting the structure of political and economic life in Europe. Career diplomacy was out of place, and our reference material was eagerly used by other governments than our own. But in preparing it at the Inquiry, I arranged a series of meetings with representatives of European governments or factions, held for the most part in the evenings and in a private dining room at the Columbia University Club.

The most important of these were the "seminars" in which President Masaryk expounded his ideas for middle and south-eastern Europe, with a map which he had prepared for us. That is now only a sad memory, but it should be said that even then not all of us thought his Jeffersonian democracy would work where it was understood by so few. This, however, was by far the best of our contacts. Sometimes they were absurd. The Syrians had a banquet in the old Waldorf Hotel to celebrate "the liberation of Syria" from the Turks. But no mention was made of Allenby or of the British, which became clear when the French Consul General acted as host. The speeches began with the soup and kept up throughout the dinner. I asked why, and was told that each speaker stood for a different organization and needed the distinction of speaking "in the presence of the representative of the United States Government." Only one spoke in Syriac, and when he spoke to me in good English I complimented him on it. He was the editor of the most important Syriac paper in Brooklyn, and next day came out against France and for Great Britain in Syria, because the dinner committee told him his English was poor and I had said it was good! I give this incident in full because it was a sobering reminder of the need for care in applying "self-determination" in the Peace Treaty.

Naturally the State Department was not happy at the way the Inquiry was apparently supplanting it in the preparations for the Peace Conference. Men whose lives had been spent in diplomatic service could hardly be expected to regard favorably the creation of a temporary body of so-called experts as the President's advisers in so many important aspects of the negotiation of peace, nor to look forward with equanimity to the prospect of having this improvised organization take any formal part in the work of the Peace Conference. Although the Inquiry might be regarded as simply an "ad hoc" commission to deal with a single problem, the State Department properly felt that the problem in this particular case covered practically the whole field of our foreign relations at the most critical, and even revolutionary, turning point in the history of American diplomacy. In their eyes it was one thing for the President to have a personal adviser in Colonel House, but widely different for the Colonel's staff to develop to the point of displacing the established governmental organ for foreign affairs.

So long as the Inquiry was simply preparing memoranda for future use it did not create for the State Department the problem of a rival organization. Throughout the war the whole world had become accustomed to regard President Wilson as his own foreign minister. The State Department, however, knew only too well that this had been the case from the very first days of his presidency. Owing to Colonel House's personal relations with the President, the Inquiry was, in this sense, the President's personal staff. It became this more definitely at Paris, where the President almost completely ignored his Secretary of State, Lansing, a fact which Lansing bitterly develops in his memoirs.

But the Colonel had no idea of supplanting the Secretary, having always avoided any office that called for administration. He had a gift for personal negotiation, a gift to the point of genius, shrewd in his judgments on men and naïf about the possibilities of international organization. The very simplicity of his mind enabled him to get behind the façade of any man he might be dealing with and think through his mind. There were times when his judgment was wrong, but he was right on many important matters. Although a Democrat, in the full Texan sense of that word, he tried to prevent Wilson from his head-on collision with Senator Lodge and his fellow Republicans. In this he failed, but his choice of Foch as Supreme Commander of the allied forces was a turning point in the war.

This was made in a meeting of the Supreme War Council at Doullens in northern France in March, 1918. Pétain, the head of the French army, struck House as too cautious, afraid to risk attack-

81

ing the Germans at a time when Ludendorff was launching his great assault. Foch, whose courage was a legend since the first battle of the Marne, offered to undercut the wing of the German army, convinced that it was not so strong as it looked. House convinced the Council that Foch, although a divisional commander—he was never commander in chief of the French army—should be given the supreme command. His strategy was followed and was justified by victory.

It was inevitable that at Paris there were those in Wilson's entourage who were bitterly opposed to Colonel House's influence and power, telling the President that the Colonel was betraying the Wilsonian program by secret dealings with the allied leaders. This came to a head one afternoon when the President called unexpectedly on the Colonel and found Lloyd George with him. Then on his way out he met Clemenceau coming in. From that day on, as the Colonel himself told me, House never got to see the President on any matter of importance. House always felt that if he could have had five minutes with Wilson to explain the situation, the breach could have been healed. It never was.

It is not too much to say that today's generation and the future generations will never be able to know what Woodrow Wilson meant to the world throughout the year 1918. At a time when the moral forces of humanity were surrendering to bleak despair, he summoned them again to action. When the war had become mere meaningless carnage, he stated the purposes of nations in terms which won homage on both sides of the front. In the darkest hour of disillusionment, he rallied the forces of civilization from their helpless involvement in universal destruction to a task not of rebuilding the outworn structure of the past but of creating a world community of which mankind had, until then, hardly dared to dream. Never before had any single individual in secular history been able to exert an influence like this. It was a world leadership, for which he himself had not been ready in the earlier years of the war, and from which, by heredity and training, his mind at first had sought to escape by insisting upon America's isolation and tradition of neutrality.

The only hope for the permanent establishment of peace on the Wilsonian terms lay in securing the co-operation, first on the part of the Allies, and then upon that of the Central Powers, to make these terms substantially their own. Neither Wilson nor House expected to find a full measure of this co-operation in the wartime governments of Europe; their faith was in the outlook of the common man, a faith which linked their ideals with those of the American and French Revolutions through Jeffersonian democracy. In any case, Wilson was always on his guard when dealing with his European colleagues. Indeed, the records show that he even distrusted them unjustly at times; it is an utterly wrong perspective of history which presents the American participation in the Peace Conference as the only liberalizing agency there.

No one nation has a monopoly on the ideas of progress. There were those in the American Delegation who interpreted the "new freedom" in terms of reactionary nationalism and whose concern for democracy failed to include that of the Central Powers. On the other hand, there was liberalism to be reckoned with in French and British opinion. France, it is true, was represented at the Peace Conference by Clemenceau, with Foch in the background. But when the delegations really came to know one another, they discovered men like M. Fontaine, a true citizen of Europe, who framed the program for France in Part XIII of the Treaty, and some French colonial experts, who, while they held a different theory of colonial administration from that of the British, were proud of a tradition of successful local government. Other elements were there as well, representing the traditional liberalism of the Third Republic, based on a sincere regard for "the rights of man and the citizen." Still larger was the proportion of those in the British Delegation who were in agreement with the fundamentals of the American position.

Although Lloyd George had fought his December election with the slogan that Germany must pay to the last pfennig and that the Kaiser should be tried, the British Delegation was largely composed of statesmen sincerely bent upon making a peace which would be a lasting bulwark against the recurrence of European wars. This applies to Lloyd George as well, in spite of his pronouncements in the election campaign. Indeed, when the Treaty began to take concrete form in the shape of boundaries and the terms imposed on Germany, it was Lloyd George who, on more than one occasion, upheld the cause for moderation even against Wilson himself. At the very last, the protest against a "Punic Peace" reached such dimensions in the British Delegation and the Ministries in London as to threaten the disruption of the Conference itself.

To the new states as well as to the old, Wilson presented a challenge which accepted nationalism but turned it against itself. Had Germany triumphed, the "pax Germanica" which it would have imposed upon the conquered would have resembled in some degree the "pax Romana," a peace held down by garrisons in the danger zones of Europe, or at least a Holy Alliance with William in the place of Alexander. Wilson's conception was the opposite of this. There was nothing in it of universal empire, no effort to retrace the processes of history. Instead of this he accepted the historic heritage of the modern age, with all its diversity of states and government anarchy by applying a device familiar to American thinking, a "Monroe Doctrine for the world," which would give a corporate guaranty against interference by reactionary and imperialistic powers. The supreme tragedy lay in the renunciation of this endeavor to apply its experience to solve the disorders of an unbalanced world.

It is time now to turn back to the story. For it I plunder my Diary:

The Voyage of the *George Washington*
Tuesday, December 3, 1918

My career as a Peace Conference official began at nine tonight. I got out of the Tube at Hoboken and was dragging my parcels along with me through River Street when a soldier challenged me, and then I discovered that the whole pier-front was closely guarded by troops. Pier 2 was at the far end of the street—as it is sure to be if you have a heavy lot of bundles. There my passport was waiting for me; and after twenty minutes or so an army officer came along and escorted a little group of us through to the ship. Of course, it was down at the other end of the piers, and we trudged along like very humble representatives of a great Republic, with our baggage jostling against our legs. The wharf itself had been turned into a series of reception halls by flags draped from the beams and bunting festooned along the walls of the passageway. At the gangplank our passports were examined by an army officer and our names verified. Then we went on board—to be met by a row of young naval officers, who at once challenged us again—and were listed as we showed our passports once more. A lieutenant then showed us to the executive officer, who turned us over to his adjutant, who again looked at the passports and then told us which rooms we had been assigned. Every aisle has a sentry pacing up and down it, and at every turn of the stairs a marine is posted, so that officers and men are eternally at salute. It is very military and the total effect reassuring, if a little bothersome.

When its former German owners named the ship *George Washington* to attract American passengers, they little thought that that would make it one day the flagship of our navy at the close of a war with theirs. For, apart from its name, the ship has no particular distinction. It is comfortable and large enough, but is not in the front rank of ocean liners. It is admirably fitted, however, for such a journey as this, a sort of ocean-going *Mayflower,* or presidential yacht, with ample room for the official party and quarters for several hundred more of the Expeditionary Force. Not much has been done to it, apparently, to fit it up for this voyage, beyond transforming the library into a working room for Military Intelligence with a large blackboard and maps, which fail to impress our geographers. The State Department has had the assignment of the rooms, but there are likely to be some changes before long.

Wednesday morning, December 4, 1918

The President has come on board. Secretary Baker came with him. He is a very unassuming, quiet-mannered man, and breakfasted with us instead of with the presidential party, but has now left the ship, which is casting off.

Later

As we slid out from the dock and headed south, the President's flag was broken out on the mainmast, and five destroyers, waiting in the river to escort us, fired the presidential salute of twenty-one

85

guns. We replied, and the din was terrific. But that was only part of it. The river was full of craft; it looked as if all the tugs of the harbor had come to see us. The water was thick with them; and each one blew as long and loud a blast as it could. We could see people on the shores as well, especially at Battery Park, where there must have been ten thousand people or more along the sea-wall. Then we slowly pulled away from the crowded upper harbor, passing the Statue of Liberty, in procession, with two army airplanes playing around us. At the Narrows we were given a return salute from the guns of the old *Monitor,* which was anchored at the open end of the net that had been placed there to block the channel against submarine attack.* As we passed through the gate in the submarine net, which brought us close to the Staten Island shore, we saw hundreds of school children waving flags, and that was the last clear glimpse we had of those on shore. At the tip of Long Island, on the east, there were crowds almost like those at the Battery, but we were already too far out to recognize those whom I knew were there, so we waved back a symbolical good-by and turned to watch the pageant ahead.

Out on the lower bay the battleship *Pennsylvania* was waiting for us, and the destroyers took up positions before, beside and behind us. There were eleven of them, a whole flotilla. Airplanes kept circling around us, much as in the river and bay, until we were almost out of sight of land, and a navy balloon from a guard ship looked down on us until another dirigible came up and gave us a final Godspeed, and then sailed off to the Long Island shore.

The President was on the bridge as we backed out into the Hudson, but went down to his quarters before we were out of the harbor. The ship is tossing lightly on heavy rollers from the south-east.

Saturday, December 7, 1918

There is little to record, even on a presidential ship. In spite of having every comfort that goes with such official state, the trip is beginning to be monotonous, one day like another.

* This was part of the wartime defense of New York harbor. An iron net was fastened to the shore by the Narrows to be drawn completely across the channel in case of need. An ancient battleship was stationed alongside, close to the forts.

86

We are now in southern seas and the air is as warm as June. We have windows wide open and sit out on the deck without overcoats or wraps and are too hot when in the sun, protected from the wind. We are said to be about four hundred miles due west of the Azores now. We expect to get to Brest on Friday the thirteenth—a date to land on!

I have a single room on the promenade deck. The presidential suite is on the deck below, only a few feet away from the stairway. A guard is on duty at the door all the time. He, or another marine, follows closely behind the President whenever he takes a walk along the deck. Mrs. Wilson is not guarded. The President does not mingle indiscriminately with the rest of the party, although others join him from time to time. The presidential dining room is the small sitting room adjoining the bedroom. The Secretary of State, the Ambassadors and personal advisers of the President eat in the rear lounge. This leaves the main dining room free for the Inquiry and the lesser officials of various sorts.

The President has not called in any of us as yet or paid any attention to our presence. But this aloofness seems to apply to his Secretary of State as well. It was only yesterday (as I am told) that he began to hold conferences with Lansing. We are all perfectly in the dark as to how useful we may be when we get across. Meanwhile we are taking it easy, although with some restiveness and grouching. But it won't be long before we'll all know about our job and be hard at it. I suppose the President is busy at his now.

Tuesday afternoon, December 10, 1918

Today I saw St. Michael of the Azores and missed an interview with the President at the same time. The President chose this moment to send for a few of us, including me, to come to his cabin and have a very confidential chat, the first on the trip. Bowman sent his secretary, Storck, to find me. He hunted high and low for twenty minutes but failed in his quest, as I had gone up to the bow to see the guns they used at salute to the Azores. It was no one's fault but my own, as I should have left word with my marine at the cabin door where I had gone. The President talked with some seven or eight of the group for an hour, and they got on splendidly. Everyone feels very much cheered and also begins to see a chance of being called on for really useful work at the big conference ahead of us. The President was very frank and very cordial, so they tell me. If I hadn't been watching the Azores fade out of sight on the northwest horizon, I should have a historic interview to record. However, my colleagues were properly sympathetic, and I hope it won't be the last chance.

After dinner I saw the President again at close range as he sat watching the movie. He conceals his emotions very well, but he was very much absorbed in the emotional scenes and seemed to enjoy them rather intensely. The silhouette of his face against the sidelight across the room showed a very determined-looking man. His front face is much more pleasant than his profile, which is very severe. He has a pleasant smile and his eyes are kindly. Mrs. Wilson sat in front of him and he was very attentive to her comfort. After the show Beer came to my room and we gossiped until midnight again.

December 11, 1918

This afternoon as I came out of the map room of the Military Intelligence for a stroll on deck, one of the men from the State Department came hurrying up to me with the news that word had come from the presidential quarters that I was sent for. Great curiosity! I hurried into the corridor and was accosted by each sentry in passing with the news that the orderlies had been hunting for me for twenty minutes. I went over to the presidential quarters and found that it was "Mrs." Wilson who had sent for me! The mystery grew. Then I found that she was aft, in the lounge, playing bridge. On my way there I met another State Department official who told me it was George Creel who had been asking for me—and the situation was less interesting. However, I found that Creel had the message which the President had written to be given as a greeting to the President of France on landing and wanted me to turn it into French. There was nothing to do but to accept, and I got with Haskins for part of the job and went at it by myself for the rest. Before risking giving it back to the President, however, we turned it over to Ambassador Jusserand for his suggestions, and I have seldom seen a school theme more marked up than the corrected document that came back to us. The incident is not without historic interest, for M. Jusserand, in conversation, made the point that Wilson's phraseology had become so familiar to French-speaking people that it was necessary to keep as closely as possible to the original English in order to give the flavor of Wilson's own speech.

Friday morning, December 13, 1918

Last night after the movie, which the President seemed to enjoy, we sang "God be with you till we meet again" and "Auld Lang Syne." At 4 A.M. the engines slowed down. It is now 7:30 and I'm up on the upper bridge looking out over a rather smooth but gray sea, with about eighteen destroyers in a great horseshoe around us. One has already brought out a pilot, and away on the horizon to the east, just visible across the stretch of water, lie at least eight of our battleships in line waiting for us.

Later (from notes on the train)

The battleships which preceded us took up a double line in the harbor, with the destroyers behind them and at their sides. We slowed down and came on majestically up to the first of the line. Then the President came up to the bridge, where I had been writing the previous pages of this account, and stood not ten feet away from me as he reviewed the fleet. (Later, he was on the top bridge for the last of it.) The guns on our ship gave their deafening salute as we nosed up to the great line. Then each of the battleships had its crew standing in a long line all around the deck, at attention, and as we passed, ship by ship the crews cheered, so that you could hear the voices distinctly across the little stretch of water. Then each ship's band played the national anthem, and we stood with bared heads.

When the last battleship had been passed, our ship dropped anchor. Then the fleet of destroyers passed in review before us, all the crews at salute. One after another in a long line they came up the alleyway between the big men-of-war and swung around us. If you have seen them battling big seas and crossing the whole Atlantic for a week, you know how to appreciate the men who sail these little craft—and who saved the war for us by destroying submarines. They are the real heroes of the sea.

The President, however, was not given long to view this pageantry. Down on the deck and in his stateroom, two delegations had already assembled to greet him, having come on board from launches as we were slowly entering the harbor. There were the high dignitaries of France, M. Pichon, Minister of Foreign Affairs, and M. Leygues, Minister of Marine, along with the heads of our Expeditionary Force and the civilians in charge of American interests in France, Generals Pershing and Bliss, Admirals Sims and Benson, Ambassador Sharp, and others. The greetings over, it seemed only a few minutes until the launches were cutting loose from the side of the ship, with the President and his party in one of them. It was the end of the voyage.

The First Days in Paris
Paris, Saturday, December 14, 1918*

I slept little on the train and was dressed as we drew up by the siding south of Versailles and, looking out, saw the great château. A hurried cup of coffee and a slice of bread made breakfast, and by the time it was over we were in Paris. As we stepped off the train, David Hunter Miller and Frank Warrin were on the platform, also Walter Wanger, a cousin of Beer's who took us and a journalist friend, Bullitt, to the hotel. We hesitated a little at accepting the army car, but Lieutenant Wanger, a very jolly boy, assured us we were going to have "major-generals do our laundering," and all things on a similar scale! We were the first car out, the first of the Peace Commission to arrive.

Place de la Concorde! You can't imagine what a sight it was. Every part of the square not needed for street was packed with captured German cannon. We caught a glimpse in passing of the Champs Élysées, with miles of cannon on each side of the driveway. France's trophies.

As we came along, people were already hurrying in throngs to get good places to see Wilson arrive. His train had been run onto

* This description of Wilson's arrival in Paris is from a letter home.

a siding out in the country (at Plouart in Brittany) to give him a night's rest, and he was due to arrive at ten.

Colonel House and his associates have already established themselves in the Hôtel de Crillon. After a survey of our quarters there we went up to the International Law Section(Mr. Miller's) of the office building to look out over the Place de la Concorde on the crowds which were packing every inch of space to wait for the coming of Wilson. We were at the windows at the corner of the Place and the Rue Royale up which the President was to come, so we had the best view in Paris of this historic sight.

The tribute of respect which Paris paid to Wilson was one that I never saw the like of and shall never see again. As one of the papers put it, it was a "pious privilege" on the part of the populace of Paris to see the man who is in their eyes and in the eyes of most of the oppressed of Europe the first moral force in the world today. The tribute was more than a casual one; it was obviously heartfelt. In spite of the size and density of the crowd, which moved in swirling eddies between the piles of cannon and the twisting, narrow files of the Garde Républicaine and the regular troops that were keeping the roadway open, there was almost no sound of voices loud enough to reach the third story of the building.

Already the long lines of horizon blue poilus stretched away across the Place and over the bridge. In the crowds the dominant colors were the black of the women, and the blue or khaki of soldiers on leave—little else, except where a red turban of an African showed like a single point of contrast. Horizon blue is the most beautiful color you can imagine. It is a tender blue, like that on distant hills. And when you recalled that those poilus, slouching at ease in typical French soldier fashion, were the very men who had taken from the Germans the cannon which were parked up behind them in the great spaces of the square, you got a queer feeling in your throat just watching them there, waiting for Wilson, "Wilson the Just" (le juste), as they have called him on one big placard.

Soon troops of artillery moved into position at the angles of the square. People jumped up on the gun carriages, the soldiers helping them up. Looking down from our windows we could see the crowds converging down the different streets into the square like a solid black stream, filling the streets from side to side. The soldiers tried to keep a single trackway open for the President from the bridge over the Seine through the Place de la Concorde and on into the Rue Royale. But the pressure of the crowd was so great that the line of soldiers was moved in and out until the space which they were to keep clear was all indented and twisted instead of being a straight line held in place by an immovable row of soldiers. There may have been anywhere from fifty thousand to a hundred thousand people in the square before Wilson came.

Then guns started booming over by the riverbank, a little to the southwest, by the railroad station of the Luxembourg, where Wilson's train had arrived. We could see the smoke. The crowds began to strain against the guards. Over the river we soon saw the bright helmets of the Garde Républicaine, the same old splendid-looking guards on very fine horses—the war has left some—and behind them, first a closed carriage, then an open one, and in it Wilson and Madame Poincaré. We saw him very well. He was bowing and raising his silk hat all the time. The people cheered wildly. Then Monsieur Poincaré and Mrs. Wilson—also cheered by the crowd, but less. Then files of carriages and soldiers, and it was over.

As for the crowd, it was out for all it could see, and our well-decked quarters got much attention. It was a public holiday. Everything was closed up tight. All Paris was on the boulevards, and that afternoon and night they were packed. I never saw more people. In the evening five of us took an army car and drove through the boulevards until we were finally unable to move, and then slowly turned off into a side street. A funny side to it was that in the shadow of the interior of the car, Beer was taken for Wilson in disguise by people in the crowd—not only once but half a dozen times. They caught his profile; and then, as Haskins said, the rest of us looked like strong-arm men—with the exception of me, whom Haskins proposed for a counterfeit House. Soldiers and officers in the crowd were having their caps stolen (snatched from behind for souvenirs), and most were bareheaded; but they stayed on—sometimes, I'm afraid, following their caps. There was a good deal of rather more than cordial fellowship, but none of the boisterous quality of the New York crowd at the celebration of peace.

We edged our way bit by bit along the great boulevards till we came to the Boulevard Strasbourg, which cuts off at right angles, and turned down it to the river. In a few hundred yards we had gone six hundred years, through the silence of deserted streets, by the Palace of St. Louis over to Notre Dame, standing out massive and almost spectral in the darkness. There were only a few street lights at long intervals, except on the boulevards, and, even there they seemed to be only about half power. The side streets were almost pitch dark. We turned south from Notre Dame and up the hill of Ste. Geneviève by the old Roman road, the Rue St. Jacques, which still bears the mark of the Roman engineer, past the site of the church where Clovis was baptized, and swung around the Panthéon, which crowns that hill with its tribute to France's immortals—*Aux Grands Hommes la Patrie reconnaissante,* as the motto reads across the architrave above the pillars of its façade. There were no crowds here; it was absolutely still and quite dark. We turned the search light of the car upon Rodin's *Penseur,* standing out in front of the great shadowy mass of the façade of the church—and that was the last impression that I carried away from Wilson's day in Paris.

Monday, December 16, 1918[*]

I began my duties as Librarian of the Delegation by a visit to the Bibliothèque de la Guerre, the library which has been established to gather every book, article, or scrap of paper that is of any importance for future historians of the World War. It is housed in a street that runs north from the Champs Élysées, and not far from the Hôtel de Crillon. The Librarian is Camille Bloch, a historian whose volume on the care of the poor in the old régime on the eve of the French Revolution was one that I had reviewed at length in the *Political Science Quarterly* years before, and had sent him a

[*] The diary from this point on was dictated each night to Dr. Preston Slosson (now Professor of History at the University of Michigan). Dr. Slosson had taken his doctorate in history with me at Columbia, and I was fortunate in having him with me throughout the Conference. He did not have shorthand, but was an expert at the typewriter, and each night he sat by my bedside taking down the record of the day. Some items, of course, were not recorded.

copy of my review. It was a fortunate coincidence, for it opened the doors of French bureaucracy, and he set about getting the wheels started which would permit us to have free access to all their documents. I came back to the Crillon very well satisfied with the first contact with the French.

Then came the reception for Wilson at the Hôtel de Ville, to which I had received an invitation. The drive from the Crillon to the Hôtel de Ville was through streets with crowds at least eight deep or more all the way on either side behind the long row of regular troops that guarded the driveway down the center of the street. The ceremony in the gilded hall of the Hôtel de Ville was stately enough, with the guards presenting arms along the corridors; but the unforgettable part, once more, was the silence of the crowds along the way. Except for the uniforms of the soldiers, the only color anywhere to be seen was black. I dismissed the army car at the door of the Hôtel de Ville, for I wanted to get the feel of the situation by walking back; and besides I distinctly felt that there was something wrong in my riding past the long line of those sorrowful, war-stricken people. If anyone wants to feel the full measure of the tragedy of war, he will find it here.

By December 24 the books and documents of the Library were unpacked and checked, and consultation with it could be left to the competent hands of the staff. I then got in touch with French statesmen, and on December 24 I had a long talk with M. Albert Thomas, who had been French Minister of Munitions the last year of the war. A firm supporter of the Wilsonian program he had broken with Clemenceau, who then turned bitterly upon him. I found him a winning personality, forceful but with a keen sense of humor.

New Year's day began with a conference of the heads of the Inquiry at which Dr. Mezes explained that the President wanted our conclusions with reference to every problem. As I was not working on any political question, I decided to submit a statement on the need for a clause in the Peace Treaty on child labor, arguing that in the settlement of the major issue this important subject might be lost sight of.

94

MEMORANDUM OF LABOR LEGISLATION

The main interest in the Peace Conference seems to be centered upon divisions of territory, possession of colonies, popular self-determination and self-government, and upon such economic topics as indemnities and questions of trade.

All of these subjects to a large degree are nationalistic in character. They call for maps on the one hand, or statistics on the other. But there is a whole series of questions which lie outside these, and which are of vital interest to as many people, although not so definitely before us—the questions which are associated with labor, with the demands of the great masses who are suspicious of this assemblage of diplomatists. . . .

The Congress of Vienna banned the slave trade. The Congress of Paris-Versailles must save the children. For the future upbuilding of democracy this is essential. Singly, nations cannot be allowed to depend upon themselves; they are too near exhaustion and are calling on their children to help. Little boys of seven or eight are dragging great carts through the streets of Paris—little boys with a strip of black on the arm. They must not be permitted to lack the education which would make free men of them. France alone cannot deny herself their labor, if Germany is using them, for she would lose the industries they make possible. Belgium and Italy need even more the moral and joint support of the League of Nations. Fortunately England, by the great Education Bill of last winter, has laid down a program for us all. Unfortunately, the United States Supreme Court, by its decision of last June, declared the child labor law there unconstitutional—having regard to southern mill-owners. That one decision now stands in our way like a mountain, for it makes it difficult for the United States to take the lead. Besides, the only way to enforce the legislation would be the way the American law attempted it, by control of commerce—forbidding trade in articles made by children. We'll have to do tall fighting to get it repealed!

Think what it means to put into the acts of this Conference a charter of liberties for the children of the world. They, alone, are not citizens of any one nation with obligations, they are the wards of us all; and the strength of the moral forces of the League would be placed at the one common task of ensuring their liberties. The one hope of democracy is education; it has no safety but through intelligence; here is a guarantee for the future, as well as a security for the present, through the association of the great Powers and the progressive minor peoples in a single purpose.

A glance at this memorandum will explain my colleagues' lack of interest in it, limited as it was to child labor. Yet it had a weight of history behind it. It had been the conditions of child labor even more than that of women in industry, which in the days of the Chartists had called for the first social legislation in England to curb the evils of the factory system. The Parliamentary reports on which Karl Marx had based his attack on capitalism in *Das Kapital,* dealt largely with this situation; yet it was the one aspect of social reform which most clearly avoided the question of class warfare, based as it was upon humanitarian principles.

In the following months, negotiations on labor questions proceeded along an entirely different line from that of presenting problems for specific reforms to be embodied in the Peace Treaty. In building up a permanent organization to deal with the changing and developing programs for labor legislation in the future, I did not lose sight of this interest in child labor legislation, and in spite of a feeling in the Labor Commission that this was not a pressing issue like the eight-hour day, I had the satisfaction of carrying it through on to the program of the first International Labor Conference, that was held in Washington in the autumn of 1919.

My memorandum fell flat in the American Delegation, but the British at once took it up. Lord Eustace Percy, in his capacity as liaison officer of the Foreign Office, put me in touch with Edward Phelan of the British Ministry of Labor, who had arrived in Paris that very day, and I was given complete documentation on the British plans. With the customary efficiency of the British Civil Service they had gone much farther than merely to outline a program of labor clauses for the Peace Treaty. The problems of labor legislation, as they pointed out, could never be wholly settled at any one time and would need for future development the erection of some sort of international organization, capable of carrying on the work from year to year. My own tentative beginnings had not gone beyond the idea of having the League of Nations assume this continuing responsibility. This had also been Lord Percy's point of view and would seem to have had some support in the trade union circles with which Sir Eric Drummond had been in contact. On the other hand, the officials of the Ministry of Labour and Home Office

96

had combined to propose a definite international labor organization which would eventually form part of the organization of the League of Nations but would be set up at once without waiting for the full establishment of the League. None of this inside story of the formation of the British program was known to me at the time. But Mr. Phelan argued effectively that the League of Nations would not be able to mobilize as efficient instruments for actually securing social legislation as a body especially appointed for that purpose.

In the weeks and months that followed, Mr. Phelan and I were destined to work together intimately and at high pressure in the negotiations which led to the creation of the International Labor Organization, and I found him a loyal colleague, fertile and creative of suggestion, one who was never lacking in the understanding of the difficulties confronting the American Delegation, perhaps aided in this by his Irish sense of humor. The International Labor Organization owes more to him than will probably ever be widely known, for both as planner and negotiator he worked impersonally in order to work effectively. The immediate outcome of the talk with him was that I set about the preparation of a more serious and enlarged study of the problems of social legislation, the result of which was summarized in the memoranda of the following days.

The British proposal on labor legislation was not for any special reform but for an international labor organization which could keep pace with the progressive changing conditions and demands of labor, and so secure not one single Labor Charter, but a never-ending series. The idea was a large and fruitful one. So far as labor was concerned, the Paris Peace Conference would be but the first step in a process, the beginning of a continuous co-operation on the part of Labor, Employers and Governments in an International Labor Organization, empowered to draw up international legislation which would go into force without having to pass through foreign offices or parliaments. In the long reaches of political history there is nothing to match this experiment in international legislation on matters which have hitherto lain exclusively with national control. But it was too much of a World Government for acceptance by the United States, even if, by any chance, the British themselves would come to accept it, which strangely enough, did seem to be the case, for it was Balfour who proposed its construction in the Peace Conference.

Wednesday, January 8, 1919

Beer, Young and I were invited by Lord Robert Cecil, British Minister of Blockade during the war, and now head of the British "League of Nations" section of their Delegation here, to dine with him and Lionel Curtis, the brilliant young (forty or over) statesman of the "British Commonwealth" plan of British federation. It was a quiet dinner in Lord Robert's room, and the only other person present was his private secretary, Captain Walters.

We took an army car and got there at eight o'clock. The British have taken two big hotels, the Astoria and the Majestic, and they have a group of very solemn butlers and detectives at the door to look you over—or look over you, as they mostly do—with British imperturbability and in a calm, quiet, efficient manner. There was some reluctance on their part to taking us up to Cecil's rooms, which made the butler apologetic when he discovered that it was all right. Cecil is a very tall man—six feet three or more. When he sits down he slides into the chair and lets his body get under the table, so as he and I sat opposite and looked across at each other, we were both comfortably fixed with our eyes above the tablecloth. After all, Lincoln used to like to sink to his shoulder-blades, so why shouldn't we! He has a massive forehead with a curiously thick shock of brown hair back of it. In some ways he reminded me of Moberly Bell, of the *Times,* especially in the play of a smile on a rather stern face—the sternness entirely contradicted by kindly blue eyes. A modest, quiet man, very serious and very thoughtful, religious in tone, but not without a keen sense of humor. His father, the Marquis of Salisbury, had a much heavier face, to judge by his pictures. His secretary, Captain Walters, is a very lame young veteran, with the quiet manners of England at her best.

We had a simple English dinner, served by English girls—for the British haven't left a single Frenchman in their building, having brought over servants and all—the simple fare being as elaborate as the Crillon menus, with champagne and port in addition! It may have been that which made the subsequent conversation so entertaining. But in any case we handled the League of Nations and settled derelict peoples' fate to our mutual satisfaction. There is no time like this for political philosophy.

Wednesday, January 15, 1919

I am afraid the British may pull out before some of the most important items are settled.

I did not appreciate, at the time, the speed and precision with which my British colleagues were working. It subsequently appeared that the War Cabinet had that very day finally discussed and agreed to a "Joint Memorandum" of the Ministry of Labour and the Home Office on International Labor Legislation which sanctioned the creation of a Commission at the Peace Conference for Labor Legislation. Lord Curzon, Foreign Minister, telegraphed to Mr. Balfour in Paris a summary of the Cabinet decision, and that night the Right Honorable George N. Barnes, representative of Labor in the War Cabinet, crossed over to Paris.

Thursday, January 16, 1919

Bibliothèque Nationale. Introduced Slosson to work there.

Evening—Dinner with Beer, Mezes, and Hornbeck, and Sir Valentine Chirol, Lionel Curtis, and Philippe Millet of *Le Temps*. Millet speaks English so well that Mezes took him for an Englishman, and even at the end of the evening Millet had to remind him that he was "only a poor Frenchman after all." Beer and Curtis waded into Millet on French foreign policy. Millet reacted very strongly but had some caustic comments to make about the French Foreign Office. Chirol, in a reminiscent mood, told his memories of Bismarck's days in Berlin and especially of the man who pulled the wires in the German Foreign Office and to a large degree controlled its policy, Holstein, *"l'éminence grise"* of Wilhelmstrasse. Holstein once said to Chirol that William II would either lose his crown or die in the madhouse. Holstein had secret correspondents in the European capitals and kept spies watching the German ambassadors. Everyone was afraid of him. Von Kuhlmann's share in ruthlessly forcing the Brest Litovsk treaty upon Russia makes impossible his being sent as an envoy to the Peace

Conference, where he would have been a powerful figure. Chirol said that Lichnowsky's tribute to Kuhlmann was due to the fact that he did not want to show how much he had been taken in. Beer and I told Chirol that he should write his memoirs for the public, especially the history of the Entente diplomacy.

A cable from Professor John Bates Clark, Director of the Division of Economics and History of the Carnegie Endowment for International Peace, announced my appointment as editor of the *Economic and Social History of the World War,* which the Carnegie Endowment proposes to publish. It is the same plan which I was offered two years ago. It will involve spending at least three months of every year in Europe.*

Saturday, January 18, 1919

In the morning routine library work with a visit to the Bibliothèque Nationale, where Slosson is hard at work.

Afternoon—First meeting of Peace Conference in plenary session. In the scramble for tickets, the State Department won out over the Inquiry group!

About five o'clock I had an urgent telephone call from Ray Stannard Baker, in charge of American publicity work, that at this first meeting of the Peace Conference, to the surprise of the American Delegation, Clemenceau announced that next to placing responsibility for the war and for crimes committed in it, the third item on the agenda was for labor legislation, on which I have been working, and which, only at three o'clock this afternoon, Dr. Mezes placed in my hands.† Great panic in the newspaper world, as no one knew what was meant; so with the assistance of Frank Warrin, I prepared for Arthur Sweetser, of Baker's staff, a detailed story of Labor's demand's which is to be given to the press. Finished about midnight and continued legal study of the situation with Warrin until about one.

---

* During the Peace Conference the only work I did on the History was to deliver a lecture on its problems at the Sorbonne, under the Hyde Foundation.

† I have no notes of my interview with Dr. Mezes at which this took place. Mr. Gompers was landing in England on this day and did not arrive in Paris until the twenty-second or twenty-third, and spent the first days of his visit with the French labor leaders.

It was not only this one point of the announced program of the Peace Conference that puzzled the journalists, but the fragmentary and apparently hastily improvised program of the meeting as a whole. It gave the impression that somehow or other things behind the scene were not going well, and the inference was quickly drawn that the meeting had been staged more to distract public attention from the real progress of negotiations than to furnish a proper clue as to what was actually taking place. The three points mentioned first on the "Order of the Day" were those which engaged no differences between Allied and Associated Powers, and therefore could be undertaken without long negotiations. But on territorial, financial, and economic questions it looked as though the small Powers were to have to plead their case with the great Powers, and this meant that the storm signals were already set. Although the program announced that the question of the League of Nations would be the first to be taken up at the next session, the way in which the announcement was typed in at the bottom of the page seemed almost to suggest an afterthought. This impression of haste and improvisation was accentuated by the fact that the program itself was not printed, but only mimeographed, as if done at the last moment.

Sunday, January 19, 1919

Slosson and I working on labor questions in my room.

Breakfast with Sweetser at which I read over his mimeographed account of what I had prepared for the press. This was then passed to the Commissioners and given to the press in the afternoon for cabling home.

Baker brings in M. Léon Jouhaux, of the Confédération Générale du Travail, who had drawn up the program of labor of the Leeds Conference of 1916, which has been taken over largely as a basis for suggestion by the Chamber of Deputies. A man in early middle life, forceful but rather quiet, letting the other man do the talking, but able to express himself with moderation and clarity.

Monday, January 20, 1919

Dinner with Feisal and Lawrence—His Royal Highness Emir Feisal, son of the King of the Hejaz and Sherif of Mecca, and

101

Colonel Lawrence, of the British army, the conqueror of Damascus. It was a small dinner arranged by Beer. The other guests were Bullitt, the young journalist who clips the day's news for the Commissioners and sometimes edits it orally for them; Bowman; Westermann (as the specialist on Turkey); and two lieutenants, Wanger and Osborne, who work with Beer.

The Emir wore a long black gown with sleeves, like a professor's gown, with no embroidery except on the shoulder, where there was a network pattern of thread of gold. He wore over his head a light silk cloth that hung down to the shoulders and was tucked away inside the gown in easy folds. Around his head, on top of this simple substitute for a turban, were two rows of large, white braid, bound together by a single gold string. The effect was singularly like a crown.

His face was most attractive, beautifully shaped, with clear, dark eyes that struck us all as being those of a man who, although he has been facing constant danger for many years, retains an irresistible sense of humor. He carries a golden dagger in his girdle, which is woven of gold thread, and when someone remarked on it, he said jokingly that the Parisians said he was only half civilized because he carried a dagger—but their officers carry swords!

This descendant of Mohammed was cracking jokes all evening, even in the midst of his most serious argument for the Arab cause. When he was asked what his right title was, he said that the Western Powers were imagining that they had conferred a favor on his father by calling him king; but his father was only amazed at their impertinence, seeing that a man who was the descendant of the Prophet and Sherif of Mecca bore so proud a title that it could not matter to him whether men called him, in addition, King, Emperor, President, or Donkey. His ancestors had been Sherifs of Mecca for nine hundred years, and no other title in the world compared in splendor. One hundred and eighty million Mohammedans share his view.

Later, when he was presenting the Arab case, he interjected: "You know that out in the desert we often tie the camels head to tail in a long row, and then we put a little donkey at the head to lead the line. Lawrence has been that little donkey."

102

But here were present not one American donkey but seven! What might they not be able to do for Arabia! If they would go out to Arabia they might see for themselves the justice of his demands. Then there would be statues erected to them all over Syria! Noting that we were seven, he recalled the Arab proverb: "When seven agree, the world will become heaven or be utterly destroyed."

His story of the Arab independence movement kept us till about midnight. Colonel Lawrence had to do all the translating, for when they were together in the East, as Feisal jokingly said, Lawrence was so set on learning Arabic that he couldn't be got to talk English, and as he, Feisal, distrusted and disliked the French and so would not learn their language, there was no way to talk except through Colonel Lawrence. But all the same he caught on to what we were doing, and when Bowman asked for his autograph on the dinner card he remarked that everyone of us wrote backward and he alone wrote forward. He asked for Bowman's dinner card in return, and then, bubbling with laughter, asked for a fountain pen and wrote just above his name a line of Arabic and showed it to Lawrence, who said that it read, "I agree to all of Feisal's demands."

Lawrence came in the uniform of a British colonel but wore his Arab headdress to keep his friend company (they wore them through the meal and all the evening). His veil over his explorer's helmet was of green silk and hung down over his shoulder with a tassel or two of deep red. Around his head was a similar double strand of big, corded braid, as in the case of Feisal's, about three-quarters of an inch in diameter and looking much like a crown. He has been described as the most interesting Briton alive, a student of medieval history at Magdalen College, where he used to sleep by day and work by night and take his recreation in the deer park at four in the morning—a Shelley-like person, and yet too virile to be a poet.

He is a rather short, strongly built man of not over twenty-eight years, with sandy complexion, a typical English face, bronzed by the desert, remarkable blue eyes and a smile around the mouth that responded swiftly to that on the face of his friend. The two men were obviously very fond of each other. I have seldom seen

103

such mutual affection between grown men as in this instance. Lawrence would catch the drift of Feisal's humor and pass the joke along to us while Feisal was still exploding with his idea; but all the same it was funny to see how Feisal spoke with the oratorical feeling of the South and Lawrence translated in the lowest and quietest of English voices, in very simple and direct phrases, with only here and there a touch of Oriental poetry breaking through.

Among the experiences which Lawrence recited none was more interesting than his description of what the motorcar and the airplane have done to the desert. He got in his airplane out east of the Jordan one morning, crossed over to Jerusalem to see General Allenby, flew down to Cairo to lunch with the Sirdar of Egypt, then on to Alexandria for a call and back to Jerusalem for afternoon tea (it once took forty years to make the Egypt-Jerusalem trip), and had time before dark to write out his dispatches and plan the next day's campaign, having flown a thousand miles in one day in addition to the day's work. He says that after airplaning in the desert one doesn't want to fly anywhere else. One can land anywhere at any time in safety. The British have established a three-day route across the Arabian Desert from India to Cairo, with one stop at an oasis for lunch in the Arabian desert, passing the night at Basra, and making only one more stop en route to Delhi. He explained the change in desert fighting which the airplane has brought about. The Arabs have to come to water holes, with their camels; an airplane with a machine gun sets out for each water hole and settles down to wait. . . .

Automobiling also is a rare sport and there are two ways of doing it. One is to have a Rolls Royce and put it through at fifty miles an hour, so that it just catches the tops of the dust bumps and almost goes like an airplane. The other way is to have a series of Ford cars stretching across the desert, so that as soon as one breaks down another can be taken. Either one beats camel riding.

Feisal invited us all to come to within ten miles of Mecca to visit him. His father wouldn't mind our coming all the way, but some fanatics in India would think that the Sherif was an unbeliever too, so he guesses it would be best to meet us some miles out from the sacred town. The story of his demands, the serious part of the

104

evening, is being jotted down by Westermann in another chronicle, but Feisal completely won his audience.

Tuesday, January 21, 1919

A visit in my room from Dr. C. T. Wang* who, although technically in rebellion against the Chinese Government, has joined the Chinese Delegation. Nothing could be more typical of China. Formerly head of the Chinese Senate in the short-lived experiment of a Chinese Parliament, he had joined his Cantonese friends in revolt against the coup d'état of the Peking Government. A convinced republican, he came over to the United States during the war to carry on propaganda against the Peking Government. I met him first in the apartment of Francis Sayre, President Wilson's son-in-law, and he visited me once or twice in my own house in New York. He is working with those who are his enemies in China; but the incongruity of the situation seems less evident to them than to us. The Chinese Delegation is at least united in opposition to the Japanese in Shantung and also in the expectation that the United States will not let China down.

From China to Yugoslavia! Dr. Bogumil Vosnjak came to discuss the Slovene question and to renew his acquaintance from New York days. He will supply us with the official documents, particularly with reference to a plebiscite which has been held in the country of the Slovenes and which shows a great growth of Yugoslav feeling. A copy of a second plebiscite taken in the districts bordering Italy will be on hand, to try to meet Italian claims.

Saturday, January 25, 1919

The second session of the Peace Conference met at three o'clock, the session at which Wilson made his great speech. I had a ticket and was all ready to go when Dr. Bowman rang me up to say that Admiral Trowbridge, the British Admiral who had been in charge of Danubian shipping, was coming to his office with Mezes, Seymour, and Day to discuss free waterways and especially the Danube, and they needed me to join in, with a refreshed knowledge of Danubian history. So there was nothing to do but swallow my

---

* Later the well-known Foreign Minister of the Chinese Republic through some of its most critical years, whom I met in Nanking in 1929.

disappointment and forget about the Quai d'Orsay. I had a ripping headache and treaty clauses did not appeal to me, although Dr. Slosson had sat up the night before to prepare Chamberlain's monograph* for speedy consumption by Commissioner Henry White, Mezes, Bowman, and myself against the Admiral's coming.

Trowbridge is the man who let the *Breslau* and *Goeben* escape at the opening of the War but was acquitted by the court-martial by proving that his actions were controlled by the code instructions he had received purporting to come from the Admiralty, while in reality they came from the German warships. In any case, he had more decorations sewed on his coat than he could get on one side and had started a bright patch of color on the other. A British admiral has yards of gold lace on his sleeves, about twice as much as ours. He was a quiet-mannered, unassuming talker, set upon presenting his case as the main thing. He is now in command at Belgrade, and after having directed the water-borne transportation of the eastern Mediterranean during the war, is very keen on developing the river systems so as to open up those countries. He has some eighty-three ships at present running cargoes on the Danube, and pointed out that he could put behind one tug ten barges with as much in them as in three hundred train loads.

When we asked him who owned the ships, he said: "I don't know, I'm running them. This is wartime. When you fellows make peace, then someone will have to find the owners. At present I am running the Danube, and for the first time in its history I am sending ships to any port, free of embarrassing harbor dues, tariffs, or any other of your political devices. There are tons of food up in Hungary and thousands of starving people in Serbia, so I send up ships and get the food to the people who need it; the same with coal. The Bosnian farmers have tons of plum marmalade they can't eat and need to sell. I am going to move that plum maramalade before you fellows make the peace."

Then he went on to develop his vision, which was that of free

* Professor Joseph Chamberlain was the American authority on questions of river transit, especially on the Danube and the Rhine. The reference is to his memorandum covering the legal history of European waterways which was prepared for the Inquiry. This is a good example of the way in which the studies of academic colleagues were put to practical use during negotiations.

waterways all over Europe by which goods could be shipped from British ports and sent up the Rhine or the Elbe and across canals to the Danube. The Germans have a cross-country canal now. It does not draw much over six feet of water, but somehow boats from the Krupp works came under his guns at Belgrade. He sank two of them and got the German sailors, so he knew what he was talking about. But at present territorial boundaries have to be crossed and tariffs paid. All the great waterways should be free.

He said that this vision of free riverways is forced upon a man who sits in Belgrade and sees that wonderful river practically unused. He wants to connect the Morava with the Vardar and so get a waterway to Salonika. He knows the Serbs well, having served with their army during the war, and hopes they will not be too modernized, as they have a complete farming democracy. Only three men in Serbia own more than a hundred acres. But the Danube must not be their northern frontier, as there are Serbs for sixty miles north of it. When he crossed the river into Neusatz (Novi Sad), the inhabitants were so Serb that in an hour's time business was going on as usual in spite of changed sovereignty; and when he was at Belgrade, before the Austrians took it, and had heavy guns that could shoot into villages north of the river, the Serbs would not let him shoot because they said, "Those are our brothers and mustn't be disturbed."

Anyway a river is a bad boundary line, because you don't know what the other fellow is doing across it. The best line is a row of white stones across an open country where each can see the other and you have no misunderstanding of what they are doing. A row of these white stones now marks the line across Macedonia between Greece and Serbia, and it has been there long enough for the people to get used to it, so it is accepted as permanent. Moreover, the Serbs are not so keen about Macedonia now that they have lived there; it is a barren country with meager possibilities, and all the Serbs were eager to get home to the more smiling landscapes around Uskub and north. They will be satisfied with the arrangements made at Salonika, where the Greeks are to allow them separate shipping facilities in the harbor. The Serbs and the Greeks refuse to be drawn into a conflict which one of the Allied leaders, whose name I withhold, seemed to want to foment. As for the Bulgarian boundary, it might stand where the Bulgars had it before the war except that the Bulgars should not be allowed to control the railway by having territory so close that they could cross the line to attack a bridge at night. The railway is now running as far as Uskub, but from there on the destruction was carried out thoroughly by the Germans on their retreat. The southern part of the railway is not completely destroyed, the Germans were driven out too quickly; but when they had time they perpetrated a crime not in the laws of war. In the week of the armistice they so wrecked that part of the line, blowing up tunnels, bridges, culverts, embankments and all, that it will take a year to rebuild it. As this had no military value, it simply prevents the country from peaceful rehabilitation.

Meanwhile the Peace Conference was getting organized for work, with a whole series of commissions (13 in all) for the major problems, such as territorial arrangements, in Europe, Asia (especially China) and Africa, colonial settlements, especially Mandates, Reparations and Labor. I was offered the secretaryship of the Commission on Reparations but took an alternative place on the Labor Commission while Reparations went to John Foster Dulles, the first experience in treaty making of the future Secretary of State.

The Diary record for those busy days is too full to quote, but a red letter day was that of my visit with Lord Milner. The entry for that day runs as follows:

Monday, February 10, 1919

Morning—Worked in my room as usual. Beer and I had a luncheon engagement with Philip Kerr, Lloyd George's private secretary,* at the Premier's house in the Rue Nitot. It turned out to be overlooking the quiet square of the Place des États-Unis. We were met at the door by Kerr and taken into a sumptuous apartment. In the reception room there was a gorgeous full-sized figure painting by Hoppner. Along the walls of the drawing room were Gainsboroughs, Lawrences, and other old English masters, along with rich tapestries—exquisite pieces. Kerr explained that it was the Paris flat of Lady Mitchelham and was loaned by her to the British Prime Minister for the Peace Conference. Lloyd George had been

* Later Marquis of Lothian and Ambassador to the United States.

called back to London to open Parliament, and Lord Milner had come to take his place.

We were shortly joined by Sir Maurice Hankey, a slightly built, quick-motioned, clerical-looking soldier, who has been secretary of the Imperial War Cabinet since the creation of that body, about 1907. It was known first as the Committee of Imperial Defence, an obscure antecedent of the supreme body now in command of the entire resources of the British Empire. He has been present at every Imperial and Inter-Allied Conference, and I learn from others that no one else knows so much of what has taken place. He has kept a dairy.

Soon we were joined by Lord Milner, and after chatting a few moments before the fire sat down to lunch in the adjoining room. Everyone recognizes that Milner is the ablest brain in the Imperial service dealing with genuinely Imperial problems. He reminds one of Elihu Root, both in manner and to some extent in appearance, though with a fuller forehead and less irregular features; quiet, but forceful, not reticent in comment but carefully choosing his words when giving an opinion, much like a philosophical lawyer. Naturally we discussed the League of Nations as it is taking shape in Paris now. There was some doubt expressed as to the exact function of mandatory States under varying circumstances, and the advisability of bringing under one general system of political philosophy the government of the whole world. One thing I can quote, as it does not apply to the realm of diplomacy. Milner said that Britain had succeeded well where it had really tried hard in handling primitive peoples, but that was an entirely different job in colonial administration from the co-operation in government necessary where the people governed were of about the same grade of intelligence as their governors. He indicated that in his mind this second task was so different from the first as to be hardly in the same category of colonization, and said that it was so difficult a job that he wondered if the British or any other nation could ever succeed at it.

The question which required the greatest wisdom in statecraft was to determine at what stage, and how far, a people of capacity but immaturity should have their rights of self-government admitted. I asked him if there was any way for knowing when that time had arrived. He said that the dividing line seemed to be reached when the governed people began to express themselves in abstract terms, that is, in the demand for constitutions and institutional bodies, instead of in terms of personalities. Colonial administration could be highly successful as long as it was a question of personal confidence in the administrator and personal rule by him. For this type of government what is needed is not so much technical knowledge as dependable character and good common sense. This is what the British public school system has developed in the young men who go out to savage tribes with training only in mathematics and the humanities, especially the classics. The strange paradox of their success in colonial administration is not so inexplicable after all, for both by position and by racial prejudice they naturally take a position of aloofness and have an innate sense of their own superiority which primitive peoples readily recognize as a sign of leadership.

Milner said that this stage of the colonial problem was rapidly narrowing down with the growth of education and he did not look for a long continuance of the old British colonial system. I asked him if he would be a little more definite about the second stage to which he referred—that in which the natives were thinking in general or abstract terms. He said that there was no exact way to define it, but that as nearly as one could state it, it was about when a people began to demand written or formal safeguards for their rights. He said that the turning point sometimes came before the native people were really ready for the reform for which they were asking, but that even if they were not ready or able to take on constitutional government, they were likely to cause the old personal type of government to fail as soon as they ceased to look to the personal qualifications of those governing them as the essential basis of relationship*

Naturally, the luncheon passed rapidly, but although Kerr told

* This was, of course, before Milner's famous report on Egypt, but it is a clear indication of the fact that he had already come to the conclusions which became the basis of that report. The visit to Milner made a great impression on me, for it completely changed my impression of him. I had always thought of him as the outstanding exponent of British imperialism, which shows that I wasn't even at the time fully aware of the statesmanlike outlook of the man. For it was Milner who more than any other left his impress on the group of young men, most of them his former assistants, who through the Round Table did so much to transform the British Empire into a Commonwealth of Nations.

us Milner had an engagement or two, it was two-thirty before we left the table, so I imagine that we did not bore him overmuch, for he is not of the tolerant type of social diplomat.

After leaving we drove to the British headquarters at the Astoria for a conference with Lord Percy and straightened out some African matters Beer had on his hands.

The most difficult problem was one of the first to be settled. By February 12, the draft of the Covenant of the League of Nations was ready for the printer, largely due to the work of David Hunter Miller and Sir Cecil Hurst. The printed text had to be ready for a ten o'clock meeting of the commission next morning and Mr. Miller and I had the responsibility of getting it set up correctly. The one most puzzling problem was how to list the signatory nations. Should the British Dominions go in alphabetically or under a single caption. I suggested the caption should be British Empire and the Dominions be listed under it, slightly indented to show they all belonged to the Empire. This seemed natural, because they were all members of a "British Empire" delegation. Neither Mr. Miller nor I was bothered by the fact that there was no British Emperor and therefore, legally speaking, no British Empire. The symbol of empire had been a royal, not an imperial crown. But no one paid any attention to this quiet revolutionary act of two Americans at midnight, February 12. The League of Nations itself managed to ignore it, although the United Kingdom never signed the Covenant! It was only later, at the Imperial Conference of 1926, which created the British Commonwealth of Nations, that Balfour called attention to the fact that somehow, no one knew just how, the term British Empire had been used in the Treaty of Versailles. It was really due to Miller and me.

The next Diary entry of interest is a description of the Big Ten, the heads of State with their foreign ministers, on February 13. The subject, the future of Syria, was of less interest to me than my first glimpse of Clemenceau as president of the Peace Conference. I quote the entry for the whole day.

Thursday, February 13, 1919

At quarter to three I was getting into a car to go to the meeting of the Big Ten, which was discussing the fate of Syria. The little

111

Army Dodge car slipped through the sentries at the gate of the French Foreign Office without a challenge, and we drove up to the steps at the west side, where the porters were in wait for us.

The most interesting figure in the conference room was Clemenceau. He is by no means the rugged, venerable figure pictured to us during the war, the *Père Victoire* of the trenches, much less *le tigre* of the Chamber of Deputies, but a comfortable-looking, well-dressed bourgeois, with what seems like a touch of foppishness in wearing all the time fawn-colored gloves.* Settled back, half-sunk in his armchair, with his eyes on the ceiling, he gave the impression of not listening more than half the time, but if there was any point worth noting he was always on deck. This apparent, but deceptive, listlessness may be a self-protective mannerism acquired in Parliament; in any case it is more than shared by Balfour.

Two things about Clemenceau particularly strike one, his eyes and his voice. The eyes are large and dark and kindly but inscrutable; they seem to be trustworthy and yet to suggest that perhaps there is something concealed beyond the thought expressed, so that one hardly knows at what stage of agreement one has arrived—puzzling, deep-set eyes. The other thing most noticeable is the timbre of his voice. I had expected a shrill, metallic voice, but Clemenceau, has a rich, sad note in his voice, hard to characterize, musical but not resonant, suggesting somewhat the broken voice of an old man but sufficiently rich to carry perhaps further than any other in the room. He is a man without frills.

He had hardly sat down before he declared the session open, and, after some formal business, stated that President Bliss of Beirut College would address the representatives of the Powers on Syria. Then he rose from his chair to greet Bliss in person and escort him to his chair. President Bliss, a distinguished-looking college president of the long, thin Yankee type, gave his evidence with a quiet but forceful and convincing manner, calling for a commission to visit Syria, Balfour at first seemed rather bored with the whole proceeding, much as he must have acted in Parliament through debates. At times he was apparently asleep, yet when something was said affecting the interests or honor of England, he was suddenly

---

* I never found out the reason for this. Albert Thomas said jokingly that it was to conceal his tiger claws!

112

on the job, showing that he must have been listening all the time. His intervention was at first phrased in a suave, almost apologetic tone, but when he did not get the answer he was after, this quality disappeared as he persisted, and finally, when the incident—rather a trivial one at first—seemed to him of sufficient importance, a distinctly different note rang in his voice. He was no longer the complacent, thoughtful auditor, but there was a touch of iron which was quite a contrast with his usual casual way of talking and showed for the first time the element of command. Milner then added something very similar to what Balfour had said, in much the same tone, but one would imagine that it was more in the line of Milner's habitual manner of getting his way.

The incident here described had to do with Dr. Bliss' effort to discount the evidence concerning Syria which would be given in Paris by those he regarded as being in reality agents of the French. To make this point he said that as Syria was under martial law, it was impossible to get an accurate statement of the Syrian point of view except by an examination on the spot by commissioners authorized by the Peace Conference. This mention of martial law was what stirred Mr. Balfour to protest, as General Allenby was in control in Syria. He wanted Dr. Bliss to explain what he meant. Dr. Bliss refused to, because he said they should find out the situation on the spot and not take his word for it; but then Balfour retorted that the honor of the British Government was at stake in this because it implied that British martial law was preventing the Conference from getting accurate information. Dr. Bliss tried to head off the attack by saying that he wasn't talking about British martial law in any country, but Balfour wouldn't let it drop and finally asked Dr. Bliss point-blank if the British were using martial law to prevent the Conference from getting anti-British evidence.

By this time Dr. Bliss had had enough and blurted out, "Quite the contrary." This was all that Balfour wanted, and he sank back satisfied. Clemenceau took no part in this dialogue. After all, the proponents of French claims in Syria were the clericals.

After President Bliss, a Syrian commission appeared, and the leader, Chekri Ghanem, an Arab-looking gentleman with a long, forked, gray beard, read through his horn glasses a long account and plea which took two hours and a half to deliver and translate.

Just as he was starting, Westermann slipped a note to Wilson to tell him that Ghanem had not been in Syria for the last thirty-five years, having spent all his time in France. This hint was enough to destroy Wilson's interest in the long, ineffective outpouring of pathetic eloquence which followed. Before long he got up from his chair, wandered over to the other side of the room, and stared out of the windows, with his hands in his coat tails, clearly disconcerting the French.

Clemenceau spoke over his shoulder to Pichon in a stage whisper, which carried to me as I was directly in line behind, asking savagely, "What did you get the fellow here for, anyway?" Pichon, spreading out his hands in impotent protest, said, "Well, I didn't know he was going to carry on this way." It was a complete give-away.

Even at best it was a long waste of time, for when the Syrian was half through and suggested apologetically that perhaps he was taking too long, Clemenceau interrupted the hearing to discuss with the members of the Commission whether they should listen to the whole report or not. While the discussion was going on, the old Syrian, looking anxiously at the faces around the room, let the pages he had just been reading slip back nervously through his fingers on to the pile of manuscript below. Finally, when Clemenceau courteously informed him that he had better finish it, he gathered them up again and began about three pages back and read them all over again, apparently without knowing the difference. As it had been a particularly gross section, in which he stated that the Syrians would rather be delivered back to the Turks than live under British rule, it was a test of the patience of the Commission.

The reason they allowed him to go on was, obviously, the need of conciliating that particular group of Syrians by giving it the satisfaction of having talked to the Commission. When you think how many such groups there are in Paris now, you can see how difficult it is for the main business to get done; yet in these last ten days the Commission on the League has succeeded in turning out the most important document in the international history of Europe or of the world, and in such a way as to win almost universal approval.

After the Syrian hearing was over, Clemenceau was about to

close the session when President Wilson rose and in a somewhat tentative way said he would like to bring something to the attention of the Commission; he hardly knew whether they would think he was justified in doing so, but he had promised a delegation of women that he would ask the peace conference if they would make provision for a consideration of problems of especial interest to women. There was a moment's silence and then Clemenceau said, "But we have provided for such questions in the Commission for International Labor." Wilson said that this was not just what he had in mind.

Clemenceau interrupted with a sharp little exclamation, "Ah, it's the suffrage?"

Wilson admitted that that was one of the problems proposed. Then Clemenceau explained how deeply interested he was in woman suffrage but that this was not the place for it, that it belonged to domestic legislation. Wilson said that he would not urge the point, but he felt in duty bound to bring it to their attention.

Then a funny thing happened. Each of the members of the Commission seemed to feel that it was his duty to say something. Balfour began by telling how long he had fought for woman suffrage, but both he and Milner emphatically endorsed Clemenceau's point of view. Orlando hadn't much to say, but Sonnino protested that he had stood out for woman suffrage in Italy under the most difficult political conditions; but of course the matter was purely domestic and should not form a part of the Treaty. When everyone else had spoken it was evident that the Japanese, seated away toward the end of the row, felt called upon to say something too, and Makino made a little speech in English, expressing his appreciation of the part played by women in civilization; but he, too, agreed that this was not the place to recognize their political rights.

Clemenceau understands English but not Japanese English, and as there was a little buzz of conversation at the close of the incident he turned to Pichon and said in an aside, *"Qu'est-ce qu'il dit, le petit?"* (What's the little chap saying?) in a tone like that in which one would inquire what a young child was saying at the end of a table, when it didn't much matter what he said so long as he hadn't made a break. But Clemenceau's voice is very penetrating and I'm quite sure Makino heard it.

When they took up the question of presenting the report of the League of Nations at the next meeting of the plenary session someone asked whether it was really before the whole session or not, and Balfour informed Clemenceau that it was "The whole caboodle!" which needed an explanation from the translator before Clemenceau got it. A little phrase like that will show how informal some of the discussion was; although, of course, when the Commission is really at work it is quite impressive. Clemenceau is not a dignified figure but a very energetic one and keeps things moving as rapidly as possible. He has no ceremony about him at the opening or closing of a session.

On the way out Lansing, who has all along quite ignored the group of specialists except when thrown in personal contact, showed some surprise when Lord Milner reached across to shake hands with me and chat about the session.

I walked home. The moon had risen, though it was only half-past six, and misty reflections of lights on the wet pavement of the Place de la Concorde recalled the tones of Edwin Scott's pictures of twilight in Paris. There is little traffic on the Seine now, but at the moment of crossing the bridge a tug was pulling up against the current a row of barges, with their long tillers manned by two or three bargemen to swing them clear of the bridge abutments, and a few Seine fishers still remained on the bank patiently waiting.

One of the most interesting of my callers at this time was Professor William Rappard of Geneva, arguing the claim of his native city as the seat of the League of Nations. He won easily over the Belgians, who wanted it at Brussels, not only on account of the history and geography but because, although a Swiss, he had been born in Brooklyn and spoke American—as he also spoke German and, of course, French—without the slightest accent. Colonel House was so taken with him that I had to warn him twice that he was not an American.

Meanwhile things were going badly in the Commission on Labor Legislation. The American members, Samuel Gompers representing Labor and Henry Robinson, a Los Angeles banker, were raising obstacles; Gompers because he was a simple trade unionist and was afraid that working with governments might bring socialism; Robinson because of his opposition to labor legislation in the United States. The British proposal for an international Labor parliament working independently of foreign offices was really a kind of super-state and had no chance of final adoption. On the other hand, the ominous threat of Bolshevist revolution in Budapest and Berlin was already reaching us in Paris, and before long much of central Europe was in flames. Professor, later Supreme Court Justice Frankfurter, who was in Paris on behalf of the Zionists, agreed with me that it would never do for Wilson, who had been hailed by Labor as the champion of freedom, to fail on it when it had been announced as one of the first aims of the Peace Conference. So I wrote a note to Colonel House, pointing out how serious the situation was, especially in view of the threat of Bolshevism.

The Diary again takes up the narrative at this point.

Sunday, March 9, 1919

A note was waiting in my room to say that Colonel House would see me at five o'clock on international labor legislation, in answer to my request for an interview. When I spoke to him I found that he had been led to share fully the view of the American delegates on the Labor Commission that nothing could be done with the British proposal because it looked so much like a super-state. I argued that this was not the way to view the situation, that if there was anything in the idea of international labor legislation at all, then the United States ought to have a point of view of its own and not merely come forward as a negative critic of European plans. I said that Wilson's championship of democracy would make a sorry showing at the Peace Conference if his delegation were to be blamed for failing to set up a common-sense plan which might be put through as a compromise between American ideas and those of Europe. I told him I was sure it was possible to secure a compromise and in addition we might even have a special concession for the United States, in view of its constitutional limitations. The Colonel placed the matter in my hands, telling me to get in touch with Major Berry, head of the Pressmen's Union of America, who has been the Colonel's liaison with the American labor leaders while in Paris.

Although Colonel House placed the solution of the labor negotiations in my hands, the position in which I found myself remained irregular and at times embarrassing. His instructions were entirely informal and I had no written authorization from him, still less from Mr. Lansing or the President, to undertake the task. Fortunately, the purpose of my intervention was so well understood that it was never questioned by the other delegations. So far as the American Delegation was concerned, all that happened was that Colonel House informed the American labor leaders of his wishes; this was quite evident two days later when I met Mr. Gompers for the first time, for I found him fully informed about the situation, and he at once cordially accepted my position as technical adviser. The anomalous situation was never entirely corrected, and when I found myself seated on the Labor Commission I had no other credentials than the invitation of Mr. Gompers in the first instance and of Mr. Robinson later. In reality, however, my task was that of technical adviser to the whole Commission rather than to the American Labor Delegation, for unless I could procure acceptance of the British to a modification of their plan, there was still no hope of agreement. This situation was recognized when the Commission appointed a sub-committee on March 17 to study the text of a possible compromise, and explains my appointment to that committee not as a delegate but as technical adviser to the committee as a whole.

My first day's work was therefore with the British, in an effort to get them to accept a modification of their plan for a labor parliament which would not give the appearance of a super-state making labor laws for all the world. This was the impression which their first plan had made upon those of my colleagues with whom I had spoken. There was no use going to Mr. Gompers until I could secure a new formula as a basis for negotiation. The formula, however, had to be one which would fully recognize the fact that the United States could not undertake any obligation to accept labor legislation in the form of treaties, because, as had been so forcibly pointed out by both Mr. Gompers and Mr. Robinson, the Constitution of the United States placed labor legislation under the states and not under the Federal Government.

A tentative proposal that the states themselves should be repre-

118

sented in the international conference and thus negotiate directly with foreign governments was equally unconstitutional; and on the surface of things the impasse seemed insurmountable. For the Europeans on their part would have regarded the plan as a failure if the powers of the international parliament were to go no further than the expression of "pious opinions," as Mr. Barnes, the British Minister of Labor, called them. This would have been a complete disillusionment to the European labor world, however much such meetings might resemble the annual conferences of the American Federation of Labor.

I at once set to work, therefore, and got the British to accept a dual procedure, starting from the point that if the International Labor Conferences would vote recommendations for labor legislation so carefully drafted both in form and content as to be capable of enactment into law, an enactment could follow immediately in the case of those States that had no such technical difficulties as the United States, and the same text would furnish a program of legislation for federal governments. Ultimately these two alternatives were openly recognized in the Treaty, and the United States procured in that way exceptional treatment by having it understood that any convention adopted by a labor conference would be treated as a recommendation for labor legislation by the United States instead of as a treaty obligation. A detailed study of this whole incident shows how an apparently impossible situation can ultimately be solved if there is sufficient good will and patience on both sides, combined with a real desire to see the result attained. Negotiation of this text was the most important work on the agenda of the Labor Commission down to the time Mr. Gompers left Paris on March 27, for the issue at stake was the existence of the International Labor Organization itself.

The next few days were the busiest ones of my life, drafting texts by night, with the aid of colleagues and especially of Dr. Slosson, who was more than a secretary, then taking them around to the British, French, Belgian, and Italian delegations to make sure of their support in the Commission. This was old-fashioned diplomacy after all! The chief difficulty naturally was the objection of the British to my proposal which left the United States free to treat

119

draft conventions of the International Labor Organization as merely recommendations for the Federal Government.*

But there was more to this incident than the rephrasing of a single clause. I had never liked the elaborate provisions for foreign inspection of labor conditions in a country and for applying penalties against a violator of the treaty. The British and French Delegation had emphasized the need for such measures, because in their past experience they had found that even some of the European Governments would sign obligations of this sort and not carry them through, and they did not wish to assume the obligations of the draft conventions on their own part unless there were adequate assurance that they would be observed by all the signatories. The result of this way of thinking had been the insertion of a whole series of clauses calling for inspection and creating an international sanction for international labor legislation.

In spite of the logic behind this reasoning the result was unpalatable to an American, because it bore a specious resemblance to a super-state. Therefore, I proposed that all of the sanction clauses should be boiled down to a general statement, placing the responsibility for final action upon the Council of the League of Nations. If, however, my proposal for the treatment of draft conventions as recommendations in the case of nations like our own were accepted, then I was willing to waive my objection to the sanction clauses, because they would only apply after the enactment of labor legislation by States in which there would be full provision for enforcement. To this extent it seemed to me that my objection to the sanction clause was very largely met by the treatment of draft conventions as resolutions in our case. I, therefore, yielded on that point, on condition that the British yield on the other.

The constitution of the International Labor Organization would not in reality have lost anything, but would have gained in coherence and simplicity, if all of the complicated provisions for

* The proposed clause is Article 405 of the Treaty of Versailles. "In the case of a federal state, the power of which to enter into conventions on labor matters is subject to limitations, it shall be in the discretion of that Government to treat a draft convention to which such limitations apply as a recommendation only, and the provisions of this Article with respect to recommendations shall apply in such case."

enforcement had been boiled down to a provision for inspection and reference to the World Court for any charge of violation of the Treaty. But at the time it was quite impossible to secure this concession from a Commission the leading members of which had had years of experience in dealing with evasions of the law and who wished to make sure that this labor legislation would be a reality. In particular, Sir Malcolm Delevingne, as an official of the Home Office, had spent much of his life dealing with such questions, and his interest in labor legislation was too genuine to permit him to accept anything short of a well-rounded system of enforcement. So strongly did the British feel about the situation and so completely had they given up hopes of reaching agreement with the American delegates, that they had their trunks packed to leave for London, and were ready to go immediately in the event of the failure of our conference. To prevent such a collapse of the whole labor section of the Treaty I told Delevingne that if he would accept my proposal for recommendations instead of conventions I would agree to sanctions, believing that they would never be invoked. They never have been.

There were still details to be ironed out, and it was not until April 11 that the Report of the Commission on Labor Legislation was up before the Fourth Plenary Session of the Peace Conference. For me it was a date in history which I, naturally, recorded in full.

Friday, April 11, 1919

A beautiful warm April day, although I didn't step into the sunshine until I left in the afternoon for the session at the Quai d'Orsay. In the morning I was at the telephone talking with Sir Malcolm and learned that things were going well at his end. I saw Robinson and got him to move in on Lansing. Then I prepared a further memorandum for the President through Colonel House.

At luncheon Oulahan, of the *New York Times,* and Sweetser, of the Press Bureau, discussed the Treaty. The journalists are much depressed. In a treaty of this size it is hard to see the woods for the trees. If the terms are decent enough for the nations to get along with one another for the time being, then the good work that is being done in other lines may make this Conference one to be proud of after all. But it has managed to put itself in the worst light with the public, the newspapers are down on it, and nobody knows what is going on, so that all the dismal gossip circulates in Paris in a blue and sulphurous haze. At the last moment before going to the Conference I dictated directly to the machine an additional suggestion for the President.

At 2:45 I was in the car with Beer (to whom Frank Simonds surrendered his newspaper pass) en route across the bridge to the Foreign Office for the Fourth Plenary Session of the Peace Conference. Driving up to the steps of the Foreign Office, we arrived just as the official British moving picture man was taking a picture of Barnes and his colleagues standing chatting on the doorstep. They hailed my arrival and dragged me forward into the picture, and so the incident is preserved in the records of the British history of the Peace Conference. There were other pictures taken in the course of the session, but the light was poor and the crowd too great. There were also several sketching, among them a Japanese and a Hungarian artist, Ivan Sors.

Meanwhile, the audience began to filter in. The Labor Commission was assigned a row of chairs close beside the horseshoe table toward the head, so I had a very fine point of vantage. It happened strangely enough that the man behind whom I was seated was Sir Robert Borden, who got very busy with the other Dominion Premiers in the course of the debate, trying to make sure that the Dominions were not being dragged into obligations in the labor field unless they were represented in the League of Nations. Balfour sat a few feet away and this time was anything but asleep.

His colleague Bonar Law beside him looked like a rather ordinary businessman, with none of Balfour's intellectual power and none of Lloyd George's quick comprehension, at least none written on his face. The three men at the center of the table, Lloyd George, Clemenceau, and Wilson, are fundamentally alike in their ability to apply a principle immediately to any given situation. All three certainly came to the room without fully knowing what was ahead of them, and yet they did what I imagine was exactly the right thing to do, that is, if they follow up the situation where they left it.

Perhaps the private discussions carried on from Balfour's end of the table drove all else out of Wilson's mind when he rose to speak. I should explain that all this discussion around the head table, which brought the veins out on Balfour's flushed face and the twinkle into Clemenceau's eyes, was carried on while speeches were being made. As Walter Weyl said later, the chief use of speeches is to enable the leading statesmen to discuss matters among themselves while the audience is being entertained.

The previous sessions had been held in the Room of the Clock (Salle de l'Horloge), so called from a marble clock on the mantelpiece, a room large enough for the Conference but very poorly provided with room for the journalists. The session of the Ten which I attended before was in a still smaller room, which is the official office of the French Foreign Minister. This time we passed through a suite of elegant antechambers to the banquet hall of the French Foreign Office. There are three windows on each side, with mirrors interspersed in the usual French way. The ceiling has Renaissance frescoes (of the late nineteenth century), and there are some eight enormous electroliers which when lighted gave a real touch of magnificence to the otherwise businesslike assembly. A huge table covered with green baize was fitted like a horseshoe around the southern half of the room at which the ministers plenipotentiary were seated. At the north end, chairs for the journalists were arranged in regular rows with room for those behind to stand up if they should get interested, which they mostly did.

At three o'clock Clemenceau rose and in very rapid French said: "Gentlemen, the session is open. The first thing on the program is to pass the minutes of the last plenary session. The minutes are passed. Then the Report of International Labor Legislation Commission. Mr. Barnes has the floor."

Say that as rapidly as you can in French and you can see how quickly we got into action. Mr. Barnes then made his speech. It was a very fine presentation. The only trouble with speech-making at a diplomatic conference is that the translation makes one listen twice over to everything said so that the fine effect of the original is sure to be pretty well lost. Colliard, the French Minister of Labor, followed with a little written speech which I have reason to believe had been prepared by Max Lazard, perhaps in conjunction with

Mr. Fontaine. But the finest speech of the day was Vandervelde's, who was speaking both as a Socialist and as Minister of State in Belgium. He hailed the document as one of the most notable steps in history ever taken by organized governments. His speech was extemporaneous. He told me afterward that he has no copy but that the Socialist paper will print a full text and he will send me one. The English translation was not very happy. Then followed desultory speeches.

While the talk was going on, I had a good look at Paderewski, the great pianist, now a statesman, who sat across the table from me. He has a very strong face, more powerful, however, than delicate, but with great distinction. I met him at the end of the session and had a little chat with him. I was talking to Patek, our Polish member of the Labor Commission, and when Paderewski came up to us he took me for a Pole! When he heard my French, however, he addressed me in good English.

The speech-making went on. Lord Sinha, for India, said almost exactly what I had suggested to Delevingne. The Maharajah of Bikaner spoke for the princes of India in a choice little speech in which he pointed out that his fellow princes would be the "competent authorities" in their states to whom the matter should be referred. The thing I regretted most was that Japan did not speak, for, as a matter of fact, it was Japanese acquiescence in the plan as a whole, when modified by the amendment that the proposed labor treaties should be drawn up in conformity with varying civilizations, which enabled India to come along. In a word, the Japanese have enabled the convention to become a world treaty and they are not getting the credit they deserve.

After the South Americans had finished, the chairman rose and said, "Gentlemen, you have heard the Report and the British amendment. [He had previously put an amendment by Sir Robert Borden.] The Report is now to be adopted." There was an instant's pause and then he quickly added, "It is adopted unanimously. The session is over."

Everyone rose and there was a general hubbub. We were congratulated on all sides; but in the midst of our success felt that something had been put over on us. The quick adjournment after

124

the passage prevented us from bringing up that part of our Report upon which Mr. Gompers set much weight—the Labor Charter. This was the nine-point statement of the right of labor, based on the text "labor is not a commodity or an article of commerce," a text in the Clayton Anti-Trust act of 1914 which exempted labor unions from its prohibitions of trusts.

Mr. Gompers sincerely and earnestly held that this declaration marked the last stage of the liberation of labor from slavery. In Lincoln's day man himself had been made free; in the Clayton bill his labor as well was declared to be a part of himself and not the property of other men, to be bought and sold in a "labor market" as the slave himself had been bought and sold in the slave market fifty years before. But the issue which seemed so important to American labor did not interest Europeans.

At dinner Walter Weyl and I decided to spend the evening celebrating by going to the opera for the first time. The French Government was giving a gala night at the opera in Wilson's honor, an honor not given to any other government, but the opera chosen was Berlioz' *Damnation of Faust*. If, as I was told, it was Clemenceau who chose the opera, it showed him at his most diabolic. On the other hand, he should be given the credit for the fact that they planned Wilson's departure for midnight through the empty streets in order that the changed attitude of the Paris crowd, which had greeted him three months before would not be noticeable.*

The opera house was full from cellar to garret and we took the last two seats in the orchestra. Many uniforms, and especially American, gave a distinctive note to the audience, but France is beginning to throw off the pall of the war, and Frenchmen were there in full dress, which they did not wear when we first came to Paris. Marguerite was sung by Chenal, the most famous of French prima donnas, and the staging far surpassed anything I ever saw at the Metropolitan. The Labor Charter was a long way off, and yet perhaps the work we have just finished at the Quai d'Orsay may help to bring these creations of art into the lives of more of the

* The reference here is to President Wilson's return to Washington for a few days to survey the situation there and carry out some of the essential duties of the Presidency.

125

workers of the world, when it is recognized that the rebuilding of civilization depends fundamentally upon Labor.

The International Labor Organization was the alternative to the Communist revolutionary movement which had spread out from Russia to incite violence in Budapest, Vienna and Berlin. There was no sign of it in Paris until May 1, "Labor Day" in Europe. Then, to anticipate mob violence, Clemenceau massed sixty thousand troops in the city and once more, as in 1919, I saw how panicky the ordinary policeman acted while the soldiers—perhaps because there were so many of them—behaved with the utmost coolness, and even with good humor.

From my window on the Place de la Concorde I watched a cordon of horse, stretched out across the street below, open up to let infantry march through them from the square behind. These troops started moving up toward the crowd, with their rifles ready for use, gave us a tense moment. Fortunately, when face to face with the crowd they halted, grounded arms, and merely stood on guard. Along the garden of the Tuileries there was a whole regiment of cavalry and another along the banks of the Seine; but nothing really happened after this first skirmish, and half an hour later I walked across to the river through a practically empty square over to the Pont Alexandre III. There was an army kitchen serving hot coffee to the troops there, and one of the soldiers with whom I had a little chat told me that they had been ordered out from Versailles at two in the morning. He didn't mind it for himself, but his horse had had nothing to eat all day. He told me that the cavalry was drawn from central France. He was from Lyons and it didn't take much questioning to see that he had little sympathy with the police.

I walked around among the horses for quite a distance with a growing feeling of depression at seeing so much preparation for civil war. Between sixty and a hundred thousand troops were concentrated on Paris. It gave an unexpected turn to the historic suggestions of captured German cannon along the Champs Élysées to see French troops quartered among them in anticipation of a renewal of the commune. They were seated on the park chairs and making themselves comfortable in that complete abandon of which

126

the French soldier is capable. Some had thrown a tarpaulin over the barrels of the large German guns and made a roof that way to shelter them from the rain. Practically all were smoking, and they looked bored but still good-natured.

Toward midnight I looked out over the roof of the Crillon and saw against the sky the dark figure of the sentry posted there, walking up and down with his gun on his shoulder. It gave a queer sense of a beleaguered city, in the midst of the unsettled social forces of Europe today.

The harsh judgment which was registered against the Treaty of Versailles in Germany was repeated in the anti-Wilson campaign in the United States. But the fault lay not in vindictiveness on the part of the representatives of the Peace Conference of the Allied and Associated Powers. Even Clemenceau stood out against Foch's demand for the left bank of the Rhine. They were, upon the whole, fair minded, well-intentioned men; but they were given an impossible task, that of writing a charter for Europe without the presence of half of it—the ex-enemy states. The German delegation received only a printed text and replied by written memoranda. This led them to make as great a blunder as the Conference had made. They found fault with every part of the hundred-page treaty and so united the allied delegations which had become very unhappy when they had put the thirteen parts of the great treaty together and realized that though each section might be justified if it stood by itself, the Treaty was more than the sum of its parts.

It was only after the labor section of the treaty was adopted by the Conference, that, on reading the whole treaty for the first time, I discovered that there was no guarantee of social legislation for the sections of Germany given to Poland. I hastily got a meeting of the members of the Labor Commission still in Paris. (Mr. Gompers had left it in March) and they readily accepted my draft of what became Article 312 of the treaty, which safeguarded the savings of workers and all others in the territories that passed from German, Austrian or Hungarian sovereignty, so that their old age, accident and sickness insurance would not be taken from them under any pretext by the new government under which they would have to live. The International Labor Office was to look after the enforcement

127

of this article. I was happy to have inserted the one article in the treaty to which no one could object. Incidentially, I took some risk in doing so, for I couldn't reach either Colonel House or President Wilson to get their consent to my calling the Commission together; but both of them, later on, were quite appreciative of my violation of protocol.

THE SIGNING OF THE TREATY

The only time the Conference of Paris met at Versailles was for the signing of the treaty, on June 28, 1919.

The Secretariat had taken immense pains to make sure that the signing of the Treaty would be witnessed only by those who in some way or other had had a share in its making as plenipotentiaries or commissioners. There were several kinds of tickets admitting the bearer to different parts of the Palace of Versailles, and the bearer himself had no idea of the exact meaning of them.

When the hour came to leave the hotel, there was a whole company of American army cars waiting in line in front of the Crillon, each with a huge colored label on its windshield and hood and a special list of its passengers. Beer, Haskins and I had a car together. Just as we were getting into it a well-dressed civilian American stepped up to us, pointed to the empty seat, and asked if he might go along. We explained how impossible this was, but he told us how equally impossible it was to find a taxi and that all he wished was a ride to the gate of the city of Versailles. He was a businessman and was merely sight-seeing for the day. There was no reason under the circumstances why he should not ride with us that far, and when we reached the city gate and showed our credentials to the guard posted there he quietly left the car and disappeared. When the ceremony was over I found him on the terrace at the doorway to the grand staircase of the Palace. I asked him how he had managed to get in and he pulled out of his pocket a Pall Mall cigarette case, bright red with a coat of arms in gold at the corner and said that had been his *"laissez passer."* It was the only touch of comedy in the high drama of the day.

Our road lay through the forest of St. Cloud. Perhaps it was the contrast with its shadowy avenues and restful glades which lent an

128

added magnificence to the military pageant that stretched out before us in the sunlight from the city gate to the Palace. On each side of the broad avenue, as far as the eye could see, regiment after regiment of cavalry stood motionless in line with lances upright, their spear heads glittering in the sun and little blue pennants fluttering from the shafts. Horizon blue is as fitting for parade as for battle; it forms an indistinguishable mass, and while it lacks the gay rich note of the old red uniforms of French soldiers it gives a tone to the picture that is entirely lacking in the business-like drabness of the khaki. It must be over a mile to the Palace gate and on either side the troops stood in exact alignment.

Inside the grille of the Palace there were other regiments more gaily caparisoned, until finally the climax came at the main doorway. Here we found the Garde Républicaine, who are in France what the Horse Guards are in England. Dismounted, but in full regalia, they reached in long lines from the doorway up the grand staircase to the Hall of Mirrors, where the Treaty was to be signed. There was something that reminded one of the days of the Grand Condé, who had been greeted by Louis XIV on this same stairway in that other victory over the Germans three centuries before. For these troops still wear the shining cuirass and the great crested helmet with its long black and red horsehair *crinière* and huge black riding boots with spurs. Step after step up the grand staircase they stood in double line with their swords at rest in front of them ready for salute. Draped on the walls behind were the flags of all the Allies, with the Tricolor to the fore, giving a richer glow than tapestry to the great gilded hall itself.

It was, as everyone knew, the moment for the *revanche* of France, to force Germany to sign its treaty of defeat at the very spot where Bismarck had had its triumph proclaimed in 1871. But Bismarck had chosen the spot for Germany's *revanche* of war and of a civilization so largely based on war. The one thing that seemed incongruous in the event ahead of us was not the humiliation of a conquered Power, for that was a commonplace in the past of Europe, but the fact that this Treaty proposed at last a way of escape from such a vicious circle.

The seats in the hall were all low, red-upholstered benches without backs, giving as clear a view as possible of the proceedings. The seat assigned to me was close to the front and over by the wall, so I stood during the ceremony itself against the embrasure of a window and saw everything close at hand.

The Allied leaders came up the grand staircase through the central aisle of the hall escorted by military attendants to their seats behind the table where the signing was to take place. Then there was a pause and the hall grew absolutely still as the two German delegates were ushered in and given their places at the side of the table, more like men facing sentence at a trial than the representatives of a great Power at an act of sovereignty. They were both deathly pale and nervous, and the nervous tension grew while the Treaty received the signature of the Allied Powers. When the turn finally came for Dr. Bell and Herr Muller to sign, one of them found that the pen wouldn't work. One of Colonel House's secretaries stepped over and pulled his fountain pen from his pocket and handed it to him, and I suppose has the pen as a souvenir still.

No sooner had the Germans completed their signatures than immediately, as from some electric signal in the hall, the guns of St Cyr on the southern slopes of Versailles began to boom the announcement to the world outside. Then, from fort after fort on the hills around Paris, the heavy guns broke into a salute in a vast reverberating chorus. With a stiff bow, but not exchanging a word of greeting with anyone, the two Germans left the room by the same side door which had admitted them. It seemed to me an added and unnecessary humiliation, but perhaps it saved them from embarrassment.

Out on the terrace below, the crowd now came to life like a lawn party in the gay afternoon sunshine. The great fountains had started playing at the same moment that the guns had begun to boom. There were hundreds out there who had not been admitted to the ceremony but who could nevertheless tell their friends—and record for their descendants—that they had been invited to the Palace of Versailles for the signing of the Treaty that closed the World War.

I had no time to stay and look around, for I had to finish packing, have an early dinner, and catch the presidential train.

I never expected to leave any city again in such state. Red carpet reached down the stairway from the street, and all the ugliness of the station was hidden by a forest of high palms. There were troops at salute and a band playing the national airs of France and America as President Wilson left Paris at the Gare du Luxembourg.

Once home, I paid a visit to Washington, D.C., which lasted only a few days, for it was so full of the dust of battle against Wilson that the I.L.O. was almost lost to sight.* I tried to see the Secretary of Labor, William B. Wilson, but was told that he had fallen ill the day I arrived. I later learned that his illness ended the day I left Washington to return to Europe. The situation was more than disconcerting, it amounted to a national disgrace; for, urged by the British to meet the threat of Bolshevism then menacing Europe, President Wilson had, incautiously issued a call for the first International Labor Conference to meet in Washington in October, 1919. This was ignored by Congress which alone had the power to vote the money for it. To prevent a complete fiasco, the British Government paid the cost of the Conference—a far-sighted action of statesmanship as the event was to prove, but which neither then nor later received adequate recognition.

After a short visit to my parents at Strathroy, I sailed back to Europe on the *Leviathan,* the largest American ship, which was still equipped as a transport with iron stanchions for beds along the decks. However, we had Mrs. Herbert Hoover and her young son along as fellow passengers and had a good time together in the almost empty ship. The reason we were going on a transport was that, in spite of the omens in Washington, Secretary Lansing, although utterly out of sympathy with the League and the I.L.O. was too much of an international lawyer to go back on obligations already assumed, and I was sent over to London to meet with the Organizing Committee of the I.L.O. for the conference which the President had called. After this was over, I was to settle down in Europe as General Editor of the History of the War for the

* Yet Senator Lodge said that the I.L.O. was the worst part of the Treaty. However in 1960 the Department of Labor published a "salute" to the I.L.O. on its fortieth birthday, which the great grandson of Senator Lodge, as Assistant Secretary of Labor asked me to write. The I.L.O. had lasted through a second world war and had become an organ of the United Nations.

Carnegie Endowment, and that is why our whole family went along.

The Organizing Committee of the I.L.O. held its meetings in the Treasury building, on Parliament Street, just around the corner from the Prime Minister's house at 10 Downing Street.

There were difficult problems to solve and no precedents for the framing of the Rules of Procedure, so this important work was referred to both M. Fontaine and me. But he was called back to Paris and it was left to me.

To those who have not taken part in international conferences and to many who have, the framing of the Rules of Procedure may seem like a mere technicality, but the history of the United Nations has shown only too clearly how governments (like the U.S.S.R.) can use the rules of procedure to make sure of having their own way against the will of the majority.

Pioneering alone in this almost unexplored territory, I fell back on the rules of the House of Commons and Chamber of Deputies and the Labor Economic Conference and drew up Rules of Procedure designed to prevent the break up of the I.L.O. Conference and the Trade Union Units and to make it supreme over the governing body. My plan was modified only slightly and has remained the structure of the I.L.O. conferences ever since. Sir Eric Drummond, Secretary General of the League, sent Major Abrahams to see how it worked, and the I.L.O. rules were largely taken over by the League at its first meeting. The rules of the United Nations are more complicated but they too are based on this pioneering work of mine in London.

Our Committee also had a major problem in framing a rule to apply "the principles of the eight-hour day" to countries where there were industries working on a forty-hour week, without lessening the safeguards of labor which would be contrary to the terms of the Treaty. On the other hand there were countries where some of the work was carried on the basis of a fifty-six or sixty-hour week and the sudden change at the behest of an international body might cause a major dislocation in national economy. While the differences in conditions of labor among the Western powers were not too difficult, the contrast with the Orient at once raised almost insuperable questions. Japan, as the most industrialized of the Asiatic powers and an ally of the Entente in the war, needed to have some

132

concession if it were to take part in the Washington Conference and become a working member of the I.L.O. The Japanese delegates were visibly impressed and for several days kept telling us that, owing to the breakdown of telegraphic communications they were unable to report the adherence of their government. When, however, the concession in working hours was made sufficiently high, the telegraph and cable communications with Japan were reported to be working next morning.

The granting of this concession to Japan turned out to be one of the most important events in subsequent months. Already at the Paris Peace Conference Baron Makino, speaking for the Elder Statesman of Japan, gave it as his measured view that the betterment of labor conditions would be a dominant problem for the future in the Orient, for it would affect not only industrialization at home, but immigration abroad. The bearing of this upon Japanese-American relations was obvious, although little attention was paid to it at the time. Japan, however, took the matter very seriously and when the Conference met in Washington, the Japanese delegation was the largest of any nation there, coming with many newspaper correspondents and other observers. Their disappointment at the failure of the Washington Conference played a large part in their disillusionment with reference to the American policy. For it was at this very time that Mr. Wilson was being accused of selling out China to Japan because Japan was to be allowed to retain its hold of the Chinese ports which it had taken from Germany in the war.

The Japanese Government finally instructed their delegates to accept all the principles laid down by the Conference, with reservations to meet the special conditions prevailing in Japan. Convinced that this had far-reaching implications I wrote a letter to the *Times* (November 21) calling special attention to the clause dealing with the prohibition of child labor, a matter of great importance in the industrialization of the Orient. The *Times* paid tribute to this letter in a lengthy editorial, and I was, therefore, not surprised to receive a warm note of acknowledgement from Dr. Nitobe, then residing in England, one of the finest gentlemen of any nationality I have ever met.

CHAPTER 8

The History of World War I

The I.L.O. having been launched (however inauspicious the circumstances), it began its career of greatness, and I turned back to history. But this time it was something entirely new, a co-operative history of the impact of the World War on the economic and social life of nations, not merely a study of its cost but of the way in which it had affected the life and thought of a generation. For the next six or seven years I lived most of the time in Europe, gathering evidence at first hand of the far reach of the cataclysm.

As early as December 1914 I had submitted a plan for an Economic and Social History of the World War (a weird title but a real one!) to the Carnegie Endowment for International Peace at the request of Professor John Bates Clark, the Director of its Division of History and Economics. After the war and the Peace Conference were over, I was invited to undertake the general editorship of what turned out to be the greatest co-operative history ever written. Ten years later there were a hundred and fifty volumes covering fifteen countries. Over two hundred collaborators in sixteen countries worked on it, among them thirty-five wartime cabinet ministers.*

I hesitate to invite the reader to follow me in the story of the

* *Economic and Social History of the World War* (New Haven: Yale University Press, London: Humphrey Milford: Oxford University Press, for Carnegie Endowment for International Peace, Division of Economics and History, 1924-1940). The Endowment distributed this work to 300 of its 750 depository libraries, and yet, with over 300,000 volumes given away, the publishers realized some $90,000 in sales.

making of this work which took so much of my life, for with World War II intervening and the ominous threat of nuclear war still haunting us, World War I seems almost as far away as the War between the States. Yet the First World War was more revolutionary than the second. Three great, historic empires passed away —the Hohenzollern, the Hapsburg, and the Romanoff—and the United States emerged not only as a world power but as the greatest of them all. Its impact on the mind of the West was unparalleled. In spite of the fact that it was preceded by a series of crises, when peace seemed to hang by a thread, the actual outbreak struck with a tragic force unparalleled by any event in Western history, at least since the wars of the French Revolution. To the military mind there was something supremely inspiring in this spectacle of men marching to a rendezvous with death; but the death that was waiting for them was not that of the high drama of war, but of multiple assassination in the sordid, vermin-infested setting of trench warfare.

The moral and social displacement of the war was matched by its economic cost. In the first three months of the fighting, its cost had run greater than that of all the costs of England's wars in the eighteenth century—wars which had won its world empire. It would seem as though no nation would be able to bear up under it, and yet they were keeping up, though exhausting investments and resourses the world over and piling up debts—to be liquidated ten years after the war was over in the Great Depression.

Wars of peoples are not so easy to stop as those waged by princes or governments, as was already shown in the first war of nations, that of the French Revolution. Even Napoleon had known when to stop—as at Leoben—if only to gain an interval before a renewal of the struggle. Bismarck could call a halt to his policy of blood and iron when, for the purposes of statecraft, he held the army of von Moltke, after its victory at Koeniggratz, from marching into Vienna. But there were no Bismarcks or Napoleons in 1914. The deadly drama had escaped control, a fact already apparent before the end of the year. Evidently it was becoming a test, not merely of the endurance of the warring nations, but of war itself.

It cannot be said that these ideas were either clearly seen or widely held in these first months of the war. On the contrary, the greater demands of the war, the more it became the duty of governments to maintain morale by obscuring costs or offering a glowing, imaginary balance sheet of the prize of victory. The fallacies of war economics are familiar now, but in wartime when everyone is employed and wages are high, the coming day of reckoning is lost sight of. More fundamental, however, is the fact that war economics is a totally different thing from the economics of peace. Its purpose is not prosperity but security, a possession without price in the market place, but priceless in the other sense of the word. From this point of view, therefore, a mere balance-sheet of loss and gain is meaningless, for the competition in destruction may be the necessary, and therefore, the valid insurance of survival. The categories of normal living no longer apply.

There was no one in the academic world better qualified to deal with these questions than Professor John Bates Clark, the Director of the Division of Economics and History of the Carnegie Endowment for International Peace. A philosopher capable of exploring the intricacies of economic theory, he was free from the dogmatism which, from the days of Ricardo and Mill, had so largely colored economic thinking and made of liberalism an apology for things as they are, instead of an instrument for liberation. On the other hand, he was not carried away by the new trend toward statistics, which, while furnishing a valid basis for analysis, became in second-class minds a mere science of accounting. Conscious that the problem of human conduct is more than a mathematical equation, and unwilling to accept John Stuart Mill's traditional discounting of the costs of war, Professor Clark decided that the fundamental analysis of the problem of war lay more in the field of history than of economics; that it called for a sensing of the tides of public opinion and of the mechanics of governments as well as a weighing of economic facts. Therefore, he conferred with his colleagues in the Department of History at Columbia University, and especially its then head, Professor William A. Dunning, and they, in turn, suggested that he make a beginning by inviting me to prepare a memorandum for the consideration of the Carnegie Endowment.

My memorandum of December, 1914, and another a few months

136

later turned out to be a blueprint for *Economic and Social History of the World War,* upon which I was now engaged. It had been recognized that nothing on it could be done during the war, but even before the Peace Conference was over, the Trustees of the Endowment had approved the plan and sent word to me that I was appointed Editor in Chief with authority to nominate editors and workers in each European country.

This meant that we would have to live in Europe while the *Economic and Social History of the World War* was being prepared. From every point of view London was the place to begin my war history, and I chose as the Chairman of the British Board of Editors, Sir William (later Lord) Beveridge, the head of the London School of Economics, for this greatest of all co-operative histories was not a task for historians. Its authors had to be those who had held office in wartime from which they could watch how things actually were done. Research at second hand in the documents of the war—the orthodox way of historians—was ruled out by the enormous mass of them. The British Government needed thirty-five miles of shelving for theirs alone, and I later found that the Continental governments had even more, so that the total shelving would be over two hundred miles in length. I then amused myself by calculating that giving one minute to each page a researcher could look them all over in some five thousand years, and that would not leave any free time to consider what it all meant!

The only board member who had been with the Endowment before was Francis Hirst, the former editor of *The Economist,* a close friend of John Morley and an outspoken Liberal in the great tradition of Gladstone and Cobden. He was, naturally, as critical of wartime controls as Professor J. M. Keynes was in favor of them. Keynes, the next choice, had been the financial genius at the Treasury and was supposed to open up to us the story of Great Britain's war finance; but he not only contributed nothing, he stated in our last meeting that he had obstructed our efforts as well. Beveridge and the other members were deeply shocked at this, especially as Keynes had all along accepted the regular editorial stipend of the Endowment. Very different was the loyal collaboration of Tom Jones, the Secretary of the Prime Minister, who opened

137

up to me all the documentation his office could supply. I recall one incident. He showed me the list which the War Cabinet had of the unofficial or quasi-official bodies that had grown up during the war to deal with wartime emergencies. There were only two typewritten pages, and the incautious historian of the future who relied upon this list would be entirely misled. So with Jones' help a competent researcher was put on the job, and our history published a *Dictionary of Official Wartime Organizations* which disclosed that there were over three thousand wartime organizations.

I should, perhaps, explain that this incident was typical of much of the confusion of wartime. The Socialist economist, G. D. H. Cole, said in one of his volumes that the picture he had of labor during the war was that of a constant series of organizations to deal with situations which shifted so much from time to time that in order not to complicate things and not to waste time no one bothered to go through the motions of dissolving them. It was more practical just to start something that fitted a present need.

This is worth pausing over. It could never have happened in bureaucratic France or Germany, where things were done tidily. The saying that the British built their empire in a fit of absent-mindedness just misses the point. The absent-mindedness was only on the things that had become unimportant or obsolete.

I had thought that I knew the British, but my first talk with Beveridge showed me that I still had something to learn. I proposed, in one of our first talks, that we should draft outlines of the volumes the contributors would write. Beveridge turned to me in alarm. Did I mean that the editor was going to prepare detailed directions for the authors? I explained that I wanted to make sure that there would be proper co-ordination between the volumes and also that the author was covering his whole field. Beveridge said: "That's not the way we edit a volume in England. The British method is to choose the right man, make quite clear what is wanted of him and let him bring out his own story and interpretation of the facts. Don't interfere with him after having clearly stated the problem at the beginning, how much of it he is to cover, what other studies there are alongside his. Then leave him freedom to do the job as he sees fit."

138

That is the way the volumes of the British series of the History, some twenty-four in number, were edited. The result is what might be expected. The British series has more individuality, more resilience, more vitality than any of the Continental series. Each volume is the testament of a man; his personality shines out in it. This is also true of some of the Continental volumes, of Gide in France, Einaudi in Italy, Mendelssohn-Bartholdy in Germany and Pirenne in Belgium. But as editors they thought it was their duty to outline the other volumes of their colleagues in detail.

France came next. Fortunately Professor Charles Gide,* the outstanding French economist, accepted the editorship of the French volumes. No one could speak with greater authority. A Huguenot from southern France, he shared the stern realism and puritanism of the Huguenot tradition. Along with him came his former pupil and colleague Professor Charles Rist, later Vice-Governor of the Bank of France. Professor Rist was also a Huguenot, coming from Alsace. Associated with them were Professor Henri Hauser, also from Alsace and Arthur Fontaine, with whom I had worked so intensively at the Paris Peace Conference, and who was Director of the Saar mines.

At once the contrast between the method of the French Editorial Board and that of the English Board became evident. Instead of proceeding, as the English Board had done, to assign a subject to a competent colleague or collaborator and allowing him to work out his monograph as he saw best, the French Editorial Board, with Gide watching carefully over every item, went into details and prepared a blueprint for the author before actual writing. This kind of work, which as I shall indicate later was Continental in character, was not followed on one occasion when a former Prime Minister was asked to work and preferred to have his own freedom. The result was that I threw his book out and *refused to have it as a part of the War History because* it was too jingoistic, political and apologetic and thus wouldn't do in a Carnegie Endowment history.

Next to the British and French series came the Belgian. I chose for my colleague in Belgium, Professor Henri Pirenne, Rector of the University of Ghent. Professor Pirenne was not only the greatest

* Uncle of André Gide, the novelist.

historian that Belgium has ever produced, and one of the greatest in Europe, but he also had a distinguished record during the war. He preferred exile in Germany to co-operating with the invaders, although they did their best to inveigle him into that position. While in his exile he was relatively well treated by the professors of the university town in which he was imprisoned. After his return he became, of course, a national hero.

Professor Pirenne accepted the position of editor for the Belgian series, and he turned out one of the best series in the whole History. The best way to appreciate the importance of Pirenne as a citizen of Europe is the fact that when Oxford gave its honorary D.C.L.— Doctor of Civil Law—to General Douglas Haig, and Marshal Ferdinand Foch, it chose Professor Pirenne to be the representative of Belgium.

The volumes of the Belgian series did not escape the criticism of Herbert Hoover, however, who felt that they did not give enough credit to the work of the Belgian Relief, which he had so ably directed. Professor Pirenne's reply was that, while the American Relief had done a magnificent job, it had been matched by the quiet but efficient work of the Belgian's neighbors, the Dutch and British. In any case I had to tell Mr. Hoover that I could not rewrite the Belgian History or question the judgment of so great an historian as Pirenne, based on the national collection of documents in *The Archives of the War,* which he had created, and I saw no reason to question his choice of collaborators. The volume on food supply during the German occupation was written by the Belgian official in charge of it, and I pointed out to Mr. Hoover that a revaluation written by an American would be open to criticism in Belgium.

Until December 11, 1920, I lived in Vienna preparing the organization of the most complicated of all the History series—that of the Austro-Hungarian monarchy. Fortunately, there was at hand a great economist of the old Austrian school, Professor Wieser, who had as high a standing as a philosopher and economic theorist, as he also had in statesmanship. During the war he had been Minister of Commerce, a position which made him intimately familiar with the personalities in high places. Representing as he did the best traditions of Austrian cultural life, of the interest in music, art, literature, and philosophy, I found in his home, where we were frequent guests, a revival, as far as one could have it in the intellectual sphere, of those elements of Austrian culture which had made Vienna, next to Paris, the intellectual center of Europe.

Wieser was the leading economist of Austria, but not without a tragedy in the family, because the war had touched them closely with the loss of members of the family itself.

He chose as his Hungarian colleague, Dr. Gustav Gratz, formerly Minister of Finance, one of Wieser's own former pupils many years gone by. Along with him he chose Dr. Richard Schüller, the former economic head of the Foreign Office of the Austrian Empire, who had lived through the whole war at the Foreign Office and watched the monarchy disappear. I asked Schüller if it had not been a tragic experience and got from his answer some of that light-hearted spirit of the Viennese when he said he found it so interesting he never had time to be sorry. That gives some idea of the outlook of public servants of the Hapsburg monarchy. No wonder it disappeared!

Professor Wieser reminded his colleagues that this was an occasion where Austrians could show once more the high quality of their scientific work by being objective in the discussion of a calamity that had affected their lives so deeply and so tragically. To each collaborator was reserved freedom of opinion with regard to measures taken by the government, whether they agreed with them or not; setting forth his ideas about the causes of the economic disaster that followed the war; describing in detail the war phenomena as they appeared to him at the time, uninfluenced in this regard by any editorial oversight. This was in line with the best traditions of liberal thought of the nineteenth century, and Professor Wieser emphasized it at length.

One of the qualities of Austrian writing, as I found out in the course of my work later on, was simply the word, "length." Everything was long; even the sentences were long. The Prussian sentence is quick, clear, well-organized and logical. The Austrian sentence begins at the top of a paragraph and rambles on down the page—the same leisurely, casual way in which life was organized in the old regime.

This description is perhaps unfair because after all there was a clarity and a direction of effort in the Austrian editorial control which ranked well with that of any other country. The result was ultimately an Austrian series of the first quality.

There was one part of the old Hapsburg monarchy that could not be treated from Vienna—that was, of course, Czechoslovakia, the newly formed state that had arisen under the aegis of Thomas Masaryk. Although Professor Wieser had been professor of political economy at the German University of Prague from 1884 to 1905, and his scientific reputation in academic circles in Prague was untouched by the war, still he agreed with me heartily that the Czechoslovak history—if there were to be a volume—would have to be done by a Czech.

So I went to Prague and talked it over with President Masaryk, who greeted me as an old friend, from the days of our work together in New York. We succeeded in getting the man who was then in charge of the financial policy of Czechoslovakia, Dr. Alois Rasin. He had been responsible for keeping the Czechoslovakian currency at par when everything around him was going into a terrible sweep of inflation. He did this by the strictest laws maintaining control over prices. He was assassinated by a Communist just at the time of the triumph of his financial policy. When all the rest of the old Hapsburg monarchy was on the downward spin toward worthless currency, Czechoslovak money remained at par.

This was my first visit with President Masaryk in his presidential office in Prague, in the old historical palace of Czech kings on the Hradcany hill. From his room one looked down over the bridges across the river to Vltava, the busy city on the east. He was especially keen to show me his library, with shelf after shelf of American books—for example, everything to date of Willa Cather. He had a lovely home in the suburbs at Lany, where he insisted that I come to spend the night. He had already found that the nationalism which he had evoked in creating the new Czechoslovak nation was restive under his political philosophy, built after the model of Thomas Jefferson. But he was not discouraged. Czechoslovakia had done better than its neighbors in the post-war period.

Professor Wieser was an Austrian of the old school—a very cultured gentleman—and had a generous outlook on the world as a whole. However, he had no confidence whatever in the Magyar. He warned me when we started to work together that it would be impossible to find any Magyar collaborator one could fully trust, unless he had been so long in Vienna that he was sufficiently in touch with the broader culture of the Viennese. Nationalism and a sort of Oriental streak ran in the Magyar blood.

That reminded me, of course, of the saying of Metternich that the Orient began at the Ringstrasse—the Ringstrasse being that great avenue around Vienna where the wall had formerly stood and along the side of which the university buildings and city hall had been erected. The Foreign Office itself was on the Ringstrasse. From there on down the Danube, Magyar, Slav, and Romanian were all races that the German-Austrian was never fully able to comprehend. This was certainly borne out in the history of the Hapsburg monarchy.

Wieser had been professor in Prague for several years. He had known Thomas Masaryk and had admired his qualities. With reference to the Yugoslavs, the Serbs, there was nothing but disdain for these Balkan people, who he said, like all Slavs, were really incapable of self-government, in the sense in which the Germanic people had worked it out. Naturally this affected the whole set-up of the Austro-Hungarian Editorial Board, and I found it necessary to assume the chairmanship myself as an outsider and ask Wieser simply to act as executive secretary of the Austrian section itself, and of the Austro-Hungarian Board, while I, myself, presided at it.

My Austrian colleagues understood the situation perfectly and co-operated with good will. But I could not have carried out so great a responsibility if I had not been able to share it with David Mitrany, who not only aided in the editing of the volumes on all the countries of southeastern Europe but wrote the final volume summing up, in a masterly survey, the effects of the war in the Danubian countries. Mitrany was Romanian-born but had been correspondent of the *Manchester Guardian* in Germany and then served in the British Foreign Office during the war. His intimate knowledge of men and events never influenced his critical objectivity, for his advice, like his writings, was in the best traditions of English Liberalism. He also worked with me on some of my adventures in peace-making during the years that followed. Finally his contributions to political thought won him the honor of a professorship in the Institute for Advanced Study in Princeton—Einstein's colleague.

After the organization of the Austro-Hungarian series of the War History came the organization of the Italian series. My family and I went down to Italy in the early winter of 1920.

We settled down in Rome and I got in touch at once with Professor Pasquale Panteleoni, who had been the economist on the research committee of the Carnegie Endowment. One of the most brilliant of European economists and sociologists, he was, however, a very erratic and unaccountable person with an emotional complex that kept showing itself in the most astonishing ways. He was completely carried away by Gabriele D'Annunzio and became Finance Minister of D'Annunzio in the Fiume episode.

Obviously, it was impossible for me to continue using him as a member of the Endowment Editorial Board, which was a very embarrassing situation. However, I frankly explained to him my embarrassment as it was obvious that he really had no sympathy with the aims of the Endowment and was already a thorough-going fascist. The result was that on January 1, 1921, I left Rome for Turin to see the Italian economist most highly thought of in England, Professor Luigi Einaudi.

His library was filled with English literature, not only in the field of economics but of history and philosophy. I have never found any where else on the continent of Europe anything to compare with it. He was a follower of Alfred Marshall, and that meant that his ideas were not completely mid-nineteenth century with John Stuart Mill, but that he had liberalism of that adjustable type which showed itself in the rich philosophic thought of Marshall, one of the greatest of English economists.

Einaudi, at that time, had been appointed Senator on the basis of the old Italian constitution where a number of distinguished men were appointed to the Senate because of their intellectual attainment. As Senator, he had been responsible for some of the financial legislation of the Kingdom prior to the war. But during the war he had held no high office, so far as I can recall. I found him quiet,

modest, forthright, thoroughly informed on all the European eco-
omic questions, as well as those of Italy, and he gathered around
him a little group of his former students and friends—Professor
Pasquale Jannaccone, professor of Statistics, and Professor Um-
berto Ricci, professor of Political Economy at the University of
Bologna and an honorary member of the London Cobden Club,
which showed his point of view in politics and economics. These
together formed the little group of the Italian Editorial Board.

Professor Einaudi was, of course, subsequently to reach emin-
ence as the man, who, after the Second World War, was in charge
of the finances of Italy in the provisional government following the
war. In that interval he not only saved Italy but saved Western
Europe from communism. I make that statement without any quali-
fication, because before the English had thought of it, he had set
up a policy of austerity in the insistence that the industrial capitalist
class pay very heavily to make up the deficit which the war had
left Italy. By this stern action, which was recognized by the Italian
workingmen as giving a fair and equal chance for them and the
employers, he undercut the propaganda of communism in Italy. It
was definitely to Einaudi's credit that Italy threw off the communist
trend which started in immediately after the war. That was, in a
way, a greater contribution to Europe than Einaudi, President of
Italy, could even bring , and it has not received adequate recognition.

In 1932 he came from his home in Turin to visit me in Milan
during the international conference which met under the auspices
of the League of Nations. We had a grand time together. He smil-
ingly remarked that the corporate state in which the Fascists
claimed to have brought labor and capital into co-operation did not
really exist. The Podesta, as an organ of the central government,
was kept under its control and obliged both labor and capital to
act as puppets of the government. This was my last personal contact with Einaudi, although we kept up an exchange of letters from
time to time even after he became President of Italy.

What he did after the Second World War was exactly what he
recommended should have been done after World War I in the
volume in the War History which he wrote. So that it was his study
of the economics of the First World War which in this roundabout

145

way paralleled the work of the Marshall Plan in Italy, preventing the possibility of the communist political victory in the years immediately after the war.

With the British, French, Austrian, and Italian Editorial Boards all organized, and the plan for the War History in each country under way, I then returned to America in the winter of 1920-1921 to present my report to the Trustees of the Carnegie Endowment, and to find out especially from Root how strongly the whole plan would be endorsed. It met with complete and enthusiastic endorsement and I was able to return in the spring of 1921 to Europe to continue the organization of the War History in the countries not yet organized, with the financial support not only of the Carnegie Endowment for International Peace but of the Carnegie Corporation as well.

By good fortune on my voyage back to Europe I had for a daily companion Colonel House, all to myself. He laid the chief blame for Wilson's defeat to the fact that he had no longer been able to reach the President and win him over to conciliatory measures, which, he insisted, were not a betrayal of Wilson's ideals but the practical way to realize them. Next to his personal concern was his fear, a real one, that the chaos left by the failure to organize the peace would mean another world war. He was as clear on this as Wilson was in his last public utterance.

The British and French volumes of the War History were already appearing. The most difficult of all, those on Germany, came next.

A visit paid to the permanent head of the Foreign Office had been facilitated by Dr. Riedl, who by this time had become Austrian Minister in Berlin, and the conversations in the Wilhelmstrasse seemed at the time to remove all difficulties of an official character, but we were to learn later on that the government of the Weimar Republic, however ready it might be to blame its imperial predecessor for political and military mistakes, was by no means equally ready to have historians reveal the economic situation the war had created. It was not the Foreign Office, however, but the Ministry of the Interior which ultimately blocked the publication of the history of German industry during the war. In the initial stages of

146

the preparation of the German volumes there was no hint of anything but friendly and full co-operation. It was only when the reparations problem came to dominate all others that the German Government decided not to reveal the history of its war time industry and commerce.

Then I called on Dr. Walter Rathenau, Minister of Reconstruction, and the most important man in Germany at the time. As a great industrialist, the head of the Electrical Trust, he had been the first to see that war had undergone an industrial revolution and could be won only by the mobilization of the entire economic energy of the nation—in short, total war. His Raw Materials Division of the War Office, which he had begun with a chair and desk, finally became larger than all the rest of the War Ministry. I found him at 62 Wilhelmstrasse, almost exactly opposite Bismarck's house; but, whether designedly or not I do not know, it was in bad repair, with bits of plaster chipped off the entrance hall, dingy walls and cheap stair carpet. Only the minister's own room had been refurnished.

Dr. Rathenau was a tall, strongly built man of middle age, with a bald head, the baldness accentuated by the closeness with which he had clipped the little hair left. Only close observance could discover the lines where the baldness stopped and the fact that his hair was almost white. It could hardly have been blond, for his eyes were dark brown and there were traces of dark hair in the closely trimmed whiskers, reminiscent of his Semitic blood.

The shaven skull was of a peculiar shape, rising almost to a ridge-like bump on top, almost like some of the heads of those northwestern Indians one sees in the museum, heads distorted by pressure during infancy. The face was hard in outline and would have been noticeably so if it were not that the brown eyes, while keen, responded so quickly with the gleam of intelligence to the points of conversation as to relieve with a certain touch of something approaching friendliness the otherwise reserved and forbidding expression. This quick intelligence did not affect the manner of the man, however, which was reserved and deliberate. Whether or not it was that we spoke English instead of German, he seemed to weigh every phrase he uttered and rounded off his expressions to

147

logical or literary conclusions, speaking with deliberate care, as through he were dictating a formal article. Throughout the interview it was clear that he was weighing not only what I had been saying to him but the implications of the whole enterprise with a complete concentration upon it for the time being. It was not one of those interviews which one sometimes has with busy men in which one feels that the listener's mind is wandering from the subject from time to time. Although our talk touched upon a subject which naturally suggested to him other types of treatment—he was impatient of all mere academic enterprises and classed with that the gathering of historical data—yet he did not fail to keep to the main thread of the interview and was able to re-phrase for himself my own problem in clearest possible form.

He met me with a cordial handshake—a strong grip of a muscular hand—and told me that Dr. Riedl had told him enough of the enterprise that we might dispense with preliminaries and proceed at once to consider what means should be used for the carrying out of the history in Germany. I indicated briefly the type of collaborators we had secured in other countries and what I had done so far in Germany, including the account of the War Office History under Sering and a visit to the Reichsbank. Instead of commenting upon these items separately he then restated the plan in his own words, dividing the subject into two major divisions—Production and Finance.

To these he said there could be added a third section which I had not mentioned, dealing with the economic policies of states as affected by war and also those which tend to bring war. I pointed out that this third division carried one over too much into the field of politics for my present plans; if I were to take up such subjects now, the scientific and impartial study of the more strictly economic facts might suffer from the suspicion that I was undertaking the history in the interest of some one political policy or was at least not detached and free to make impartial judgments on the economic side. He admitted the justice of this but said that the history would fail of its full significance if it were always kept to the analytic side of the problem. Its chief merit would be in the ultimate synthesis. With this I agreed but insisted that the value of the synthesis must rest upon the adequacy of its control of the detail upon which the synthesis would rest and that the chief justification for the history itself would lie in the fact that its conclusions would bear the mark of authority and not simply of probability as in the case of premature or journalistic surveys. He said, however, that as far as he was concerned he had lived throughout the war so closely in touch with the facts that for him it was rather a case of summarizing his conclusions than of massing his data.

When I asked him to nominate others, he said that the best advice he could give was not to use either professors or bankers. I said that I thought I knew what he meant about professors, but why not bankers? He said that they were experts on the money market but few of them had any philosophical insight into economic processes. Then I recalled that, like Henry Ford, he had carried out his organizational plans in the face of opposition from the banking world. It shows how little I heeded his warning when I made a partner of the Warburg Bank firm, Dr. Carl Melchior, chairman of the German Editorial Board, and Professor Albrecht Mendelssohn-Bartholdy, executive secretary in charge of research. Dr. Melchior, had been high in the financial circles in German administration during the war, and was one of the official delegates of the German Delegation at Versailles. Prior to the making of the Treaty he had played a decisive part in the negotiations at which had ended the food blockade of Germany by the surrender of its ships.

The British delegate with whom he had chiefly to deal, John Maynard Keynes, has written in bitter and contemptuous terms of some of the leaders at the Peace Conference, including, of course, President Wilson, but he has reserved for Dr. Melchior the highest possible praise, respecting not only his unshakable integrity but the clarity and directness of his thought. Although the Weimar Government had twice offered him the position of Minister of Finance in the new German State, he had refused public office and had gone back quietly to his banking house at Hamburg. Modest and retiring in demeanor, he was little known outside the field of his competence, which was nothing short of financial statesmanship. His acceptance of the chairmanship of the board was a guarantee that

149

the purpose of the History would be faithfully kept in mind as the work proceeded. His conception of editorial control was about halfway between that of the Austrians and the British. There should be no undue interference with the actual writing but a careful supervision to make sure that the German series would not be a glorification of German military achievement, but a well-balanced, objective study of the whole effect of the war upon Germany.

In all of this Dr. Melchior relied upon the executive secretary of the board, Dr. Mendelssohn-Bartholdy, Professor of International Law at Hamburg University, and one of the outstanding leaders in German liberal thought, who was chiefly responsible for the best contributions in the German series, among which was his own study, *The War and German Society—The Testament of a Liberal.* Dr. Mendelssohn was at the same time editing that great series of documents supplied from the Foreign Office, *Die Grosse Politik der Europaischen Kabinette,* which opened to the world the documentary evidence for the diplomatic history of Germany from the war which created the Empire to that which brought its downfall.

In his mind and in that of the German Editorial Board, the Endowment's *Economic and Social History of the World War* was a parallel undertaking. While the full implication of this conception would not be evident in the early days, namely, that the War History was to furnish a test of the validity of Clausewitz' theory of war as an instrument of policy, yet it was a great conception which fired the imagination of my German colleagues, one worthy of the tradition of German scholarship and science.*

This much has been said on the significance of the effort made to secure a well-rounded German series in the *Economic and Social History of the World War* because it reflects the spirit in which Professor Mendelssohn-Bartholdy approached the task of writing this final volume. A descendant of Moses Mendelssohn, the philosopher of enlightenment and the friend of Lessing, grandson of Felix Mendelssohn-Bartholdy the composer, and a son of Karl Mendelssohn-Bartholdy the historian, he brought to the study of

* The full rebuttal of the Clausewitz theory was not made until my address in Berlin in March, 1927, given below.

jurisprudence, of which he was a distinguished leader, the many-sided gifts which made him an outstanding exponent of the best traditions of German culture. It was a tribute to his impartial and judicious outlook that he was chosen to represent Germany on the Arbitral Tribunal at the Hague, set up in connection with the administration of the Young Plan of reparations. He was honored by other countries as well as his own and held the honorary degree of Doctor of Laws of Harvard University; but in the autumn of 1933 he was obliged to seek asylum from the persecution of the Jews in Germany, and Balliol College, Oxford, created a lecture-ship for him. His sudden death in November, 1936, prevented a revision of his volume which would have brought it up to date and filled some of the lacunae, especially in the sections dealing with the economic effects of the war. Happily, however, the volume combined with fundamental objectivity the clear personal note of one who could rise above the warping prejudices of his time because of his fundamental interest in life itself. It was thus given to the public under the dual caption of a historical survey and "the testament of a liberal."

The German volumes covered every aspect of the impact of the war upon Germany, except one, that of industry. For this all-important subject the Reichsverband der Deutschen Industrie (the German parallel to the National Association of Manufacturers) prepared an elaborate survey, but after all the research on it was finished and the manuscript ready for the printer, the government, then in the midst of its controversy over reparations, refused publication.

Dr. Duisberg, the head of the great chemical trust, who was a loyal member of our editorial board protested in vain that the politicians were merely hurting Germany's case by refusing to open up the economic and social costs of total war. He was determined that I, at least, should see that a revolution in chemistry could not be held back because of its poison gases or high explosives. He had me visit two of the great chemical works, Leuna Werke near Halle in Saxony (now in Communist control) for the fixation of nitrogen for fertilizer as well as for explosives, and the wonderful works at Leverkusen on the Rhine, where the coal from the river barges is made over into all the coal-tar derivatives, from medicines (such as aspirin) to dyes. There was a museum of all the richest colors anywhere in nature—quartz, flowers, feathers from the bird of paradise—and alongside them the perfect parallel in the coal-tar dye.

Looking out of the window of a laboratory where a scientist was working on the cure for sleeping sickness in Africa, I asked why the adjoining building had been destroyed, leaving only a hole in the ground. It was demolished on the orders of the allies in the war, because it had produced poison gas for the battles on the Western Front. I asked Dr. Duisberg, when I saw him next, why his great organization did not take the lead in offering to open up his chemical secrets to international inspection, as a major step toward disarmament and the elimination of the fear of war. To my surprise he said that he had already made the offer to admit qualified French chemists into his laboratories, but the politicians, responsive to popular feelings of mistrust, refused the offer. This was over thirty years before a similar impasse in science happened, when solutions by the scientists of technical problems in atomic energy were rejected by the politicians.

The direct cost of the war to Germany, that of its government expenditures was the equivalent of almost two years of the nation in peacetime. The indirect cost in the business of its citizens was probably twice that. Even this was less proportionately than the total cost to Austria-Hungary, which was about five times as great as its annual income and almost four fifths as great as Austria-Hungary's national wealth. Yet, in neither country had government or economists attempted to deal with these statistics of disaster as something apart from the problem of reparations, until the analysis was made in *The Economic and Social History of the War*. There, it was pointed out by the English economist, Francis Hirst, that the best index to the costs of the war was to be found in the tax rates of the post-war years. The British taxation was four times as heavy as that of Germany at the very time when Germany was beginning to show signs of going bankrupt.

It was while working on these problems that I ran upon a surprising incident in Vienna. From Berlin I had gone back to Vienna to deal with the problem of publication. I have not said anything yet about this, although planning and carrying it through in each country was a full job in itself. I mention it here, however, for another reason. When I visited the University Press in Vienna, in its palatial quarters, I was surprised to see some printers printing by hand alongside the most modern presses. On inquiry I found that they were setting Arabic type because the University Press had the monopoly of printing the school textbooks of Egypt and, I think, Turkey.

That touched on the problem of Austria's economic resources, some of which evidently were "hidden." Mr. Hoover was saying that Austria was an economic vacuum. So I went over to see the executive head of the Austro-Hungarian Bank, Dr. Alexander Popovics, who was writing a volume on War Finances for me, and asked for a memorandum on other sources of income from eastern Europe and Asia. I found that the ownership of railways and utilities were not all lost.

Coming back to New York for a meeting of the Trustees of the Endowment, I laid the matter before Mr. Root, and he got me a subsidy from the Carnegie Corporation of $10,000 for research on Austria's resources. I persuaded Professor Rist, an outstanding specialist in finance, to go to Austria and investigate what could be done to strengthen its economics. I then turned over his report to Sir Arthur Salter at the League of Nations, and from this came the League's effort at financial help for Austria. Professor Rist's expenses amounted to less than $790! Incidentally, however, it was his first step out of academic life, opening a career which ended with his becoming Vice-President of the Bank of France.

My work in Vienna made me sharply aware of the economic problems of the Danubian countries. In November, 1921, the successors of the Hapsburg Monarchy—Austria, Hungary, Yugoslavia, Romania, and Poland—had met with Italian representatives at Porto-Rosa to discuss a lessening of customs barriers between their respective countries. The Conference helped to open the transnational railway service and the Danubian shipping, but tariffs and other obstacles still crippled trade. Therefore, on my next journey to America, I proposed to the Trustees of the Carnegie Endowment that in co-operation with the International Chamber of Commerce the Endowment should call a conference of the chambers of commerce and other commercial bodies in Austria, Hungary, Yugoslavia, Bulgaria, and Romania to restore normal conditions of trade and commerce in southeastern Europe.

The Trustees readily voted $10,000 for such a meeting, and at my suggestion Frederick Keppel, then Executive Secretary of the International Chamber of Commerce, with offices in Paris, undertook to organize it. On my return to Europe I also visited President Masaryk and found in him and Dr. Benes strong support for the proposal; but although Mr. Mitrany mobilized business support for it in Romania and Dr. Gratz in Hungary, it met with opposition from the vested interests, both political and economic, and nothing came of it. In a last letter to Keppel I said that the experience gave me an added sympathy for those who try to get anything worthwhile done in a world so surcharged with political intrigue and personal ambition.*

I shall not describe the Russian series of the War History because I had little to do with it. The editor was Sir Paul Vinogradoff, Regis Professor of Jurisprudence at Oxford, and he had a competent assistant in Michael Florensky, now professor at Columbia University, whose own volume, *The Fall of the Russian Empire,* covers the whole tragic war and revolutionary periods.

For the same reason, the concentration of the History on Western Europe, the editor was unable to give adequate study to the two nations which seemed to have profited from the war, Japan and the United States. The Japanese series was left under the guidance of Baron Sakatani, the correspondent of the Endowment in Japan.

Fortunately the fragmentary American series contained one essential volume, *The Cost of the War to the American People,* by Professor John Maurice Clark, son of the economist John Bates Clark, under whose direction the History was originally planned. The writing of this volume was delayed until 1931 when the false

* A fuller account of this effort to use the International Chamber of Commerce is given in the first edition of George L. Ridgeway's *Merchants of Peace,* (New York: Columbia University Press, 1938), Chapter XI.

post-war prosperity of the 1920's was being liquidated in the great depression. The immediate effects of the war are analyzed statistically, showing a loss in goods, services and government expenditures of somewhere in the neighborhood of fifty billion dollars, after making all allowances for the gains from increased war-time production. But, as Professor Clark points out, the final economic impact of the war is beyond calculation. It reached too deeply into the very processes of civilization to reveal its full effects until long years afterward; and by that time so many new elements will have entered into the economic life of the nation, that the traces of this great convulsion will become impossible to follow.

But if the statistician may never be able to register the exact extent of war costs, the historian can describe the nature of the catastrophe of scientific war. And that was the fundamental purpose of the *Economic and Social History of the World War*. In the course of the work it became clear that the most important fact of the war was not the extent of its destruction, incalculable as that was, but that in the era of science and industrialism war had ceased to be that controllable instrument of politics, which had been the excuse and argument for it in the past.

CHAPTER 9

Glimpses of History in the Making

The making of the History of the War and my contacts at Geneva gave me a privileged seat at the great but confused drama of Europe, during the post-war years, keeping me in close touch with governments and leaders of thought. Some thirty-five members of wartime cabinets were working on parts of the History alongside professors and government experts. How richly rewarding these contacts were will appear from excerpts of diaries and letters, which follow in a rambling sort of way, along with one or two extracts from my writings.

Of all the historic incidents with which I was associated in one way or another, there was none more important than the Imperial Conference, which met in London in 1921 to remake the Empire into a Commonwealth and to shape its new policies in the new post-war era. As I was living in London at that time, I had an inside view of the Conference, for the Prime Minister of Canada, Arthur Meighen, had been a fellow student in the University of Toronto, and had been a close friend of my brother. We were, therefore, on rather intimate terms, and between meetings of the Imperial Conference we got together and I learned from him and from John DeFoe, the editor of the *Winnipeg Free Press*, who was also a delegate, how the debates of the Conference went on, day by day.

The Imperial Conference, back in the days of Queen Victoria's golden jubilee, had been repeated every ten years as meetings of the Prime Ministers of the Dominions and outlying sections of the Empire. But these early meetings were little more than informal gatherings until the World War, when the Dominions played so great a part that they were represented in a new organization called the Imperial War Cabinet in which Sir Robert Borden of Canada sat alongside the British Prime Minister and the other Prime Ministers of the Dominions: Hughes of Australia, Massey of New Zealand, and Botha of South Africa.

Under the impact of the war the Empire began to take on a whole new character. The part played by the Dominions in the war and at the Paris Peace Conference made the Imperial Conference a more closely knit organization than had ever existed before. Something really "imperial" had happened. The Dominions were no longer mere guests of the mother country, but partners in government.

At the Peace Conference it had been Hughes of Australia who was *l'enfant terrible,* to the great discomfort of Balfour, but in the London Conference it was Meighen who had an important demand to make upon the British and one most unwelcome to them. He insisted that the British give up their alliance with Japan, which it had made in 1902 as a protection against Russian imperialism in the Far East. Now, Meighen pointed out, there was bitter opposition to Japan in the United States because of Japan's aggression in China, its treatment of Shantung, and its Twenty-One Demands. Meighen pointed out that if the United States were to go to war with Japan, it would mean going to war with Britain as well, and Canada was deeply concerned.

His argument won out. The Empire dropped its Japanese alliance, but not without a bitter attack by Hughes and a strong dissent from Lloyd George and Curzon. The importance of this measure to the United States was fundamental, because Secretary of State Hughes was then able to call the Washington Conference of Naval Disarmament and secure what looked like a real reduction in armaments by limiting the capital ships of Great Britain, the United States and Japan to a ratio of 5:5:3. As I have said elsewhere, I was always skeptical of disarmament by arithmetic, especially in view of the changing character of munitions. The Wash-

157

ington Conference was hailed by many pacifists as the short way to peace. I still held to the point of view that the way to peace was by conciliation and conference, especially in the League of Nations and that naval engineers would falsify the ratios.

As the rest of my documentation on the Imperial Conference is still under the seal of secrecy, I shall close off the year 1921 with two extracts from my diary which open two other doors in the drama of history, one in the British House of Commons, the other in the French Senate.

Although the date is now forgotten, at the time everyone in the British Empire regarded Wednesday, December 14, 1921, as one of the most momentous days in its annals, for the new Irish Treaty creating an independent republic was to be submitted to the British Parliament and to the Dail in Dublin in the hope of ending a century-long feud.

It was a dreary cold sky with a sharp East wind blowing, and the sun struggling through the mist hardly showed itself across the south of Palace Yard. The streets were lined with the Guards in their great overcoats and tall furskin busbies. The procession was the usual one with the Horseguards Band with the inimitable drummer with his two drums on either side and the gilded trappings which reminded me of the old files of the *Illustrated London News* that were the delight of my childhood. It is a taste for childhood in any case. After several carriages, each of them looking like the Lord Mayor's carriage with the powdered coachman in his cocked hat and the silk-stockinged footmen standing up behind, came the royal carriage with its eight black horses gaily caparisoned, and the King, Queen and Prime Minister sitting inside what might be described as a huge golden crown with glass windows. The Queen looked queenly, and as for George, he had done enough to win golden opinions, so we had best be charitable and not comment on his appearance. Had he had his father's presence he would have been a great king.

After the procession had passed, I went back into the building to see the Commons answer the summons of Black Rod and go in procession to the Lords to hear the speech from the throne. Standing by the aisle where the Commons were passing, by chance I

158

took a look toward the Lords and to my surprise saw clearly seated on their thrones facing the aisle down the Commons and therefore facing me at that moment, Their Majesties! They were sitting stiffly and were waiting for the coming of the House of Commons.

The procession of the Commons itself was a very ragged affair. Behind the Speaker and a few officers, came Lloyd George side by side with Asquith. The two short stumpy figures trudged along —both of them in apparent good humor and talking freely to each other. As they passed, one noticed that they both shared another peculiarity, for no one else in the House has such overflowing white locks as both Asquith and Lloyd George. Coming back—and the speech only took five minutes—Lloyd George was walking along with Mr. Clynes and just in front of me stopped and stooped under the rope and left the procession with Winston Churchill and some others following as if a little puzzled but bound to keep close by the Prime Minister at all costs.

I left the building for lunch as soon as the speech was over and then got back by two o'clock to make sure of a seat for the afternoon. I had the first seat in the front row beside the ambassadors and in line with the peers. The galleries were naturally full to overflowing, and half an hour before the House began its session, members started to take their places and there was an antimated buzz of conversation.

Just before three o'clock, when the Speaker took his chair, there was an outburst of "Hear, Hear" and "Oh, Oh" from all over the House and a genial sort of smile directed toward one figure in scarlet officer's court uniform. It was Sir Samuel Hoare who was to move the reply to the speech from the Throne and it is an old custom that the mover of the reply shall act as though he were in the presence of His Majesty and therefore appear in court uniform, if he has one.

On the front Government bench were seated Austen Chamberlain, Sir Robert Horne, Chancellor of the Exchequer, and all the rest of the Cabinet, so closely packed together that when a new Parliamentary secretary tried to wedge in there was no room except on somebody else's knees, so he had to stand beside the Speaker. However, they made room when, some time after the first speech had been made, Lloyd George appeared. On his appearance there was a great outburst of "Hear, Hear" all over the house. It is a custom of Parliament not to applaud by handclapping but simply to call out "Hear, Hear."

It was a cordial tribute, but not by any means as strong as I had expected. Some few members rose in their seats, but whether the rest were afraid of not getting any seats when they sat down again or not, in any case there was very little rising in honor of the greatest moment in Lloyd George's history, and he was soon quietly seated with the rest of the Cabinet listening to the second speaker. This was no other than my old friend the Rt. Honorable G. N. Barnes. I saw him in the morning and had a word with him and told him how glad I was of the honor which had come to him of seconding the reply on this occasion. He spoke very well indeed and with particular appropriateness he cited the case of Lincoln, when before the Civil War he tried vainly to appeal to the Southern states to avoid the issue of civil war. After the two speeches in reply to the address from the Throne, I had expected that Lloyd George would speak at once, but he waited until Mr. Clynes and Sir Donald MacLean had given voice to the support of the Labor and Liberal parties to the treaty with Ireland. It was now between four and five and the casual visitor might have wondered why the benches emptied while Clynes was speaking, for the Labour leader was both forceful and eloquent. But I suspect that the real situation was that the great English institution—afternoon tea—was asserting its prerogatives.

In any case, hundreds of members hurriedly left the house. Lloyd George, however, was not among them and stayed to do honor to Clynes and Sir Donald MacLean, the latter of whom spoke with that nicety of diction and almost prettiness of manner which have perhaps helped to qualify him as leader of the little group of Liberals left in the house.

The benches were still in this empty condition when, without waiting for further speeches, Lloyd George rose and began one of the greatest speeches of his life. There was a rush through the doors on all sides to fill the benches, and it was not long before not only the house below but the galleries on either side were filled with people listening carefully to every word of the Prime Minister.

I found the speech upon the whole disappointing. In parts it rose to the full measure of the occasion, but only here and there at the resounding end of a period. He seized every occasion that presented itself to keep the house in good humor both by deft thrusts at his opponents—particularly at Mr. Asquith—and by some of his allusions to the difficulty of the task itself. This sense of mere politics was accentuated by the telling and dignified phrase which he quoted from the elder Pitt, so strangely in contrast with the casual quality of his own oratory. His speech had evidently been carefully prepared. He constantly referred to the manuscript on which it was clear that he had noted all the headings of the different points, and he was sufficiently at home with the text to turn rapidly from one outline to another set of papers containing the illustrative quotations which he could insert at the proper moment. But in spite of this care of preparation, there was a sloppiness in his sentence structure and in the logic of his presentation which showed the casual character of his mental training.

The speech was rich in substance, for it touched upon practically every phase of the controversy. He carefully anticipated lines of attack which he knew would be followed in subsequent debate, but the placing of these various points lacked that systematic development which is essential to true elevation of style. There was something distinctly commonplace in his utterance which even the historic quality of the moment could not disguise. Indeed one felt sometimes as though he had distinctly failed to produce the effect he sought. This was particularly the case when at the central point of his speech he seized the text of the Treaty which was lying on the table before him and waved it in the air. There was only a little outburst of "Hear, Hear" and that of a rather perfunctory kind.

The thing I objected to most, however, in the speech was the conscious effort to claim the entire credit for the present government and to prevent the opposition from making good any claim that the freedom of Ireland could have been obtained before. It would have been far more statesmanlike to have generously paid a tribute to the work of those who have laid the basis for the Irish settlement through long struggle and much obloquy, instead of putting the question before the house as a matter distinctly of ex-

161

pediency, as the solicitor in a law suit finally comes to the conclusion that the moment has arrived to bring his unreasoning clients to agreement. This simile, which he developed at great length was all given in such a way as to bring a laugh, and particularly to turn it against Mr. Asquith, who sat uncomfortably on the other side of the desk. It was not a time for mere parliamentary fencing.

In short, Lloyd George had not lost himself sufficiently in the subject. He was always too self-conscious and one had a suspicion that the Irish settlement was not more in his mind than the question of his own power. This may be ungenerous, but it was the impression his speech made upon me.

I should, however, say that there were some moments when he spoke with great forcefulness and emotion. I could see Lady Astor, for instance, lean forward in her seat and straighten up as though electrified with the eloquence of the Prime Minister. There were some really affecting periods, and after all the greatness of his achievement should not be forgotten and he should be allowed the privilege of taking to himself whatever credit is due. It would be utterly wrong to think that Lloyd George was lacking in sincerity. When I heard him three days later address the Building Trades Council, made up of workmen and employers, I felt that even when most devious he was ready to interject a joke or a quip in the rapid flow of the talk or discussion, in order to make his point.

He used notes that had obviously been prepared for him by others and statistics which were apparently quite new to him. He showed no sign of apologizing when he had to ask the Minister of Health, who sat beside him, whether the bill they were discussing had already passed the House of Lords or not. He was as careless about logic as about the details in his notes, however. Here is a sentence I copied down: "The new spirit of brotherhood between the classes has been brought about by the war more than either class is willing to admit." Just how much of the spirit of brotherhood they can have without knowing it is more than I have been able to make out. Again in replying to criticisms later he said: "I don't always succeed in coming up to my own expectations . . . and that's all I ever hope to attain!" But no person seemed to notice these slips. The speech was clever in its homeliness; his illustrations

162

were mainly drawn from the building trades themselves so that everything he said was direct.

By a happy chance, only a few days after I witnessed this scene in Parliament, I was present in the French Senate when M. Briand made one of his most important speeches in defense of his foreign policy, especially with reference to his treatment of Germany. I was struck by a little incident as we passed through the crowded lobby of the Senate—filled with animated groups of senators—on the way to the gallery. It was just three o'clock, and we had come out into the narrow gallery back of the chair of the President of the Senate along which he was to come in a moment. It was lined with the Garde Républicaine with rifles and fixed bayonets, and a roll of drums gave notice that the President was leaving his rooms for the Chamber. The whole atmosphere was military in the extreme and reminiscent of that one outlook of France which links its history to the Revolution and the Empire. Contrasted with this were both the personality and the manner of the President of the Senate, M. Emile Bourgeois, the convinced pacifist and veteran leader in France of the World Court movement and the pacific ideals of the League of Nations.

In no other Parliament that I have seen did the presiding officer proceed to his chair down a line of shining bayonets as was the case in France. But then I had never seen a Parliament of the Central Powers in session.

The session began with the announcement from a member of the Cabinet that M. Briand hoped to be present as soon as he could disengage himself from a troublesome question in the Chamber of Deputies, and the Senate settled down to listen—or rather not to listen—to a long disquisition on the manufacture of chemicals in France by a senator who had once been a professor of chemistry, and who had hard work to keep even the casual attention of his colleagues to the question in hand. Presently M. Briand arrived and quietly slipped into the crowded Government bench on the front row and the house got down to the real business of the afternoon.

Two questioners then presented their attack upon the government. Whether by chance or design the interpellators were evidently men of little standing in the Senate—one from the extreme Right

163

and the other from the Right Centre. They launched into tirades against the government for all the things that had not materialized from the Treaty of Versailles to the present, and it was clear before they sat down that Briand would have an easy chance to demolish the attack. Indeed, without waiting for the third speaker on the program, he quietly rose and shuffled across the carpet of the stairway to the tribune. The enemy had played into his hands, for at once he seized upon the general character of the attack and turned it to his advantage by insisting upon its vagueness and the absence of any specific suggestion for bettering things.

It was easy to disclaim a general responsibility for all the evils following upon the war and for the most part he made his disclaimer in an argumentative tone without any oratorical gestures; but after having reasoned with his colleagues in a quiet conversational way he then suddenly turned aggressive, and with a rapid change of countenance and raising his voice so that it resounded throughout the hall, he called for something positive and constructive from his enemies—that the House might decide between them, instead of simply hampering the activities of the government by a general negative attitude. This permitted him to make the real point of his subject, for having carried the house along that far, he then grew definitely defiant and invited his enemies to come out with something specific and intimated that there was a lack of real patriotism in their hampering a government by innuendoes of general attack instead of contributing the constructive statesmanship of which France had so much need in its present perilous situation. The taunt was directed, as every person knew, at Poincaré, but it was clear from the gathering storm of applause that Briand had the house with him too strongly in this to make it a favorable moment for Poincaré to reply, and so as Briand felt more and more secure in his position, he attacked Poincaré, although not definitely naming him, more and more bitterly, and left the implication that the man who had attacked him in his absence was either a coward when called upon to face the issue, or else a mere faultfinder without any real plan of his own.

This was the essence of Briand's speech, and if this had been all, it would not have amounted to anything more than mere preliminary maneuvers; but during the speech he seemed to feel that the chance had come to show his own courage, and turning to the analysis of Germany, he for the first time ventured to give an official French sanction to the idea that it was possible to co-operate with that section of Germany which wanted to re-establish its name as an honest partner of the European State system. A single instance in this connection is perhaps all that will be remembered of his speech—"There are two Germanys, not simply one; the Germany of honest anti-imperialistic convictions, anxious to rid itself of the incubus of militarism is a fact, as well as the Prussianized system which brought the war."

Briand spoke without any notes whatever, marshaled his facts coherently, and presented them logically—more logically indeed than Lloyd George speaking from notes. His voice ranged from the casual conversational tone of an argument to a flourish of passionate eloquence: and the ease with which he recovered from his passion shows that the exposition as a whole hung together in his mind —argument and passion being different elements in a single expression. Yet there was something in Briand, in spite of this latent fire and appeal to the higher qualities of statesmanship, which reminded me of the native shrewdness of the French Canadian. There was something suggesting a conscious artfulness in his movements and glance. The directness of the Breton was combined with the experience of the politician and the interest of winning men. Compared with Clemenceau, for instance, he could employ that method of self-effacement which is one of the subtlest devices in debate. All in all, his mastery of the arts of the parliamentarian was so real that the Senate, although obviously by no means reconciled to his policy, gave him an overwhelming majority.

What France needed was greater courage in its leadership. Those in responsible positions knew quite well the catastrophe before the country if it persisted in demanding the whole of what was rightly due to it from the war. But both Chamber and House had a majority elected to enforce the claims of France, no matter what might happen, and so the government felt obliged to temporize, and none was willing to speak out frankly and fully. It was this fact which made the few short sentences of Briand admitting the possibility of dealing with specific elements in Germany of greater significance than the words themselves would lead one to imagine.

The contrast between France and Britain is one that was never more impressed upon me than when I returned from London this time. The continuity of outward things upon which Britain insists gives a specious appearance of conservatism to a society that is really one of the most adjustable to the changing current of events. The French on the other hand, insist upon the outward symbol of modernity while remaining at heart the most conservative people of Western Europe. As I watched the King's procession in London I was thinking how utterly impossible such a pageant with all its medieval trappings and unreality would be in Paris. On the other hand, had the French kings been shorn of their power and the people led to believe that they were imposing their own taxes upon themselves, it is possible that not only would there be Bourbons parading through the streets of Paris today, but that a much more significant political change would have modernized the French State, for there is nothing more medieval in Europe than the attitude of the French toward taxation. The tax collector of the Third Republic in the eyes of the majority of French citizens was as the tax collector of Louis XIV—the representative of an outside force imposing its will upon the people. In comparison with such a benighted attitude toward taxation the few trappings with which British royalty surrounds itself are of small significance indeed.

Briand's parliamentary success was only temporary. In January, 1922, he resigned to make way for Poincaré, who as President of the Republic for seven fateful years (1913-1920) now used all his influence as Premier and Minister of Foreign Affairs to insist on Germany's meeting its reparation payments. In July, 1922, my friend, Baron d'Estournelles de Constant, the Carnegie Endowment's representative in France, arranged for me to hear the debate in the Senate in which Poincaré made one of his major speeches. Two other senators had come forward with the suggestion that the German indemnity could be lessened by applying it only for losses to those who had suffered from the German invasion. But Poincaré refused to make any concession whatever. He struck me as a kind of political Calvin, whose rigid mind saw clearly his side of the question and argued convincingly to himself, and therefore to many of his listeners, that his case was unanswerable except by force. That meant, as was soon to be seen, that force would first be used by the French.

Scenes like this from the drama of European history fill my notebooks and diaries throughout these years. It is impossible to deal with all of it, for my work on the War History kept me constantly moving both across the Atlantic and from country to country in Europe. There were some interludes in that absorbingly busy life, however, when I looked in once more on the academic life, if only from a growing distance. I have already referred to the Union of Learned Academies, which I attended in Brussels in 1921. As there was no national academy in the United States, one had to be created, and the result was the Council of Learned Academies.

Then, in April, 1923, the World Conference of Historians which had been meeting at several year intervals before the war, was reconvened at Brussels, and I was chosen to be one of its presidents, as the head of the American delegation. There were almost a thousand people present, including the most distinguished historians of all European countries except the Central Powers. They had not been sent official invitations and refused to come without them. This had been a matter of great controversy during the planning of the conference. A number of British historians protested, and practically all from the Scandanavian countries stayed away owing to the exclusion of the Germans. I happened to get into the thick of the controversy, as I was the presiding president at the final session in which the future of the conference was decided.

My friend Waldo Leland of the American Historical Association and I drafted a resolution instructing the Executive Committee "to study the ways and means for making the Conference universally representative." As presiding officer when the vote came, I declared the resolution passed over the opposition of the hotheads among the nationalists. In this I had the strong support of Professor Pirenne, and I was fortunately able to call the vote to the attention of German, Austrian, Dutch, Danish, and Swedish historians and so to prevent the building up of two rival history organizations, which would be accentuating rival lines of European history, especially those dealing with the origins of the war.

It happened that the day I was presiding was the one on which King Albert gave his official reception, and, as I came into the hall in the palace, Professor Pirenne called out to me that the king wished to speak with me. The king turned to me with a question which could not have been more apt. What would historians do with the records of today, since there were so many of them? That, of course, opened up the very problem which Professor Pirenne and I had been working on in Belgium, the creation of the Archives of the War, and I had a few minutes to explain what was being done in other countries. He listened with close attention. Then I was passed on to talk with the Queen and the Crown Prince; and I heard over my shoulder the King's greeting to Professor Tout, the head of the British delegation, in exactly the same tones of scholarly interest as he had used with me, asking him in a puzzled way what the historians would do with the mass of documents in contemporary history. I suddenly realized what a task it would be to be a king and have the right word for every occasion. I even suspected Professor Pirenne of having given King Albert a hint beforehand. I asked the Crown Prince how many luncheons his father had been through that day. There were four, including an agricultural fair and a chamber of commerce, and at each there had to be the right line of approach. Royalty is a profession in its own right.

Although the Conference of Historians found the way to avoid a permanent rift among its European members, there still remained rifts in the social and political sciences, and the International Union of Academies kept aloof from such questions. Paris, however, still treasured the memories of its intellectual pre-eminence in the Middle Ages, and when I was invited to address the Acadèmie des Sciences Morales et Politiques of the Institute, the session was honored by the presence of the President of France.

A still more important occasion was the invitation of the Nobel Institute, the scientific organ of the Nobel Peace Prize, to deliver the Nobel Lectures in Oslo. I could not help regarding it as a justification of the research work of the Endowment on the study of the fundamental problems of war and peace that this body should finally decide to devote itself to investigation along similar lines to those of the Division of Economics and History of the Endowment,

168

to the Directorship of which I had just been appointed on the retirement of Professor Clark. In fulfillment of a program much resembling ours, it had inaugurated a series of annual conferences dealing with the technical problems of peace and war. But while recognition by the Nobel Institute was gratifying, the lasting memory which I brought away from Oslo was that of a meeting with the students of the University of Oslo, under the auspices of the student organization which turned out to be very critical of the stodgy, slow-moving ways of the older generation. It was at least a new experience to listen to speeches from the floor filled with impatience at the absence of practical measures to give effect to the ideas of peace which we were endorsing in theory. A similar meeting with one thousand students at the University of Copenhagen was equally critical although less forceful in expressing its dissent. I also addressed a meeting in Stockholm, but it was rather a formal affair and passed off quietly. I found the whole experience refreshing and stimulating.

As a matter of fact, I was already engaged in that very application of history to action which the Scandanavian students were demanding, and I had begun long discussions in London with the German ambassador about the difficulties which confronted the young German republic. The revolutionary outbreaks of the Communists in 1918 had been ruthlessly suppressed and the Government of the Reich had come out of its seclusion in Weimar to the old offices in Berlin; but, militant nationalism, supported by reactionary industrialists, gave an ominous aspect to post-war Germany, by assassinations of men like Erzberger, the Minister of Finance, and Walter Rathenau, Foreign Minister, who had advocated meeting the reparations terms, and armed uprisings, especially in Bavaria. Although the danger of a *Putsch* in which Ludendorff was involved, proved to be a fiasco, the danger of anarchy was not wholly gone. My friends in Hamburg told me of a shipment of piano cases from the English port of Hull to Munich. It did not seem quite the thing for a musical center like Munich to have to import its pianos from northern England, so the socialist dock workers opened the cases and found them filled with machine guns. They remained in Hamburg.

The anti-Semitic movement, which was soon to find its leader in Hitler, was already serious enough (as the assassination of Rathenau had shown), and the head of the great Hamburg banking firm, Max Warburg, took asylum in Holland. His brother Paul Warburg in New York, the chief architect of the Federal Reserve Banking system, had been a friend of mine and I decided to center the editing of the German volumes of the War History in his house at Hamburg. In Amsterdam I had great difficuly in persuading the hotel people where Max Warburg was staying to let me see him, and only after I had been duly certified by his friends was I permitted in. I stayed with him for two days and found in him one of the keenest minds I have ever known.

He pointed out that Hamburg would be the best center for work on the War History of Germany because as the commercial capital of Germany it had a better understanding of international problems. Before leaving Holland I went over to the Peace Palace at the Hague to see what had been done with the collection of documents I had placed in its library. I arrived there just as an international conference with the Russians was adjourning, but had no personal contact with any of the delegates. After a short stay I left on the train for Hamburg across the green interminable meadow lands where the Dutch cheese is made. As far as Utrecht the country was all alike and all under water, but from Utrecht on to the German frontier the canals ceased, except at rare intervals where a river crossed the railroad and the country was a poor waste of sand and pines.

It was midnight when I reached the frontier and had to scramble out to have the luggage examined. However, the ordeal was not very severe. Then I tried hard to sleep in a second-class sleeping compartment to the outskirts of Hamburg until roused by the porter a few miles out of Hamburg. As the train was about to cross the southern arm of the river Elbe, and then a stretch of low-lying sandy fields and market gardens, I saw the masts of ships in Hamburg harbor and the tall chimneys and spires of the city. The harbor which has been largely dug out by dredges is about half the width of the Hudson with a channel from the docks to the sea. Hamburg was an old settlement dating from before the days of

Charlemagne, and I suppose many a Viking ship started from her reedy shores on the Elbe with the emigrants from Saxony who conquered Britain in the fifth century. In any case, the port was an important one in the Middle Ages and remained a free city of the Empire. Practically all the harbor had been destroyed in the war and its great liners taken in reparation. Yet the shipping was rapidly coming back and the city itself bore no marks of destruction by airplane. There were liners from America and Africa and dozens of ships from the coastwise trade. Although it was early morning, there was a busy stir in the railroad station. The business part of the city looked as new as New York and well built and substantial. The older part of the city was not very much in evidence and it looked like a prosperous creation of modern industry and commerce.

I had decided to follow Dr. Warburg's advice and, as I noted in the last chapter, chose as chairman of the German Editorial Board, Dr. Melchior of the Warburg banking firm, along with Mendelssohn-Bartholdy, the grandson of the great musician and an outstanding jurist, as executive secretary. After a day's hard work with them I left for Berlin.

Many times since, I have made the five-hour journey between Hamburg and Berlin, but that first glimpse of Prussia remains most clearly in my mind—the planted pine forests interspersed with meadow lands increased in number as we neared Berlin. What impressed me most was the poor soil from which the Prussian farmers made their living. Yet, by the use of artificial fertilizers they were succeeding in extracting good crops from the light soil, one of the greatest achievements of the German chemical industry.

A room was waiting for me at the Hòtel Bristol on the great central street of Berlin, Unter den Linden, and I was shortly in telephone communication with the German Foreign Office for an appointment on Monday, which had been arranged for me by the Counsellor of the German Embassy in London. He had told me that Germany was not likely to enter the League of Nations in September, when invited by the Assembly of the League, because of the adverse action of the League on German claims to Upper Silesia. I told him that I thought it would be a disastrous policy for

171

Germany and the League, if it were definitely to refuse the invitation. I said that the maintenance of the existing Republican government in Germany was as important for the peace of Europe as the League of Nations itself and both of them should be strengthened by diplomatic compromise, that Germany should accept the fundamental principle of the Covenant and join in most of the activities of the League, reserving for the future the settlement on Upper Silesia.

When I saw Dr. von Schubert of the Foreign Office, he told me that he had already discussed my suggestion with the Chancellor and had drawn up documents to show how it could be carried out. In fact Germany was already started upon that road. He was very kind and encouraging and gave me about two hours of his time to go over the problem in detail. He said that he would try to arrange for me to see the Chancellor the next day, but it was just at this moment that Bavaria was defying the German Government and proposing to carry out a law which was almost like an act of cession from the Republic. There were already rumors of possible civil war and while that was unlikely the crisis was very great. Consequently, my proposal for German membership in the League came at the wrong moment. The next day von Schubert sent word to me that the Chancellor asked me to postpone my call for two or three weeks until the Bavarian matter was settled.

From Berlin I went to Hamburg to plan the German War History with Dr. Melchoir and Mendelssohn-Bartholdy, and on the following afternoon was on the train for Cologne on my way to London. Again I found myself back in the Middle Ages. The farmhouses of Westphalia were like those of lower Austria, for they had been originally built by the same German tribes. The low walls were heavily timbered, and the farmhouses, great oblong buildings with high roofs, extended up over two stories, the same as in Austria, but without central courtyards. As darkness came over the old episcopal city of Munster with its cathedral tower and spires against the twilight, we went on through Muhlheim to Essen, where the great Krupp works were. It was dark and yet the glare of the great iron furnaces shone out against the sky, and as our train went through this great Ruhr Valley past miles and miles of iron and

172

steel works and factories, one got a vision of the real source of Germany's industrial power in peace and war. It was midnight when we reached Cologne and a quarter past one when we took the night boat for Dover.

The ominous outbreaks of violence in Germany, which had alarmed my new friends in Hamburg, were the preamble to the Hitler regime, but they were less frequent than they had been in the first months after the war and were sporadic and local. What affected everyone was the inflation which began when the first milliard payment on Reparations was due in 1921 and finally by the middle of November 1923 reached the point of 4,200,000,000 to the dollar. The last height of inflation, of course, was due to the French invasion of the Ruhr and the German resistance to it. Then came the miracle. On November 15 a new currency was issued, the Rentenmark, with all German property as its security, and by an act of faith the German people held it at its face value.

Perhaps the most striking thing in this sad drama of a nation's bankruptcy was the way everyone tried to turn the paper money into goods. I was in the Ruhr one Friday afternoon when the week's wages were paid, and there was a stampede, a race from the paymaster's office to the company stores to buy something, no matter what, before the mark went farther down in value—which it did hour by hour. By the time I reached the store the shelves were absolutely bare.

From these reminders of the war—in the shadow of which I lived—I turned with relief to conversations with our ambassador to Germany, Alanson Houghton, who was also a trustee of the Carnegie Endowment. It was he who persuaded the German Government to make the "Cuno Offer" to France. He gathered around his fireside a group of the most important leaders in both politics and industrial life including Chancellor Cuno, and, by an unrelenting and vivid portrayal of the horrors of a war of *revanche* and then an insistence upon the folly of maintaining a theory of *revanche,* if they were not intending to carry it out, he got them to the point of accepting his suggestion that Germany make an offer to France of a truce for at least a generation during which neither country would go to war except upon the plebiscite of the whole

173

nation. The plebiscite idea which Ambassador Houghton so strongly insisted upon was due to his hostility to the League of Nations, which as a Republican politician he had vigorously opposed. Chancellor Cuno had been the head of the Hamburg Amerika Line and, in the Hamburg tradition, had always retained connections with England. He was, therefore, readily persuaded to make this offer along the lines suggested by Ambassador Houghton. Mr. Houghton was afraid that Secretary of State Hughes, with a mind trained in international law and diplomacy, would pay no attention to so revolutionary a proposal as this offer with its substitution of public opinion for diplomacy. Yet Mr. Houghton as American Ambassador had first to send the offer to the American Secretary of State, leaving it for Secretary Hughes to transmit to the French and British governments. This Secretary Hughes did—sending it to Premier Poincaré—but with no comment, which in the language of diplomacy is comment enough. Poincaré, therefore, took it to be only a *démarche* by the Germans to escape French insistence upon reparation payments.

In the course of our conversation Ambassador Houghton asked me if I, on my approaching visit to America, would take the matter up with Mr. Root and get him to understand and second the idea, since Mr. Hughes had failed to see what was involved. I said that this would mean making the plan Mr. Root's rather than the Ambassador's, and asked him just how it could be carried through without a certain amount of embarrassment to him. Houghton replied that if the plan was what he thought it was, one that was really destined to bring peace to Western Europe, it was so much bigger than anyone who might have thought of it merely as a plan, that it was folly to stand out for authorship or make any claims about it. I am happy to record this incident, for it was one of the very few instances that I have met with in which a politician or a man in public life readily and definitely surrendered his claim to fame for the sake of the cause itself. Houghton was ready to do this so the plan could be carried through, and he thought that Root would be the only one who could do it. I pointed out to Mr. Houghton that Mr. Root would not likely take any action which might be regarded as interfering with the activities of the Secretary of State. Having been Secretary of State himself, Mr. Root made it a rule to leave any and all of his successors unhampered by any action of his. When I returned to the United States, however, I did take the matter up with Mr. Root. But, unfortunately, I found it was exactly as I had pointed out to Ambassador Houghton. Mr. Root declined to take any action in the matter. It was, I think, a mistake and one which made Root's later years of less value to his country than might have been.

Three years later, however, the substance of the Cuno offer was incorporated into the Treaty of Locarno, minus Houghton's idea of a plebiscite.

I got back to Paris in January, 1923, and had almost given up any further idea of the Cuno Offer, when to my surprise, Tom Jones dropped by at the Hôtel des Saints Pères where I was staying with my family. He had come over to Paris with Prime Minister Bonar Law for a consultation with Poincaré in a last vain effort to persuade Poincaré not to invade the Ruhr for the enforcement of reparations. As Secretary to the Prime Minister, Tom Jones had come to ask me to get the Treasury expert, Mr. (later Sir) Otto Niemeyer, and others of his staff in touch with the French Foreign Office and other leading Frenchmen. I arranged for several meetings at dinner and lunch with Professor Charles Rist, then Vice-President of the Bank of France, and Arthur Fontaine, Director of the Mines of the Saar, and I took the occasion then to tell Jones about the real origin of the Cuno Offer.

Jones agreed with me that Germany had made a mistake in not making the offer directly to England and France, but said that it was now too late for anything to be done and that the influences on the other side were too strong. As Bonar Law left the railway station on his way back to London, having given his assent for the French entry into the Ruhr, he said to Poincaré, "We think you are wrong but you may be right, and we shall hope for the best." Bonar Law was already a very sick man and was unable to hold his own in the conference with Poincaré.

The author's parents

The author at the age of twelve

The author with Secretary of State Cordell Hull at a Washington conference, 1937

photo by Carl M. Mydans

Two historians: James T. Shotwell (*left*) and Arnold J. Toynbee on the terrace of the Carnegie Endowment, 1953.

Cosmo-Silico

The author with his granddaughter Peggy, laying the cornerstone of the
Carnegie Endowment Building

Joseph E. Johnson *(left),* President of the Carnegie Endowment, and Grayson Kirk *(right),* President of Columbia University, with the author at the dedication of the Shotwell Library, 1954

The author and his family on the porch of his Woodstock,
New York, summer home

James T. and Margaret Shotwell, Woodstock, New York

CHAPTER 10

The Protocol of Geneva

In the spring of 1923 I was in Paris working on the War History when Frank Warrin, who had been David Hunter Miller's legal assistant at the Peace Conference, called on me and proposed a meeting with Colonel Requin, who he said was much disturbed over the way the problem of disarmament was being handled at the League of Nations.

Article 8 of the Covenant had called for "reduction of national armaments to the lowest point consistent with national safety and enforcement by common sanctions of international obligations," and the Council was to formulate the plans for such reduction subjected to revision at least every ten years. The execution of this provision was entrusted to a Permanent Military, Naval and Air Committee, but the members of this Committee were drawn from the General Staff of the great powers and they had not been able to agree on any plan for disarmament.

The Assembly had from its first meeting stated that the problem of disarmament differed from that of national security in that no nation could be expected to make itself defenseless in the face of menacing danger from its neighbors. This put the problem of disarmament on the basis of politics and a Temporary Mixed Commission was established (1921), consisting partly of military experts and partly of civilians. It was termed "Temporary" because it was hoped that a solution would be found that would enable the League to solve the whole problem. The chairman of the Temporary Mixed Commission was Lord Robert Cecil, one of the founders of the League at the Paris Peace Conference. Colonel Requin, who was the representative of the French General Staff on the Commission, was disturbed because he found that the British Admiralty was thwarting Cecil's plans for a Draft Treaty on disarmament to be proposed to the League. Requin said that the representative of the British Admiralty on the Commission had stated to the French that they must not take Cecil seriously, as the Admiralty would see to it that his plan would not go through at home. Requin had become joint author of the Treaty and was anxious to secure popular support for it because it was the first time that the issue of disarmament had been definitely linked to that of national security.

While the League delayed action, the Washington Conference on Naval Disarmament had been held, based not on linking disarmament with security but on the opposite theory "that the way to peace is by disarmament, and the way to disarm is to disarm."

Compared with the apparent fumbling at Geneva the Washington Conference acted swiftly. The United States, Great Britain and Japan limited their battleships to the ratio of 5:5:3 and by a dramatic act unparalleled in history sank great warships to bring their quotas in line. It looked like a solution, but what happened was that cruisers and other war vessels took the place of battleships, and naval engineers falsified the purpose of the Treaty. Public opinion everywhere was impressed, however, by this dramatic act.

Lord Esher, a leading political figure in England, proposed applying the Washington method to European armies, allowing 180,000 men to France, 120,000 each to Italy and Poland, and 90,000 to Belgium. The unreality of such a scheme was evident when actual armaments came to be considered—the questions of high-powered cannons and chemical warfare, as well as that of the unequal lengths of frontiers. The race in armaments was not ended by arithmetic, but the stalemate in Geneva was nevertheless discouraging. I promised to have the whole question studied by a group of my friends in New York, and almost immediately after my arrival there in the late autumn I got in to see Mr. Miller, told him how the situation lay and suggested that we get together a small group in order to see if we could find a solution that would strengthen security as well as lessen armament.

The result was that we got together a group of people at the Columbia University Club with Fred Keppel, President of the Carnegie Corporation, as host. I do not recall all those who sat around the table that night, but in addition to Miller the other members of our group were: General Tasker H. Bliss, of the Supreme War Council; Isaiah Bowman, the former head of the Inquiry; Professor Joseph Chamberlain of Columbia; Professor John B. Clark of the Carnegie Endowment; Stephen Duggan, head of the Institute of International Education; Austen Fox, a trustee of the Carnegie Endowment; Dr. Pritchett, President of the Carnegie Foundation; Keppel and myself. General James G. Harbord, Chief of Staff of the American Expeditionary Force in France, also attended some of our meetings. I laid the whole problem before the group and we examined the text of the Draft Treaty proposed by the Temporary Mixed Commission.

Its opening words read like a revolution in international law, for it declared that "aggressive war is an international crime." Unfortunately, however, it did not go on to define aggression so that the opening clause was more or less left in the air.* At the very opening of our discussion Mr. Miller led with the statement that if aggressive war was a crime it involved a juridical determination and the case ought to go to court. It was a matter with which the World Court should deal directly. As he was talking, the thought developed in my mind that this willingness to go to court or refusal to accept the court's determination and resort to force instead, was the key to the definition of aggression. At once the whole group took it up as a way out of our impasse. Mr. Miller reached for the back of a menu card and drafted the text of aggression under such headings as: the willingness to go to court, in the first place, and the

---

* It did, however, furnish a clue to this in the following:

> "A war shall not be considered as a war of aggression if waged by a State which is party to a dispute and has accepted the unanimous recommendation of the Council, the verdict of the Permanent Court of International Justice, or arbitral award against High Contracting Party which has not accepted it, provided, however, that the first State does not intend to violate the political independence or the territorial integrity of the High Contracting Party."

The vagueness or rather uncertainty left in the final clause was due, of course, to Article 10 of the Covenant which guaranteed the political independence and territorial integrity of the Members of the League.

acceptance in good faith of the court's action, in the second place. In other words resorting to war in violation of the nation's previous commitment to use only peaceful means in the settlement of its disputes would be aggression no matter what the grievance. In our American approach to this problem we could not invoke the instrumentality of the League, but it was in keeping with American thought and precedence to refer the question to the court.

During the winter there were a number of meetings of the Committee, and I prepared rather extensive memoranda for the Committee members. I remember that Mr. Root had once said to me that if one wanted to see if he really had a sound proposal for international dealings he should put his idea in the form of a treaty and so it was decided that we should go ahead with the actual drafting of a treaty in order to come to grips with all the difficulties.

Nearly all this drafting was done by Miller and myself, in fact I think all of it. The Draft Treaty of Disarmament and Security which resulted had two original things in it; one was the definition of aggression and the other was what we called the "permissive sanction." This latter device was Miller's invention. I recall that we were working in my office on Memorial Day, 1924, with Miller on one side of the desk and I on the other, each of us trying to find some way out of the problem of sanctions. The point was that unless there were provisions for the enforcement of peace the League would fail to meet the demands of the Covenant. On the other hand, if there were provisions for the maintenance of peace through the League, then the United States would hold aloof. It was the old problem of Article 16 of the Covenant which was before us as a definite political question. Disarmament would be proportionate to the extent of security guaranteed by the League, but that very guarantee by the League made it of a character which would scare off American public opinion. Finally Miller drafted the alternative proposal which we put into the Treaty.

> In the event of any High Contracting Power having been adjudged an aggressor pursuant to this Declaration, all commercial trade, financial and property interests of the aggressor shall cease to be entitled, either in the territory of the other signatories or on the high seas, to any privileges, protection, rights or immunities accorded by either international law, national law or treaty.

Here was the outlawry of war in the absolute sense of the word. The criminal State lost the protection of the laws it violated, those covenants of peace which hold the international community together. We realized how horrendous this threat would seem to those who had never considered how deep a gash international war cut into the structure of international relations. Our strongest critics, naturally enough, were the international lawyers, but the alternative was in the provisions for collective security in the Covenant of the League of Nations, which our committee could not invoke.

The mimeographed text of our Draft Treaty was lying on my desk one day in June when Arthur Sweetser of the League Secretariat called to talk over the situation in Geneva. He at once took a copy to send to Secretary General Sir Eric Drummond, pointing out carefully that this had been only an unofficial work of a private committee unattached to any organization whatever. Just how much Sweetser did to further the circulation of our document in Geneva I do not know, but the Secretary General laid it before the Council of the League which then unanimously voted to have it circulated as a League document.

The news from Geneva immediately brought inquiries from New York newspapers, and in order to avoid misunderstandings, we decided that we should explain the whole situation and release the documents. The *New York Times* published it in full the next morning, and parts of it appeared in other papers.

The result was startling, for the document was headed "An American Plan for Disarmament," and became known henceforth as "The American Plan." None of us ever called it this and we were always careful to speak of it as the draft plan of an unofficial American committee and point out that it had been drafted in the shape of a treaty simply to help us be more precise and definitive in our thinking in order to meet real problems the way they would have to be met anywhere.

During the summer, discussion on the document grew to the point that we finally decided that three of us, at least, would go over to the Assembly in order to make sure that our plan was not misunderstood. General Bliss, Miller, and I were the little committee.

General Bliss had been present at several meetings of the committee, but as he was living in Washington, I had to keep him informed of our discussion by letters as well, and this was the beginning of a correspondence and a friendship which I prize very highly. Few great soldiers, I think, in the world's military history have had as philosophic a mind or as scholarly tastes. Few even of the professors of classics read Thucydides to put themselves to sleep at bedtime, as did General Bliss.

Once the document had become public our discussion and correspondence took on a different aspect. We had to take steps to make sure that our very technically phrased document would not be misunderstood either at home or at Geneva. The Foreign Policy Association published a popular pamphlet explaining the Draft Treaty and organized meetings to discuss it. The Federal Council of Churches also gave it wide distribution. General Harbord described it in public addresses. President Hopkins of Dartmouth, close friend of President Coolidge, sent him a careful analysis. I got the Massachusetts State Conference of the Congregational Church, of which Coolidge was a member, to adopt a formal resolution along the lines of our Treaty. Just before leaving for Geneva, I explained the whole situation at the Williamstown Institute of International Affairs, which at that time had become an important national institution.

Finally in the Carnegie Endowment pamphlet series, *International Conciliation*, for August, 1924,* I published a history of the whole background of the League effort at disarmament and the draft treaties of the Temporary Mixed Commission and our own. So far as I know this is the only general summary of the situation that has been published.

General Bliss, Mr. Miller and I planned to reach Geneva several days before the opening of the General Assembly, to find out what had happened to our Draft Treaty after the Council had ordered its distribution. It was well we did so, for I found that some of my best friends in the Secretariat, Madariaga for one, had taken it to be an American effort to circumvent the League by way of the

* *International Conciliation*, No. 201, August 1924, "A Practical Plan for Disarmament."

Court. To prevent misunderstanding we recast the text to make the test of aggression not merely a resorting to the Court for the settlement of disputes, but going to war instead of using a method prescribed by the Council for settling disputes. We still held to the point that the issue was not the nature of the grievance but the nature of the way for settling it, ruling out resort to war under those conditions as a war of aggression. This meant going beyond the Covenant, which had permitted war as a last resort. Stated in these terms, our proposal meant strengthening, not weakening the League. But all the same it was revolutionary, and the Secretariat didn't like it.

Meanwhile the situation in Europe had completely changed. The militarism of Poincaré in the Ruhr had proved ineffective and disastrous, and French public opinion, reacting strongly against it, overthrew his government in the elections of May, 1924, and brought to power one of the finest leaders of liberalism in the history of France, Edouard Herriot. He found in Ramsay MacDonald a kindred spirit, and together they worked to settle the long drawn-out, still menacing problem of German reparations. The agreements were reached in London on August 30, only a day or so before the meeting of the Assembly of the League.

The auspices were therefore more favorable than we had dared to hope; for we knew little of the new political and moral atmosphere which was to find expression in the debates at Geneva.

The first clear sign of it came from an unexpected quarter. On my arrival Albert Thomas, the Director of the International Labor Office, telephoned urgently for a conference. Our talks during the Paris Peace Conference, while I was working on the plans for the I.L.O. were in my mind as I went to see him, but I found the other Albert Thomas, the organizer of the munitions of France during the war, concerned, even alarmed by what he had learned from the army chiefs in Paris two days before, that they were completely misinformed on the whole question of disarmament at Geneva; he was afraid that MacDonald and Herriot would make grandiloquent speeches at the Assembly and then go away, leaving a terrible anti-climax, as no one would know what to do. The League would fail, and Washington would pick up the remains and start a separate

186

organization. He had no anti-American feeling whatever, but was fearful for the effect on Europe of a European failure. He said that he had had a little talk with Herriot, but not about our plan, which he hadn't seen. I gave him a copy and when I outlined the plans for a Permanent Conference on Disarmament, working out the technical details, he became excited, for it paralleled in the economy of war the method of the I.L.O. in the economy of peace, only reaching far beyond it. Moreover, he said, our plan was the necessary complement to the Dawes accord and that without our general arrangements for security the whole Ruhr and Rhine problem would be left unsolved with all that that implied. Then he asked me if I would be willing to rush back to Paris to see Herriot. Miller and I readily agreed.

Instead of Paris it was to be Lyons, where Herriot had gone to carry out the duties of his other office, that of mayor of the city. We found him at the *mairie*. While we waited in the antechamber, I had an interesting time watching the various types that came to consult with their mayor. They were of all kinds and no one was held back; the poorest working men and women, pathetic types of worn, old and decrepit people; burly butchers and bakers, evidently important in their districts; then the professional politician and even a dandy with gloves and cane. Daumier could have filled his sketch book if he had been sitting on our bench—for it was a bench, not a chair.

When Herriot was free to receive us, we found him at his desk with a huge bouquet of gladioli flanked by another of very simple garden flowers with the tributary note from some local admirer still attached to it. Herriot himself was a very broad-shouldered, strongly built man, with a face heavy in repose but lighted up by a pair of eyes full of humor and quickly changing, a Frenchman of the solid type touched with imagination. He greeted us cordially, and then we got down to work. I told him all about our plan, as he sat fingering documents and not replying until I came to the question of sanctions, and then he broke loose, protesting that France needed a stronger not a weaker protection than the Covenant provided. What was most on his mind was that he had stood for a settlement with Germany which was more than his country thought

187

just and had got nothing but blows from the Germans. He said they couldn't understand that they were just bringing Poincaré back into power and that he gave himself no longer than January, 1925. The Germans would drive him from power as sure as fate. He kept repeating: "Ils sont bêtes, bêtes." I recalled to him that it was he who had first bravely called the attention of France to the fact that there was more than one kind of German. Thinking it over later, I wondered if it wasn't Briand instead of Herriot, but he took the compliment all the same.

Then I told him that Mendelssohn-Bartholdy had come to Geneva on my invitation and that he brought me the assurance that the German liberals were watching anxiously the developments at Geneva. I spoke of the way in which liberals so easily become cynics and how the failure of France to meet the German advances had made the liberal German opponents cynical and ready victims of the nationalist. We might, I suppose, have taken more of Herriot's time, had we chosen to do so. In any case, he asked us if he could do anything for us in Lyons and then kept repeating as he took my hand in both of his and held it in the affectionate grasp of a trained politician, that he was counting upon seeing me in Geneva and that there we could talk over more of the details of our plan. This I took with a grain of salt, for I knew how busy he would be there.

As we left, Mr. Miller said, "This morning's work was worth crossing the Atlantic for."

By the time we got to the hotel we found that they knew all about our being at the *mairie* and we wired ahead to Geneva to Viple, Chef de Cabinet of Albert Thomas, that we would be home by seven and to make arrangements for Paul Boncour for dinner. Then we got into the car and allowed ourselves a half hour to climb a hill that overlooks the city and from the ramparts spent at least five minutes sight-seeing. It was a glorious panorama but we had other things to do.

We arrived home in Geneva at seven, and at eight o'clock we were to have dinner with Paul Boncour, Chairman of the *Conseil de Défense Nationale,* which is the Supreme War Council of France. He had under him—or was in touch with—all the admirals and generals and technical experts. He came with Viple, and we dined in our hotel salon in the utmost privacy. He was the keenest man I had met in the whole of these negotiations. He was a short, smooth-faced, angular, rather dark-complexioned man, with kindly but keen eyes and a very serious cast of countenance. His great shock of almost white hair gave him a very distinguished appearance. He had read our plan through and through. He knew it so well that he could, without looking at it, refer from one Article to another.

I did almost all the talking again and told the story of how we began our work and tried to make clear the character of our committee. He understood this perfectly (and I learned that the proper French characterization of us was a *groupe amicale*). He at first held somewhat aloof from giving an opinion, but as the evening wore on, he was struck, as Herriot had been, with the fact that we had taken so much of previous French plans and built them into ours. We emphasized the importance of not allowing a repetition of the French predicament at the Washington Conference and he at once saw the setting in French politics of the principle of the recurring periodic conferences. I was delighted to find that he was not opposed, in principle at least, to the inspection committee and the fact that we were using the language of the French at the Peace Conference didn't pass unnoticed. I was surprised that, unlike the British, he raised no objection to our definition of aggression. I wondered if he had had wind of it, and had discussed it with his second in command, Léon Bourgeois, whom I felt we could count upon, for there was no more staunch pacifist in world politics.

While we were at Lyons, Albert Thomas himself went to Paris to meet Prime Minister Ramsay MacDonald and Foreign Secretary Arthur Henderson. He had worked with the latter on labor problems at the I.L.O., and they traveled together to Geneva. So, if both prime ministers were well posted on the situation when they arrived, the credit for it should go to Albert Thomas. I had a long talk with Mr. Henderson, however, the one outstanding labor leader in MacDonald's government. He was not interested in the game of diplomacy, but was keen to get to the heart of the great issue then confronting the League. After a thorough analysis, he gave his hearty endorsement to the proposed Protocol.

The Assembly of 1924, instead of marking a decline in the

League of Nations as Colonel Requin had expected, reached an inspiring climax in both membership and achievement. It was the first "summit" meeting after the Peace Conference, with the prime ministers of Great Britain, France, Belgium, and Czechoslovakia, with their foreign ministers and those of almost every other member country. The great debate was opened by Ramsay MacDonald, speaking with all the effect of his magnetic personality. But his plea for the speedy entry of Germany into the League and his rejection of the Cecil-Requin Draft Treaty of Mutual Assistance so turned the French and other Continental nations against him that they missed the fact that he had accepted the definition—or test—of aggression.

> The one method by which we can approximate to an accurate attribution of responsibility for aggression is arbitration, the setting up of a country or, rather, countries—because one country will not suffice for the purpose. There are judicial questions. There are political questions. There are questions that can only be settled by wise and enlightened citizens. There are questions that can only be settled by the trained lawyers. A system of arbitration is a system of scanning the clouds, a system of warning when a cloud, just the size of a man's hand, appears above the horizon, and the taking of steps at once, not of a military kind but of a national and judicial kind, to charm it out of existence. The test is, Are you willing to explain? The test is, Will you come before us and tell us what you propose to do? The test is, Will you expose your commitments? Are you afraid of the world? Are you afraid of daylight, a lover of darkness or timorous lest the world should know what is in your mind? Such is the test, the only test.

There was breathless excitement in the Assembly the next morning when Herriot rose to state the case for France, and universal relief when in a few sentences he cleared away all misunderstandings and offered a program which all could accept. Inevitably it all hung on the definition of aggression, which he summed up as follows:

"We admit that it is an extremely intricate and perplexing task to determine which State is the aggressor. For that reason, France was gratified yesterday to observe that Great Britain gave her powerful support to the idea of arbitration—an idea which we ourselves recently urged in London, since we were convinced that it was the only means of attacking and solving the formidable problem of reparations.

"We earnestly hope, therefore, that one of the acts of the Fifth Assembly will be to accept the principle of arbitration, which will once again settle our difficulties, since henceforth the aggressor will be the party which refused arbitration (*arbitrage*)."

Although Ramsay MacDonald's address covered the ground more adequately than that of Herriot, there was a crispness, a directness in the commitment of France which was lacking in the more carefully elaborated statement of Great Britain, and the Assembly responded to it with enthusiasm. At last the League of Nations was going to "plug the hole in the Covenant" which permitted League members to go to war as a last resort. A revolutionary movement was on foot to recast the national state system by a protocol or addition to the Covenant, which promised to open the only pathway to disarmament, by invoking the sanctions of the League against an aggressor, and defining as an aggressor "every state which resorts to war in violation of the undertakings contained in the Covenant or in the present Protocol."

These "undertakings" were spelled out in the text of the Protocol, which, in spite of—or perhaps because of—its technicalities, still remains the best summary ever made of the test of aggression and the farthest point ever reached by the governments of Europe to block the path of war:

In the event of hostilities having broken out, any State shall be presumed to be an aggressor, unless a decision of the Council, which must be taken unanimously, shall otherwise declare:

1. If it has refused to submit the dispute to the procedure of pacific settlement provided by Articles 13 and 15 of the Covenant as amplified by the present Protocol, or to comply with a judicial sentence or arbitral award or with a unanimous recommendation of the Council, or has disregarded a unanimous report of the Council, a judicial sentence or an arbitral award recognizing that the dispute between it and the other belligerent State arises out of a matter which by international law is solely within the domestic jurisdiction of the latter State; nevertheless, in the last case the State shall only be presumed to be an aggressor if it has not previously submitted the question to the Council or the Assembly, in accordance with Article 11 of the Covenant.

191

2. If it has violated provisional measures enjoined by the Council for the period while the proceedings are in progress as contemplated by Article 7 of the present Protocol (not to increase armaments or take any action likely to extend the dispute or render it more acute while the issue is under dispute).

It will be seen at once that although our American committee played a vital part in the history of the Protocol, that document went far beyond our proposal and offered the alternatives for war, in a far-flung strategy of peace.

There were busy days and nights in Geneva before the Protocol was finally hammered into shape; but on October 2, 1924, it was passed by a unanimous vote of forty-eight members of the League of Nations. A resolution of the Assembly was, however, only a recommendation to the signatory governments, and the high hopes of Geneva were destined to be dashed by a change of government in Great Britain, when the Coalition Government of Ramsay Mac-Donald was defeated in December by the Conservatives under Stanley Baldwin, whose Foreign Minister, Austen Chamberlain, made it clear that the British would not ratify the Protocol. Then the other Powers hesitated or drew back, for if Great Britain refused, it imperiled the whole structure of collective security.

At first it looked as though everything was lost. Then, a voice was heard from Germany, which, not yet being a member of the League, had been absent (at least officially) from Geneva. It was a suggestion that the principles of the Protocol might appeal in a limited way to the relations of Germany with its neighbors. But just how this led to the treaties of Locarno is a story in itself.

We stayed in Geneva only during the first days of the Assembly. As Americans we could have no share in the actual work of the League. All we had done was to offer a suggestion for the central issue. So we were ready to leave for home. The last paragraph of my Geneva diary ends this part of the story:

"There was a telephone message awaiting me from Albert Thomas, who had just got back from Berne, asking me on a question of urgency to go up to his apartment. I was there while he was eating his breakfast and found that it was only that he wanted to get the news of the day quite straight and, of course, I was glad to thank him for all that he had done and to assure him of further co-operation on my side. We had a very cordial time together. Everyone is sorry to hear that we are going, which makes it all the pleasanter to go. He said that there was a most enthusiastic outline of our plan in last Sunday's *Observer,* and he had heard nothing but its merits on all sides. He said that a good many people didn't realize how difficult compulsory arbitration might turn out to be in practice and he said it might break down at times. And I said that the one comment on that was that there was no perfect plan in the world today and yet there were a multitude of imperfect things at work and that was the world we lived in, and then I went on to say that the reluctance to accept the plan because one could foresee situations in which it might not work was the very obstacle which reformers placed in the way of reform. I tried to put it so that he wouldn't take offense and I think succeeded, for we both agreed that this was one of the fundamental facts and he wished us all good luck as we parted. Then I ran in to say good-bye to Sir Malcolm Delevingne and Henderson at the Beau Rivage. Again reluctance on their part to see us go and very cordial greetings as we left.

CHAPTER 11

From the Protocol to Locarno

Immediately after our return to Paris General Bliss and Mr. Miller sailed for home. I stayed on in Paris, partly for work on the War History and partly for further study of the proposal for dealing with disarmament in a continuing series of conferences, like those of the I.L.O. to which non-League nations could adhere.

Again it was Albert Thomas who opened the doors for me, but the technicalities were dealt with in long discussions with René Cassin, later head of the Conseil d'Etat, the supreme court for legislative matters. Professor Cassin—he still gave law courses in the University—was a close friend of M. Herriot, and together we studied the problem of French participation in the Disarmament Conference as an annex of the League. This was the first of many years of friendship with M. Cassin, who in these last years has been the distinguished representative of France in the Commission on Human Rights of the United Nations.

From Paris I went to London to pull together the plans for rounding out the War History. This gave me the chance to tell the story of the Protocol to Herr Stahmer, the German ambassador, whom I had got to know intimately when I was living in London. He was much more interested in the movement, then under way, to have Germany invited to become a member of the League. Later it was said that Stresemann, the German Chancellor, had made overtures to Chamberlain along the lines of our draft treaty, but that was not until the following spring.

I stayed only a short time in London, sailing back to New York on September 27, 1924, and undertook immediately to assess the results of our work and to see what we could do next. One of the first things to do was to call on Secretary of State Hughes. I had not gone to see him before leaving for Geneva, for it was important to keep our committee free of all official connection. But when I called on him after the Geneva episode was all over, he greeted me with a frown and said he thought I had been guilty of violating the Logan Act—that act of Congress of 1798 which prohibits private citizens from negotiating with other governments with which the United States is carrying on diplomatic relations.

I replied that the law didn't apply to anyone working with the League of Nations, for he had not recognized its existence and had not answered any communication from it. Then, Secretary Hughes's whole attitude changed. He burst out laughing and said, "You have me there!" It was so frank and sincere that I too changed my attitude of reserve, and we had a good talk about the problems of security and disarmament. I met him several times later and it was always on the friendliest personal basis. The permanent staff of the State Department, however, remained unfriendly, an attitude I have met with in other bureaucracies. On the other hand, it was grand to have a cordial endorsement of my activities from Elihu Root, when I wrote and told him the whole Geneva story.

Having made my peace with Secretary of State Hughes, I then joined in a campaign of education for United States membership in the League of Nations and acceptance of the outlawry of wars of aggression as set forth in the Protocol of Geneva. But this attempt to make peace with the peacemakers was the most discouraging task I ever undertook. In the ten days from November 5 to 15 I gave seventeen addresses at meetings mostly in the Middle West. Until July, 1925, when I sailed to Europe, I was busy writing and speaking.

At Buffalo I spoke to over 5,000 people in a great mass meeting in an armory. The League of Nations Association and The Committee on the Cause and Cure of War organized in Washington by Mrs. Carrie Chapman Catt mobilized support; but the country was still suffering from the aftermath of the rejection of the League. The peace forces were in utter confusion, part of them almost violently isolationist—and part, following Senator Borah in his plan to outlaw all wars—not merely wars of aggression—by giving the World Court "original and compulsory jurisdiction" over all international disputes, yet refusing to give it any other enforcement than "the public opinion of mankind." The slightest knowledge of the history of either law or politics should show what a shoddy substitute was here proposed for the League; but it made an appeal to both nationalism and pacifism, an emotional compound which was at its peak in the anti-Wilson movement. The foremost advocate of Borah's alleged substitute for the League, and its joint-inventor, was a Chicago lawyer, Salmon O. Levinson, who stated it so appealingly that even a philosopher like John Dewey was carried away by it. Dewey and I had been close friends, but the friendship was strained in our disagreement.

The disagreement went deep. Although for a whole year more I tried to get what we called a Harmony Peace Program and had numerous meetings on it, there was so much fuzzy thinking among those opposing the League of Nations that I finally came to the conclusion I could not work with them without compromising my own position. I stated my objections in a letter to Sherwood Eddy (December 9, 1925) from which I quote, as it states my point of view better than I could re-state it now:

> I have been and still am opposed to an advocacy of our entry into the World Court, coupled with the suggestion that this act alone absolves us of any further method of cooperation in the organization of international peace. For in it is but the first step in a long process by which our country may ultimately assume the full measure of its responsibility.

Meanwhile things had taken a new turn in Europe. The refusal of the Conservative government of Stanley Baldwin to ratify the Protocol brought clearly to light the underlying difference between British and Continental ideas on international relations. Time and again in the debates of the Assembly, the British had shown that they regarded international relations less as a legal system than as a way of living. The fact that they had no written constitution, while

196

the continental countries were all built within set legal frameworks, now showed itself as an impediment to uniform action. Moving along "from precedent to precedent" the British had an inherent dislike of assuming far-reaching treaty obligations that would limit their freedom of action in the unforeseeable crises of the future. Yet Baldwin's action in rejecting the terms of the Protocol left British public opinion uneasy, as it was strongly set upon policies of peace. The speech of Austen Chamberlain in the House of Commons was carried in news columns, not only in the provincial press of Great Britain but throughout the Continent as well, and in almost every instance there were repeated editorials, mostly critical, of the cavalier way in which the British Government was rejecting the whole idea of the Protocol.

I kept track of this mounting wave of protest. Clippings for a single week dealing with this topic alone ran into the hundreds. It is a striking fact, and one not without its bearing on the peace movement, that the negative attitude of Chamberlain procured far more journalistic attention than the making of the Protocol in the first place.

To meet this criticism Chamberlain proposed at a conference held at Locarno that the guarantee of peace of the Protocol be made the basis of peace treaties between Germany and her neighbors, pledging themselves to use only arbitration or other means of peaceful settlement of disputes and not to resort to war. It was the definition of aggression—which General Bliss, Mr. Miller, and I had taken to Geneva the year before—applied locally along the frontiers of Germany. With these guarantees of the Treaties of Locarno, Germany was admitted to membership in the League of Nations.

Behind this Locarno agreement lies a story that has never been told. During the debates on the Protocol, Professor Mendelssohn-Bartholdy came to Geneva, at my suggestion, as an observer, and I went over the whole situation with him. On his return to Germany he published a German translation of "The American Plan" and of the Protocol, and, together with Dr. Melchior, formed a German study group to keep in touch with our American group after our return to America and plan similar activities, as Germany was not yet a member of the League of Nations. This German Committee on Arbitration and Security was composed of men of the highest distinction, as even a partial list of its members shows: Ex-Chancellor Cuno, President Simons, and lord mayors of Cologne and Hamburg, Konrad Adenauer and Dr. Petersen, Professor Niemeyer, President of the German Society for the Law of Nations, Professor Hoetzsch, a conservative leader in the Reichstag, Generals von Kuhl and von Winterfeldt and Admirals Behnke and Hopmann. In the Foreign Office, Dr. von Schubert kept in close touch with the committee, but he left the actual work on it to the expert in international law, Dr. Gauss.

Mendelssohn-Bartholdy wrote me that the German group wanted to correspond with a similar French Committee on Security and Disarmament, but even before word came from him, M. Arthur Fontaine, my old friend from the Peace Conference days, had got together a group equal in distinction with that in Germany. Among its members were (in addition to himself) Albert Thomas, Paul Boncour, Chairman of the Council of National Defense and French representative on the Disarmament Conference, with whom I had worked in Geneva; Charles Rist, the economist who had become a member of the Tribunal of Arbitration of the Dawes Plan for reparations; Henri Chardon of the Council of State; Henri Lichtenberger, formerly exchange professor at Harvard, author of many books on German literature; Léon Jouhaux, President of the Confederation du Travail and member of the French Disarmament Committee of the Coal Mine Operators of France; and René Massigli of the French Foreign Office, Secretary of the Conference of Ambassadors, later technical expert in the Locarno meeting.

The purpose of the study group was clearly stated by Albert Thomas. It was to study the technical problems of arbitration and security on the basis of the principles set forth in the Protocol. It was interesting to see that the French Committee, although it included certain Government officials, operated largely as a research agency of the Government.

There was also a very active Dutch committee, headed by Dr. Loudon, who had been the Dutch representative at the League, and Professor von Wollenhoven, a leading figure in International Law.

198

There was no need of a special committee in Great Britain, for the League of Nations Union was already a national force there, and nowhere else were the problems of the Protocol more vigorously debated. The parallel to this in the United States was the League of Nations Association with Raymond Fosdick as President, and Clark Eichelberger, Director. In 1935 I took over its presidency which I held until 1939.

The treaties of Locarno became the basis of the international structure of Europe until Hitler violated them.

CHAPTER 12

The Briand Offer

In the spring of 1927 I was appointed to a Professorship of International Relations in the newly founded Hochschule für Politik, in Berlin. As this was the first linking up of academic life with the United States after the war, much was made of it in Germany. I was met on landing at Hamburg by the President of the Hochschule, Dr. Hans Simons,* and the ceremonies began at Hamburg, where I met the leading personalities of the city at a dinner given by Dr. Melchior, the chairman of the German board of the War History. On arrival at Berlin there were many functions, and my German was severely tested at banquets and conferences arranged for me by the Hochschule. First of all, there was an interview with about thirty representatives of the leading newspapers of Germany; then a dinner with parliamentarians and professors, among whom I was happy to meet Professor Meinecke, whose works I had long known. More important were long conferences with Reich Chancellor Wilhelm Marx and Dr. von Schubert of the Foreign Office.

The high point of the visit from the German point of view, however, was that President von Hindenburg gave me a personal interview, a rare proceeding at that time, as some member of his staff generally spoke for him. The conversation didn't amount to much and the most I got out of it was the impression of the man himself,

---

* Son of Walter Simons who had held the office of President of the Reich for a short time prior to becoming President of the Supreme Court.

surprisingly lacking in military brusqueness, genial in manner and speech, using casual colloquialisms. Briand, for example, was *"ein guter Kerl."* Physically the old Marshal was of great size and strength, with powerful hands laid carelessly on his desk as we talked.

I found that my academic duties were light. I had only two courses to give, a lecture course and a seminar for candidates for posts in the Foreign Office. I am not happy about those lectures for they had to be given with little preparation and I recall the weird English of some of the German exchange professors at Columbia. I am sure my improvisations in Berlin were equally hard to follow.

The one important event was the inaugural lecture, which I gave on March 1. Chief Justice Walter Simons presided, and the auditorium was filled with dignitaries: the Chancellor and cabinet members of the Reich, the Prime Minister of Prussia and members of his cabinet, representatives of Berlin and provincial cities, and the heads of the War Ministry and General Staff. This was significant, for it was the first time since the war, so I was told, that they had appeared together in public in full military regalia, with decorations and even side arms.

While my lecture was cast in the mold of a general philosophy of history,* so familiar in German universities, it concentrated on the one supreme lesson drawn from the *Economic and Social History of the World War,* that war itself had been changed by science and the industrial revolution even more than the arts of peace; that its direction was not to be determined in terms of the strategy of the General Staff but in terms of the whole mobilization of effort and resources; and since this kind of war calls for competition in the science of destruction, the discovery of new instruments and the advance of science—not merely military science but science in general—makes it impossible for either soldiers or statesmen to calculate the outcome of war, as was relatively possible in the days of what might be termed "hand labor war," when it was chiefly a contest of man power based upon local resources. I drew the conclu-

* The original text of the lecture (worked over from my German by Dr. Hans Simons) was published by the Hochschule and an English translation in the Annual Report of the Carnegie Endowment for that year.

sion that war between highly industrialized nations is from now on, by its very nature, international and not merely bi-national, for there are no nations that can wage a major war entirely on their own resources. It, therefore, tends to draw neutrals into belligerency in spite of themselves. Thus war spreads like a contagion and ceases to be directable. It is no longer that "continuation of politics by other means" which Clausewitz described. That being the case, it has ceased to be a legitimate instrument of policy in the world of highly civilized nations. In place of war there should be a "world Locarno," which, of course, would be simply another Protocol of Geneva.

As this was the most important audience to which I could bring the final lesson of the War History, and as it was soon to become the basis for the Briand offer, I quote from the concluding sections of my address:

> The new international policy, symbolized chiefly in the League of Nations must be based, not upon the rigid framework of a static world, but upon the laws of a dynamic society. The shifting of national pressures, as the conquest of nature proceeds, is no longer incidental but constant. Now constant variation calls for continuing adjustment. The problems of international relations can never be settled without creating new ones. This means that there is emerging a world community in which no single act of power is permanently effective, as used to be the case in repetitive and exclusive societies. Sound policy is henceforth that which gathers around it the accumulating force of common interest, making the interests of others contribute also to one's own.
>
> That this is the line of history which the nations of the League are pursuing is evidenced by the Treaties of Locarno. The general principles of the Covenant are guaranteed by regional agreements. The Covenant is a universal pledge of peace, but the obligations which it imposes to protect that pledge against a violator are varied according to the interests of the signatories.
>
> The Covenant had ended—for all members of the League—the old sovereign right of war; and to enforce this reform it strengthened the defenses of the weak. But defense is also war, and this emphasis on defensive measures is chiefly responsible for the first of the two chief reasons of Americans for abstention; for most aggressive wars have been camouflaged as defensive. Now in Article V of the Treaty of Locarno aggression is defined, and by implication defense as well. The aggressor is that Power which goes to war in violation of its own

202

promise to resort to the established means of peaceful settlement—arbitral, juridical or conciliation tribunal, or the organs of the League.

Two tasks are then before us. In the first place, the definition of aggressive war must be developed and applied so that automatically the machinery of international justice as a substitute for war would be enhanced and at the same time all war but defense be outlawed. As for defensive war, that would disappear of itself if there were no aggression. In the second place, neutrality must be redefined so that the neutral is no longer a potential accomplice of the aggressor, as is the case at present through the free use of its private resources in the shape of supplies.

I have touched only the merest externals of the question before me. But, if the analysis holds, we are at the greatest turning point in human history. The intelligence which has won so many triumphs over our material environment is now at grips with the human problem. Whether it is solved by us or by the generations which follow, there can be no doubt of the outcome. For science itself is working to the fulfillment of the precepts of religion.

It was only in the context of a philosophy of history that one could talk in these terms to the successors of Clausewitz and Bismarck. But I noticed what seemed to be signs of dissent by one sitting among the officers. He followed the lecture intently and when I came to the section dealing with the fact that the strategy of the General Staff did not cover the entire field of modern war but that it must cover economic problems as well, it struck me that his glance signified distinct disapproval.

The following Sunday, however, I had lunch with him, for it was no other than General Gröner, the successor of Ludendorff as head of the General Staff. He had taken over the broken remains of the German army on the West and brought them home, organizing the retreat with entire success. He subsequently became Minister of Defense, that is, Minister of War. We had a quiet lunch, just three of us, General Gröner and his friend Geheimrat Frisch. I took the occasion to ask the General to tell me frankly what his objections were to the main point of my address. He looked surprised and said: "Objections, I haven't any." Then, laughingly he added: "Oh, I know what you're thinking about. I had intended writing a book along the same lines as your lecture, and felt that you were stealing my thunder."

I mention this incident because it made a great impression on me as a justification for the solution of the technical problem I had been working at. Dr. Rathenau had had prophetic glimpses of it, but never developed his theory in detail. There was no soldier in Europe whose opinion on such a matter stood higher than that of General Gröner. The successor of Clausewitz was ready for a new theory of war.

The Berlin lecture was widely publicized throughout Germany. Parts of it were copied in the provincial press, but with little support for its central thesis. Nor was it all smooth sailing. The organization which had been created "to combat the War Guilt Lie" was still carrying on its tremendous propaganda, the strongest national protest any nation ever put out. When I refused to speak at a meeting held under its auspices, I was publicly attacked by one of its leaders, Frau Mende, a member of the Reichstag. The attack was quoted in full in the *New York Times* as well as in the German press. It left me quite undisturbed. But I took occasion to deliver an address on the completion of the great collection of diplomatic documents covering the whole history of the Empire (*Die Grosse Politik der Europäischen Kabinette*), edited by Professor Mendelssohn-Bartholdy and Dr. Thimme, in which I said that it would be a triumph of German scholarship if it could recover the objectivity of Ranke and remake the perspectives of history "by frankly ignoring prejudices" to deal with events in the light of their own times. This lecture on historical methodology was well received by the historians, but was anathema to the propagandists.

The Hochschule arranged for me to give my inaugural lecture again in Cologne on March 8, at a meeting presided over by the Lord Mayor of the city, Konrad Adenauer. There they were still too close to the war, with the Allied occupation still before their eyes, for the university professors to accept the renunciation of war as an instrument of politics, especially when advanced by an American whose government had so long refused to accept the substitute for it in the League of Nations. In a pleasant social meeting afterward they expressed their doubts as to the adoption of a "world Locarno." They had no objection to it, but were as skeptical as Senator Moses of New Hampshire. I doubt that any of them knew that Dr. Adenauer had been a member of Dr. Mendelssohn-Bartholdy's committee which had been so largely instrumental in shaping the Locarno treaties themselves.

From Cologne I took the night train to Geneva, arriving there on Wednesday, March 9. The next day I attended the Council meeting and on the 11th I witnessed the two incidents which I have often described in subsequent speeches: the treatment of the Upper Silesian school question, and that of the French police in the Saar Valley.

In the evening òf March 11 I met Chancellor Stresemann for the first time, as he had not been in Berlin when I was there. He had undergone a very heavy strain during the day, now that Germany was in the League and the Council of the League had found the solution to this head-on collision of France and Germany after the war, but was as jolly as a schoolboy out of school when Dr. Melchior, the Chairman of the German Editorial Board of the War History, and I called on him at his room in the Metropole Hotel. Nothing was said in my conversation with him that dealt with any world problem or any problem of politics. We just talked nonsense and had a jolly time together.

Although Dr. Stresemann understood and talked English, as was evident in the Council meeting, he would not use anything but German in our talk, so I had to follow suit. He told, in a very funny way, a historic incident which I imagine has not yet been recorded anywhere. He said that when he got up to make his speech in the Assembly on the occasion of Germany's entry into the League, they started filming him and threw a spotlight on his face. The glare in his eyes prevented him from seeing his paper, and he said he got so near a state of panic that Germany almost missed coming into the League at the last moment. He laughed heartily over the incident and then went on for an hour or so telling other funny stories. It was a sheer release of nerves from the long day's strain in the Council.

The reason I did not go further with the German authorities in the suggestion for a "world Locarno" than a broad statement of general principles was that I felt very distinctly that Germany was not in a position to take up this idea more than had been done at

Locarno itself. American public opinion would not have followed a German lead. I recalled the way Secretary Hughes in 1922 had turned down the proposal of Ambassador Houghton that the United States should present to the French Government, with some semblance of approval, the offer of Chancellor Cuno to make a truce with France for thirty years and not to go to war except by a plebiscite vote of either nation. There was still the delicate question, even after Locarno, as to how much initiative should come from Germany, a problem which has come clearly to the fore every time disarmament has been taken up. But the sympathetic reception in Berlin encouraged me to go ahead with an idea I had already intended carrying out as far back as the preceding summer, namely, that I should try to get M. Briand to take the definite step to inaugurate an extension of the Locarno Treaty, which had given to Europe its first positive and definite realization of the guarantee of international peace in the post-war era.

I saw a good deal more of some of the Germans in Geneva and renewed my acquaintance with my old friends there, but do not recall having gone into the matter of the Berlin speech with any of them.

On Tuesday, March 15, I arrived in Paris and for the next few days was very busy with the routine work of the Endowment. On the weekend of the 19th and 20th, I went down into the Saar Valley at the invitation of the French Administrator of the Mines of the Saar, M. Arthur Fontaine with Dr. Babcock, the Carnegie Endowment representative in Paris. It was sometime during these days—that is, during the week of the 15th and 21st—that I raised with Fontaine the problem of what Briand could do in putting the question of disarmament on a secondary plane compared with that of the renunciation of war.

At Fontaine's request I outlined the plan in a letter to him which it was understood he was to be free to submit to Briand through Léger, an old family friend of Fontaine, who was Briand's personal secretary. In this letter to Fontaine, I laid down the general thesis that the American impression of France's action at the Washington Naval Conference was as unfortunate as the French impression of the American action. France felt that its need for security had not

206

been adequately listened to or appreciated; but the Americans felt that France was showing itself to be a militarist nation, unwilling to give up its armaments. An added disadvantage to France in American public opinion arose from the fact that France was now refusing to take part in the Geneva Disarmament Conference of the coming summer.

It all looked as though France was as bad as its critics stated. Now it seemed to me that the only way to meet this was for France to state its willingness to extend the terms of Locarno to the United States first and then to all the world. The renunciation of war itself as an instrument of policy would be a much more outstanding fact than the renunciation of the instruments of war.

While Fontaine was personally in hearty sympathy with my point of view, I seemed to be making no progress with Briand and came to the conclusion that his secretary had failed to see the point. Briand had the reputation of not reading his own letters, or at least of not reading much, and I decided that Léger was, to say the least, not helpful in getting the idea through to Briand. In fact, I had my doubts as to whether Briand had any idea of what I was proposing.

Then by a happy chance my old friend, Albert Thomas, came to Paris, and I knew from his quick and intuitive reaction to the proposal which I brought to Geneva in 1924 that he would quickly see the significance and could get the issue immediately before Briand. I therefore turned to him and, as I expected, he got the point at once. He arranged that I should go with him to see Briand on Tuesday, March 22.

The interview took place at noon. I found myself sitting in the antechamber of the Salle de l'Horloge, which had been a familiar room to me in the Peace Conference days. Briand's office was on the right of this antechamber and divided with it the space that leads to the Salle de l'Horloge. Albert Thomas merely introduced me and then left the interview in my hands.

I told Briand that I had come with a suggestion which seemed to me capable of being used to advantage in overcoming certain false impressions that had gained ground in view of the French attitude toward armaments, and I did not hesitate to speak rather frankly about the opinion held concerning France in this regard. He made a half-hearted attempt to defend French disarmament policy by referring to the length of the French seacoast and therefore the legitimate naval demands of France. I told him that in all frankness this kind of argument would make no impression upon any national of any other country and rather plainly indicated that it seemed to me the kind of argument that strengthened those suspicious of alleged French militarism. I said that unless France were ready to take a decisive step of another kind, American opinion would feel that it was more and more justified in regarding the French naval and military policy as distinctly hindering pacific policies.

Albert Thomas helped me out with a very definite indication that he was on my side of things, but still left me to make the argument. Briand, as I recall, indicated with a smile that he knew that I was sufficiently a friend of France that he did not for a moment misunderstand my frankness in speaking to him this way and at once dropped this line of argument.

Then I made the definite suggestion that he should propose in a public statement in the name of France, not merely the renunciation of instruments of war but the renunciation of war itself. He did not hesitate a moment to accept the general principle of this but said that he didn't know how it could be carried out and asked me if I would draft a memorandum for him to consider as the basis. This I was unwilling to do, for I knew what a serious thing it might be for an American citizen to propose to a foreign government negotiations of this kind without the sanction of his own government. So I said that I could not undertake a memorandum of a diplomatic sort but that another way out had already occurred to me and that was that on the approaching tenth anniversary of America's entry into the World War, April 6 following, he should make a statement to the American people through the Associated Press in Paris drawing the lessons of the World War and applying them, a message which would invite the American people to join with the people of France in a definite commitment to "outlaw war."

I used the phrase, and then proceeded to explain to him that it was a formula which attained a definite place in the thinking of large sections of the Middle West through the eloquent advocacy of those in Chicago who had coined it and had become its advocates. I pointed out the importance of the fact of Senator Borah's advocacy of this principle but stated that the theory which lay behind it, namely, that there should be a readjustment of the World Court, which apparently was to take the place of the League of Nations, at least in this regard, was not a theory which could be adopted or carried out. On the contrary, I stated that the real outlawry of war lay along the lines of the Locarno Treaty and that a broad and general acceptance of this principle specifically inviting the United States to accept the Locarno principle without becoming involved in its sanctions would be a working basis for which popular support could be mobilized, and I felt that the peace movement of the United States could carry the day against all opponents.

Briand was keenly interested, but even yet was dubious, and I recall very definitely the remainder of the conversation. He said that he would not mind doing it if he only knew how to do it, but that every time he had made a speech or a gesture with reference to the United States it seemed to be taken the wrong way. He said that he did not know how to take the American people, and then he asked me if I would draft a memorandum upon which he might base a statement substantially along the lines of our conversation. I said that if it was to be considered as notes for a public address to the people of the United States there was no reason in the world why I should hesitate to offer him suggestions along these lines, and I consented to draft the memorandum.

It was understood that this memorandum should cover the main points of our interview. I should begin with a statement of what France was doing for disarmament and how it proposed to continue the problem. It was to be frankly an explanation of French politics up to date and as much a justification of them as I thought right and fitting. Then the second part of the memorandum was to deal with the proposal for outlawing war explained in terms of Locarno and the League so as to show the harmony of these two ideas.

The actual drafting of my memorandum took only one afternoon. I don't recall at the moment whether it was the same afternoon or the following afternoon, but I know that the lead pencil text, which was written on the yellow paper of the Endowment's office, is the first draft of the whole document. The penciled changes that stand there are exactly as written.

I went right back to my office in the Boulevard St. Germain, and at once sat down and wrote off my statement almost without interruption at a single sitting. It is in my safe at present. It will be found upon examination that I put a great deal of emphasis upon the disarmament problem and tried to justify the French point of view, for I was afraid that Briand would back out of the scheme and was sure that he did not see the full implications. Moreover, I wrote as a Frenchman, because he said that the whole thing would look suspicious, as though someone from the Middle West had spoken instead of the French Minister of Foreign Affairs. This will explain the somewhat overdone repetition of France's case on the armament side.

Then came the vital point in which I used the formula that Briand gave in his speech, that France was willing to make an agreement as between it and the United States to outlaw war between the two countries. "'The renunciation of war as an instrument of national policy' is an idea not unfamiliar to the signatories of the Treaties of Locarno and the Covenant of the League of Nations." This was the vital phrase which Briand took.

On Thursday, the 24th, I had another interview with Leger at the Foreign Office and took him the document. He told me that it would have to be considered with some care but gave me no inkling as to its probable fate. In fact, from that time on, I found Léger singularly hard to reach and finally gave it up and did not see him or Briand again before leaving France. I had only the one interview. I learned, however, over the telephone, that the matter was likely to be discussed at the Cabinet meeting on Friday or Saturday, but I did not learn what took place at that meeting.

In the afternoon of Monday, the 28th, I called by appointment on Poincaré, but the visit had to do with the problem of war debts, as I had been the chairman of the Columbia Committee that issued the protest against full collection in the preceding December. Poincaré took pains to reassure me as against certain critics that the Columbia protest had not in any way strengthened the opposition to the payment in France, but, on the contrary, had done exactly what it was intended to do, namely, soften the antipathies with the United States and thus make possible a more reasonable attitude at least on the part of those who had felt so deeply offended in France.

I had expected that the conversation would be entirely on this theme and the only possible reference to anything else was Poincaré's cordial remark that he was well aware of the fact that I had been "helpful in other ways" in attempting to retain the *rapprochement* between France and the United States which had been so sorely tested in the post-war days. In order not to get drawn into the equivocal position which might seem to Briand that I had turned from him to Poincaré, I did not invite him to develop what was in his mind. I wanted very much to ask him his point of view but felt that it was better to leave it in the hands of Briand, for I was anxious to have the whole proposition handled by Briand and was afraid that if Poincaré took a hand in it he would say the wrong thing and spoil it all. So I left that interview with no further reference whatever to the Briand offer.

On Tuesday morning, I left for London and went on the next day to Kingston Blount and stayed with Mitrany, in whom I reposed all confidence and to whom I told the story. Then on April 1 I went back to London and made my home with Tom Jones, Secretary of the British Cabinet, in whom I had equal confidence, as we had been through a number of incidents of this kind in the utmost intimacy. I told Jones of the plan so that if Briand's statement should appear on Wednesday, the 6th, it should not take the British so by surprise that they would give a hostile interpretation to it and so spoil it from the start.

The British papers on the morning of April 7 gave no indication that anything had been said in France, and I sailed away from Southampton that morning without any sign of fulfillment on the part of Briand. It was only when in mid-ocean a passing reference was made in one of the wireless bulletins, that I realized that something had been issued to the press on April 6 along the lines of the suggestion, but the reference was so vague as to be meaningless.

When I arrived in New York, the first thing I did on reaching my office was to call for the newspaper account of M. Briand's speech of April 6. I found it not on the front page but on one of the inside sheets. The Associated Press had taken liberties with the text, making it sound like a confused statement of good intentions based upon a sentimental memory of America's participation in the war.

211

I know of no better instance of the way in which a newspaper correspondent can destroy the force of argument of a document by trying to pick out for headlines what the correspondent thinks has news value. Fortunately, however, the Associated Press did quote enough of Briand's offer so that I could recognize the substance of my proposal. I waited with some impatience, therefore, until the next European mail brought a copy of *Le Temps*. When I had the French text before me I saw at once that Briand had literally inserted, in French translation, the most essential parts of the text I had prepared for him in Paris. The key paragraph read as follows:

> For those whose lives are devoted to securing this living reality of a policy of peace the United States and France already appear before the world as morally in full agreement. If there were need for those two great democracies to give high testimony to their desire for peace and to furnish to other peoples an example more solemn still, France would be willing to subscribe publicly with the United States to any mutual engagement tending "to outlaw war," to use an American expression, as between these two countries. The renunciation of war as an instrument of national policy is a conception already familiar to the signatories to the Covenant of the League of Nations and of the Treaties of Locarno. Every engagement entered into in this spirit by the United States toward another nation such as France would contribute greatly in the eyes of the world to broaden and strengthen the foundations on which the international policy of peace is being erected. These two great friendly nations, equally devoted to the cause of peace, would furnish to the world the best illustration of the truth that the immediate end to be attained is not so much disarmament as the practical application of peace itself.

This was the situation when I went down to see my friend Dr. John Finley, the editor of the *New York Times,* and told him the whole story in confidence. I don't recall the details of that conversation, but the result of it was a suggestion that the question be opened up again in the form of a letter to the *Times,* and the obvious person to write it was President Butler. Dr. Finley then invited me to come down on April 20 to lunch, and again told the whole story to Mr. Ochs, Mr. Sulzberger and the editorial council in the confidence which is guaranteed under the circumstances. I came away commissioned by the *Times* to go to President Butler and suggest that he write a letter for the editorial page calling attention to the significance of the Briand offer. I want to say here in the most definite terms that had it not been for the sympathetic understanding of Dr. Finley and the backing which the *Times* gave from that time on, there would have been no Kellogg-Briand Pact; for nowhere else was the offer taken seriously in those early days.

I told Dr. Butler the story of my interview with Briand. His first reaction was one of caution. He was not at the very first moment inclined to take the proposal seriously. However, when I laid the texts before him, he quickly saw the event in its full significance. It happened to be a very busy time for him, and he asked me to draft a letter substantially in the terms of my oral statement to him. I went back to my office and wrote a draft, which summarized the whole story and emphasized the fact that the French Cabinet have always visaed any important pronouncement of Cabinet members. Dr. Butler's letter rephrased this statement so as to give it his own peculiar energy of phrase.

His letter was published on Monday the 25th. On Sunday the 24th, I had gone down to the *Times* and discussed the whole situation again with Dr. Finley. Together we looked over his editorial with which the *Times* came to the support of President Butler's letter on the same page.

When the Carnegie Endowment Trustees' annual meeting was held in Washington on April 29, I took occasion to call attention to M. Briand's offer, but found no support on the part of any of the Trustees. On the contrary, ex-Secretary Lansing stated that there was nothing in it whatever, and, moreover, that it was all covered by existing treaties which we had previously made with France. There was a vigorous head-shaking by Dr. David Jayne Hill and others. The result was that the Carnegie Endowment missed the chance to take the lead in the movement for a genuine Briand Pact.

Meanwhile the use of the phrase "outlawry of war" by M. Briand brought to France the creator of that phrase, Mr. Levinson. I did not learn of this until May 19 but was warned on May 13 by Dr. Babcock cabling from Paris that M. Léger was much disturbed because the Levinson group was interpreting M. Briand's offer as an endorsement of their peace ideas. Dr. Babcock's cable stated that

M. Briand was ready with the further declaration to which reference had been made in earlier cables, but wished his appeal to go to American public opinion of all groups and not just one. Dr. Babcock's cable asked further whether President Butler could submit a new formula for a statement in Paris.

Concerning Levinson's journey I have no direct knowledge. I was told, however, that the Quai d'Orsay simply did not know what to make of his point of view. I shall have to leave it to those who know this phase of the story to estimate whether Levinson's influence on Briand was effective or not.

Meanwhile, President Butler in a speech at the American Club in Paris, summarized the Briand proposal in three broad principles: First, that France and the United States should agree to renounce war as the instrument of policy between themselves; second, that the United States accept the definition of aggression embodied in Locarno; third, that if there is a war of aggression we will not aid the aggressor.

Secretary Kellogg, however, was not prepared to accept this definition of aggression and the final text of the treaty was limited to two short articles, which after protracted negotiations, were accepted by fifteen governments:

ARTICLE 1

The high contracting parties solemnly declare in the names of their respective peoples that they condemn recourse to war for the solution of international controversies, and renounce it as an instrument of national policy in their relations with one another.

ARTICLE 2

The high contracting parties agree that the settlement or solution of all disputes or conflicts of whatever nature or of whatever origin they may be, which may arise among them, shall never be sought except by pacific means.

History was soon to show that a renunciation of war without a provision for its enforcement was nothing more than a pious declaration of good intentions, but this was as far as Secretary Kellogg was prepared to go. The final judgment on it was pronounced by

M. Briand himself, when, in August, 1928, he presided over the signing of the Pact of Paris, as it came to be called, in the hall of the French Foreign Office.

In his address on that occasion he recalled the fact that in his message to the American people on April 6, 1927, he had based his proposal along the lines of the treaties of Locarno and the Covenant and then, after commenting on the fact that the pact lacked sanctions, concluded with this warning:

> Peace has been proclaimed, and that is well. That is much. But peace has yet to be organized. For settlements by force we must substitute settlements by law. That must be the work of tomorrow.

It was to this "work of tomorrow," the organization of peace, that I then turned, and to it devoted most of the rest of my life. Naturally, my interests centered in the organization of peace at Geneva, particularly in the technique of international conferences in the Assembly and that of Conciliation in the Council and Secretariat. The Secretariat itself was an international body of experts preparing the detail for the International Conferences, and then along with it, if the question were one of extreme difficulty, there were international commissions of technical experts. It was the first great experiment in the organization of peace, and history has not given it sufficient credit.

The technique of conciliation is, of course, diplomacy at its best, solving problems without allowing them to become dangerous chiefly by the application of common sense.

I remember an incident which occurred at the meeting of the Council in March, 1927, which illustrates this point. The Treaty of Versailles had left the administration of the Saar Valley in the hands of Frence for the first seven years. Then with Germany's entrance into the League, the question came up as to how many troops France might keep in the Saar Valley. The issue had already come to the fore when I was in Berlin, and in the German newspapers there were protests against a continuation of what was called the military occupation by France. Over in Paris, on the other hand, the nationalist press reacted bitterly against the German proposal so that by implication each nation was charging the other with bad faith. At Geneva Stresemann and Briand found themselves in a deadlock, and they went into the Council unable to reach any solution. When I arrived at that meeting there were over one hundred journalists, representing one hundred million readers on the Continent of Europe, watching every step that was taken. Stresemann was presiding, never saying a word to Briand all day long, while Briand with grave, drawn face, was unable to find any formula to solve the difficulty. Then at the close of the day the Italian member of the Council, Scialoia, wrote a sentence on the back of an envelope and passed it to Briand and Stresemann. Both of them nodded assent. The settlement was that France could have the eight hundred men which it claimed were needed to preserve law and order, but must never show more than five hundred at any one time. The incident ended in a little ripple of laughter.

I recall this simply as a reminder that the organization of peace must provide for the simplest as well as for the most complicated machinery if it is to rid the world of the menace of war.

While the negotiations over the Briand offer were pursuing their tortuous course, I stated my hopes—and my reserves—in a volume, *Was as an Instrument of National Policy and Its Renunciation in the Pact of Paris.** A paragraph or two from this book will show how deeply rooted in history was the philosophy of war renunciation, which I advocated:

> The meaning of the Pact of Paris is to be found not solely or even mostly in the text itself but rather in the study of the history of civilization and a survey of the practical politics of the immediate present. If war has been with us since the beginning of time, it will only yield to forces stronger than itself; whether these really exist in the world today or not is as much the subject of this inquiry as the story of the Pact itself.
>
> The full treatment of this subject would carry us very far afield indeed; for it would call for nothing less than an analysis of civilization itself, civilization with war in it and a hypothetical future with war no longer functioning as it has throughout all the centuries of history.
>
> It may take a generation yet, or even more, before the civilized nations can be sure that they have really turned the corner in this great

* *War as an Instrument of National Policy and its Renunciation in the Pact of Paris* (New York: Harcourt, Brace and Company, 1929), pp. 4-7.

216

enterprise; for if it takes a century for nations like France and Britain to assure themselves the gains of an internal revolution, it will undoubtedly take longer for the whole world to appropriate to itself this revolution, which reaches to the very base of international relationships.

In fact, it is by no means clear that the whole world is ready for the proposal to renounce war as an instrument of national policy. Where a people is in a semi-barbarous state, force, either applied or held in reserve, is the very condition of peace itself. International peace is applicable only to responsible governments that are able to comply with the conditions of the new regime. It is a wholly false conception of international peace that makes it merely synonymous with a renunciation of war. The new regime of pacific relations is not of this negative character. It does not lessen our international obligations, but on the contrary it is in proportion as the isolation of states is given up that the renunciation of war becomes a factor in real politics.

The movement to rid the world of war is therefore one of those major changes in human affairs which in the very nature of the case can never be fully embodied in any one slight document, however much that document may stimulate the imagination or contribute to the basic ideals of a new world structure. Even the Covenant of the League of Nations is only a single chapter in the transformation now under way. Similarly, the Pact of Paris is only a part of a larger whole. Even if it be all that can be claimed for it, it still remains far short of a complete embodiment of reform. No historical analysis is needed but merely common sense to withhold assent from those who would hail the Pact of Paris as marking that single point of time in which the world turns from darkness to light.

Although deeply convinced of the validity of the peace movement—that war would ultimately go the way of the other two leftovers from savagery and barbarism, witchcraft and slavery (a faith I still hold in spite of World War II and the menace of nuclear war) —I kept emphasizing the complexity and long range consequences of the movement, in both my writings and addresses. The academic world was curious and upon the whole sympathetic, perhaps because of the underlying conservativism of my approach to the problem. I was invited to lecture at most of the universities and major colleges: Yale, Princeton, Pennsylvania, Dartmouth (six lectures on the War History), the University of Virginia (six lectures on National Security), Duke, the universities of North Carolina, Georgia, Indiana, St. Louis, Denver and Stanford. While there was one underlying theme, there were many different ways of dealing with it, and I found my most serious audiences in the national organizations of women and in the service clubs, like Rotary. All in all it was a quasi-evangelistic crusade, of which I cherish lasting memories.

In the spring of 1930, Mr. Kellogg came to New York for two or three days, and I called at his hotel to try to make sure that in his speech at the Town Hall, or in an accompanying interview, he would say that the American Delegation at the London Disarmament Conference ought to, or at least might very well, incorporate in their negotiations with Britain a consultative pact with a sanction in case of violation that would be in harmony with the Pact of Paris and really a completion of it. Mr. Kellogg was ready to do this and we drafted a statement together, but he called up the State Department and found them decidedly cold to the proposition, to such an extent that he, as ex-Secretary of State, felt that it would be regarded as hostile interference on his part, and so he dropped it.

But we got to talking about the Pact and its negotiations and reviewed the history of it. He was generously appreciative of all that I had done and claimed that his delay in taking up the offer was due solely to the fact that he had to get sufficient support in public opinion before facing the inevitable attack upon any such pacific pact both in the public press and in Congress. As I have stated in my book, it is perhaps well that public opinion did mobilize first, as it made it possible for the State Department to act with confidence that public opinion throughout the country would support this negotiation, whatever cynicism there might be in the Senate. But Mr. Kellogg had, I think, forgotten how he himself had given no sign of belief in the validity of the proposal until public opinion had had its say; and to mobilize that opinion had taken heavy and constant work.

Mr. Kellogg also told me that Mr. Levinson's claim of being really responsible for the Pact came to his attention only after the signature, and I think after the ratification. In any case, he said that he had never heard of anything that Mr. Levinson proposed until it was all over. Then as Mr. Levinson's friends were making this claim, Mr. Kellogg said that he called in the man in charge of the Western European Division and asked him if there was anything in the files of the State Department from Mr. Levinson. He found that there was a plan that Mr. Levinson had sent in, but Mr. Kellogg states that the text was utterly different from that of the treaty itself and showed that Mr. Levinson's draft treaty could by no chance have been the parent document, even if Mr. Kellogg had seen it. The two were utterly dissimilar. Mr. Kellogg asked his State Department assistant why he had not shown him this document, and he replied that there were many plans for the peace treaty and that he didn't consider this to be sufficiently important to bother Mr. Kellogg with it.

CHAPTER 13

Balkan Journey

For half a dozen years I had spent most of the time in Western Europe, but, except at Prague and Budapest, I had not gone beyond the borders of the Germanic world. The war-time history of Russia had been edited at Oxford by Sir Paul Vinogradoff and there had been glimpses of Serbia from Vienna. But Mr. Root, who never did things by halves, insisted on a first-hand survey of that part of the world in which the war began—a proposal seconded by President Butler—so that I could recommend future plans of the Carnegie Endowment in the Balkans. In accordance with the original instructions of Mr. Carnegie to the Trustees, the plan for the journey included Mrs. Shotwell as well.

The ideal starting point was Geneva, where the leading Balkan statesmen were gathered for the League Assembly in September, 1925. I met no less than ten cabinet ministers from Southeastern Europe in a few days. Even before leaving for Europe I had received a cable from M. Duca, Foreign Minister of Romania inviting me to be the guest of the government during any visit to Romania. News of this kind travels swiftly around foreign offices. I was not surprised, therefore, when in Geneva the Prime Minister of Bulgaria, M. Tsankoff, and the Foreign Minister, M. Kalfoff, also extended to me, without any gesture on my part, a very cordial invitation to go to Bulgaria as the guest of the Bulgarian Government. Then M. Nintschitch, the Yugoslav Foreign Minister, who was President of the Assembly, extended the same invitation on instructions from Belgrade. There was also a pressing invitation from the Polish Foreign Minister, Count Skrzynski, but as Poland was not on the direct line of my journey I was obliged to decline.

Plans for the visits to Greece and Turkey could not be made in Geneva because they would have to depend upon the uncertainties of two months' travel in the other countries. Moreover, I was not particularly anxious to visit Greece under the auspices of the government then in power, that of M. Pangalos, a reactionary and corrupt government. Diplomacy, however, continued to work and later on, when I reached Bucharest, I received an official invitation from the Greek Government, which, of course, it was necessary to accept. My visit to Turkey was devoid of any attention from the government, but was happily spent under the guidance of Dr. Ahmed Emin Yalman, my friend and former student at Columbia University, now a leading, liberal journalist, whose volume *Turkey in the World War,* which I then planned with him, is the most revealing study of how militarism limits and denatures statesmanship.

The Balkan journey was a very exhausting one, lasting somewhat over two months. The itinerary through Yugoslavia began on the Dalmatian coast, then by automobile to Montenegro, through Bosnia and Serbia to Belgrade. Relatively short trips were made to Neustadt in Slovenia and to Zagreb in Croatia. Then we traveled by train and automobile through old Serbia and southwest Macedonia to the frontiers of Greece and Albania. From Serbia we went down the Danube to Romania where, centering at Bucharest, we traveled many hundreds of miles through Transylvanian towns and countryside.

By this time the season had advanced so far that motor trips through Bulgaria were abandoned, as well as the plan to visit Asia Minor from Constantinople. In Greece conditions were unfavorable for a lengthy survey, and we remained almost entirely in Athens. It might be mentioned that, in order to save time, some sixteen nights were spent traveling by train or boat—a none too happy experience in that part of the world.

In the course of the journey I delivered thirteen public addresses, not including those at banquets and luncheons. Six of these were delivered in French, the rest in English with translations in the

221

native tongues wherever that was necessary. With one or two exceptions, there were no written texts of these addresses, for they had to be adjusted to situations which only became clear at the time of their delivery.

It struck me at the time as one of the strangest of chances that I should begin my work in the Balkans by speaking to the citizens of the city of Sarajevo. The lecture was translated for me by Mme. Lazarovitch, whom I felt I could fully trust. Yet I had the feeling here as on every other occasion when I spoke in the other Balkan centers that single visits of this kind could not do more than raise questions in the minds of the listeners which could not be answered without months or years of study and personal contact with those in other countries who were facing the same problems in the same way.

The murder of Archduke Franz Ferdinand was still in every mind, and the two leaders of the societies under whose auspices I spoke had both been tried b ythe Austrians on the charge of complicity in the murder but had escaped on a technicality. They had been then propagandists for Bosnian union with Serbia, and their societies are the societies for spreading Serbian culture in Bosnia. It was Mme. Lazarovitch who gave me the first satisfactory explanation of their part in the conspiracy. They were young intellectuals whose imaginations had been fired by the victories of the Serbs in the Balkan Wars and who shared the same kind of irritation against Austrian bureaucracy that was to be found in every non-Germanic section of the Hapsburg monarchy. Their reading, however, had been mainly in Russian literature and history, and it was therefore natural under the circumstances that they accepted the doctrine of Russian terrorism, which by striking at the head of the government sought to effect revolutionary changes with the least possible bloodshed. This paradox seems strange to Western thinking, but unless one understands it and the basis for it, there is little chance of understanding the Balkans and Eastern Europe. In the Balkans it fitted in naturally with the persistence of feuds among people still living in a partially tribal society. It was clear that in their minds, and I imagine in the minds of most Balkan peoples outside, as well as inside Serbia, the theory of assassination of tyrants was fully accepted.

The young women I met, who had also been in the conspiracy,

222

were devoting their lives unselfishly to a movement in adult education. Through an organization called Prosveta both men and women were engaged upon a struggle with illiteracy in the back country of Bosnia as well as in the towns. It was also part of the nationalist movement, but not in a narrow sense, because they had translated into Serbian some of the classics of Western literature as well as of Russian and were printing them in cheap pamphlets for distribution in local libraries and homes. I examined their plant and looked into some of their libraries and could hardly believe that so much could be done with so little.

The main dining room of the one European hotel in Sarajevo had been formed into a private room for our reception. The Governor of the district presided and with him was the Mayor of the town, the Commanding General of that section of Bosnia, the Metropolitan and the leading members of his clergy, the Chief Teacher in the Seminaries, the heads of the cultural societies under whose auspices the "tea" was given. I was introduced by the Governor and then spoke at some length on "Problems of Constructive Peace," indicating the line of work that the Carnegie Endowment undertakes throughout the world and the kind of work which it approves of even when it is not in a position to collaborate.

It was under these auspices that I gave my first lecture in the Balkans. The theme of my talk was geared as closely as possible to the situation. For the one argument for peace which they could understand was based upon history. The long Turkish occupation lay behind them, with its denial of freedom throughout the centuries under a military caste. Then came the occupation by Austria, with an effort at betterment but an almost equal failure to understand, because of the rigidity of bureaucratic rule and the constant threat of military action.

The next few days were spent in Belgrade, getting my bearings for the program in Serbia. This naturally began with an inspection of the Carnegie Library, which had just been completed and which, therefore, had very few books as yet on its shelves. As there was no free space for so large a building in the heart of the town where the old university stands, the library had been built along one of the newer avenues leading to the suburbs and too far away for students who had classes in the old buildings. It was explained, however, that all this would change with the rebuilding of the university, for which plans were being drawn. Already the new medical school had been built on the southern slope of the hill, with aid from the Rockefeller Foundation, and its laboratories were stocked with instruments taken from Austria and Germany on account of Serbian reparation. This was a kind of reparation payment which I never saw anywhere else, and I could not imagine anything more appropriate. The result was to provide the new medical school with the most up-to-date equipment, and, as the professors had been trained in Vienna or Paris, the school itself was certainly in the position to open a new era in Balkan medical history.

First of all, there was a formal visit to be paid to Mr. Nintschitch, the Minister of Foreign Affairs, on which occasion I was accompanied by the rector of the university. In this way the unofficial character of my mission to the Balkans was underlined, although, as will appear later, the government used to the full every possible opportunity to be of help, and I was able to see more than I had dared to hope of the country and people of Yugoslavia during the short time I was there. Unfortunately, the guiding genius of the country, Prime Minister Pashitch, was not in Belgrade while I was there. One had a strange feeling, however, that he was never wholly absent from the minds of the members of his cabinet, remaining always the dominating personality even when absent.

After a busy stay of several days we left Belgrade for Macedonia as the guests of the government. We were supplied not only with a private car on the railway, but with motor cars at every step, an interpreter, and another young man from the Foreign Office, a functionary whose services were never used and who submitted good-naturedly to constant teasing. Above all, there was the Governor (Grand Supan) of the eastern part of Serbian Macedonia. Bishop Nicolai, with a young ecclesiastic as his assistant, was the unquestioned leader of our party as far as his episcopal seat at Ochrida.

After an easy run of a night and a forenoon, we stopped at the old capital of Serbia, Skoplje. There was no escaping the obligation to deliver another lecture in the hall of the university, which we found crowded with well-dressed citizens with a group of officers in the front row, all wearing their decorations. I took as the theme of my talk that night the thought that the freedom Serbia had won would now have to be maintained by building the structure of peace, which could only happen under the regime of democracy. At the end Bishop Nicolai also spoke, summarizing the points I had made because, as he explained later, the translator had not done very well.

On arrival at Belgrade there were reporters waiting (also I imagine officially stimulated) for interviews on my impressions of Serbian Macedonia. Fortunately I was able to pay tribute to the indications I had seen on the spot of the way in which the old conditions of tribal isolation were being rapidly changed in the whole country. It was evident that the end of isolation was coming fast when we could go in a single afternoon from Skoplje to Monastir over a good motor road, whereas it used to take three or four days by mule track across the mountains.

This opening up of the country was aided by the money sent in by immigrants from America, which, although not much in terms of national finance, was enough to give a new outlook to the life of many a backward village. But equally as important as these economic facts was the new political setup when government was no longer in the hands of corrupt Turkish officials working in close touch with Turkish feudal landlords whose one interest was to exploit the peasantry. Serbian rule had brought in a revolutionary change in the whole administrative system and in a few years had completely altered conditions of life. The arrangements for rural police which I described above were all the more effective because of the advantages of new and wider markets and better communications, and by the use of the telephone the police forces could be quickly mobilized even in distant mountain valleys. The result had been that perhaps for the first time in history the local volunteers were stronger at any given point than the invading *comitadji*. These practical methods of local statesmanship mean more in that part of the world than the discussions in Parliament or the making of laws that may never be applied.

Belgrade looked good to us on our return from the gray skies

225

and rains of Macedonia, for it was literally shining in the autumn sunlight. At noon Mr. Nintschitch, Minister of Foreign Affairs, gave us an official luncheon at which he told us that he had already arranged that we should leave for a visit to Zagreb and Croatia that evening, but I very much doubt if he knew that that Croatian leader, Stephen Raditch, whom I had met the year before in Geneva, had planned to go along with us. For as we talked with Raditch on the train it soon became evident that, as a very keen politician, he would be intent upon making political capital out of our visit and that I would have to be on my guard not to get drawn into the nationalist Croatian opposition to the Belgrade Government. But I had not counted on Raditch's energy, and although I spent only three days in Croatia he made the most of them.

Raditch was the absolute leader of the Croatian peasants, a demagogue of the first order. His methods seemed to me to be those of a Tammany politician multiplied many times over. For example, he claimed that he knew every Croatian by name and all their family histories. Unfortunately, as we motored through the countryside we came upon several of them who didn't know him, and he had to tell them who he was. Then they were properly impressed. In manner he was most effusive, to an extent rather offensive to one of the members of our party. And it must be admitted that he did not help matters by insisting on talking an unintelligible jargon which he thought was English. He was known as a strong supporter of the League of Nations and used it to good effect in the Parliament at Belgrade. But in his own home city it was clear to see that he was also using the leverage of his relations at Geneva to good effect as an influence for Croatian autonomy over against the ill-advised Serbian idea of a unitary state in which they could dominate. This was one place where provincial politics helped the movement for world peace.

After a meeting in the city hall, there was a formal presentation of an album of the city of Zagreb and an artistically decorated medallion to commemorate the occasion. It was only later, however, that I understood why so much was made of the visit, for the year before Raditch had been one of the prime movers in Southeastern Europe in support of the Protocol of Geneva, having been

226

misled into thinking that it represented the ideas of the United States because of the part which had been played by General Bliss, Mr. Miller, and me at the Assembly in Geneva. Never doing things by halves, he had got together in Zagreb a great "national meeting" of something like 150,000 Croatian peasants to support the principles of the Protocol and by their support to strengthen his hand over against the Serbians in the national government. It was not until that evening that I learned how my name had been associated with this event, which helped to explain Raditch's interest in our visit.

I was to have made visits to other cities of Croatia, but just before leaving I had received word from Bucharest that arrangements had been made there which prevented any further delay. The last day in Belgrade was a busy one with formal calls and a final reception at the Foreign Office in the afternoon, which was largely attended. From there we went directly to the night boat down the Danube for Romania.

After having been comfortably established in Bucharest's best hotel, which like most of Bucharest was a definite imitation of Paris, I went to pay my respects to M. Duca, the Foreign Minister who at Geneva had so cordially extended the invitation to visit Romania. Cordiality of the official kind is not always genuine, but on this occasion it proved to be so, for M. Duca at once arranged meetings with the Prime Minister, John Bratianu, and Vintila Bratianu, his brother, the Minister of Finance, who were the leaders of the Liberal Party and the two most powerful figures in the recent history of Romania.

It was part of M. Duca's plan that we should leave Bucharest as soon as possible to visit the King and Queen at their summer residence at Sinaia in the foothills of the Carpathians and go on from there over the mountains of Transylvania.

The route north from Bucharest is level open country, but in spite of the fact that it seemed like good farming land, the houses of the peasants were poor beyond description, mere huts, distinctly inferior to those of the Yugoslav peasantry. About halfway to Sinaia we passed through the great oil region of Ploesti, with its forest of derricks and the black seepage from oil tanks. From there

227

it was by no means a royal road that led to the summer residence of the royal family, although the Ploesti oil wells are, next to agriculture, the greatest economic resource of the country. From the station at Sinaia we motored down along tree-lined avenues to the castle.

The castle itself was definitely built in the German manner, apparently under the influence of the uncle of King Ferdinand, King Carol, who came from the younger branch of the Hohenzollern family. The architecture is of that somewhat fussy, unrestful type which one sees here and there in south Germany—ornamental timbering in stucco walls with contrasting stretches of red brick or stone and surmounted by sharp belfry-like roofs. All in all, it was not a restful spot, even when seen from the long Carmen Sylva Avenue. But inside it was homelike and unpretentious, the whole atmosphere quite restful.

We were accompanied from Bucharest by a Foreign Office official who seemed somewhat disturbed by the fact that I did not wear striped trousers and a morning coat, as prescribed by protocol on all such occasions. M. Duca, however, who went along with us, reassured me that both King and Queen ran their court with informality, and that proved to be the case. As we went in, we were received by the King's aide de camp and the Queen's lady-in-waiting, who showed us our seats at a table, a little removed from the center. The Queen wore a beautiful costume with a white embroidered waist and headdress and a red skirt. The King was quietly dressed in a dark business suit. Their two daughters, the Queens of Yugoslavia and Greece, were visiting them at the time. When we got to the table, Queen Marie said, "Mr. Shotwell is to sit beside me and Mrs. Shotwell over there, beside the Queen of Yugoslavia."

The lady-in-waiting was disturbed and said to Mrs. Shotwell, as she rearranged things, "There goes the Queen again, upsetting all the arrangements, as usual." However, the change had to be made and everyone talked very animatedly, mostly to us.

The Queen of Greece was the quietest member of the family group. She was a very beautiful woman with red hair, and was inclined to be stout. The garrulous lady-in-waiting attributed it to eating candies! The Queen of Yugoslavia was much interested in our trip through Serbia and talked very pleasantly about it.

228

King Ferdinand, sitting across the center of the long table, opposite Queen Marie, at first took little part in the conversation going on around him. He seemed a little out of it, and acted as if he didn't care. But when Marie told him, with an obvious attempt at casualness, that she had invited a prominent leader of the international movement for woman's rights to have tea with them, he reacted without reserve, and she had to reassure him at length that he would not be backing a radical feminist. He held stubbornly to his point, and we were only saved from embarrassment by Marie's retreat from the proposal. The tea would be with her, but she hoped he would turn up! After this little incident such as might happen at any family table, the King grew more animated, but never quite equaled the vivacity of his irrepressible wife.

After the luncheon was over the King took me off into a corner of the sitting room and kept me there for about an hour while the Foreign Office official, much upset, walked ostentatiously by from time to time as though to relieve the King and give him a chance to escape. However, before the hour was over, he sent the diplomat away and we continued our intimate talk. There is nothing, however, to report on this except for the fact that it was a talk with royalty and that the King seemed happy to have a chance to talk about American politics, especially about Woodrow Wilson and his struggle with the Senate. I had heard critics of the King speak slightingly of him, but I left Sinaia filled with admiration for the deft way he held the conversation off the problems of Eastern Europe and yet never gave the impression of consciously doing so. The nearest we came to the subject was in discussing the Paris Peace Conference in academic terms. His bearing was modest and without a trace of formal ceremony.

Then, after about a week of motoring through Transylvania, we were back in Bucharest, where I found three tasks awaiting me before our departure: first, the delivery of public lectures at the university; second, the completion of plans for the Romanian volumes in the War History; and third, the round of official meetings and entertainments. I should have been glad to escape from the lectures, for the rigors of the Carpathian journey in November weather had brought on a severe case of grippe. But it was too late to back out and so we went ahead with the arrangements for two lectures, one at the Romanian Academy and the other at the Romanian Social Institute. The audience at the Romanian Academy was largely drawn from university circles and my lecture dealt with a description of the Carnegie Endowment efforts to make a scientific study of the nature of war today. The second lecture was a more important public occasion and was attended by the Prime Minister and almost his whole Cabinet. Professor Gusti, the President of the Institute, has a European reputation as a social scientist of the first order, and his strong endorsement of the lecture was duly noted in the Bucharest papers. It was an ordeal for me, however, because on the evening of the lecture I was running a temperature somewhere in the neighborhood of 103 and had neither time nor strength to prepare a written text, so I was obliged to speak *ex tempore*. Nevertheless, the combination of circumstances proved favorable; when, a few days later, I read over the stenographic account of what I was alleged to have said, it needed almost no corrections before printing in both the original French and later in an English translation.* It was the first rounded statement of my theory that the scientific revolution in warfare of World War I pointed the way to the renunciation of war as an instrument of policy.

The next morning we left by train for Bulgaria, the government placing an official car at our disposal.

We crossed the Danube at Ruschuk and found that the Bulgarian Government had sent down another special carriage for the night journey to Sofia, with a Foreign Office official in charge who had been specially trained for this kind of service and who bore the weirdly appropriate—or inappropriate—name of Kissimoff. He was an experienced diplomat and throughout our stay in Sofia was most solicitous and helpful. Perhaps I should add here that in none of the countries we traveled through had there been any request made for official railway carriages or any other travel privileges.

The morning of November 6 was spent in a long talk with young King Boris III. The King received me alone, opening the door

* Published in April, 1927, in the Endowment's pamphlet series, *International Conciliation*, under the title: "Locarno and the Balkans: A Turning Point in History."

himself to admit me to what he called his office, a long room with absolutely none of the trappings of a palace. Its wall were bare, lacking any kind of decoration; there were only two or three office-like chairs and a few books. The most striking object was on a shelf by the door—a telegraph instrument of the kind ordinarily found in railroad stations. When I remarked about it, King Boris explained that he had a mechanical bent and had learned how to telegraph when a boy, and that this was very useful to him because he could send messages which the telephone might garble. But he said that it was also the direct access to him from the government officials in the provinces. At that time he said that the last thing he wanted to hear was the click of the instrument, for it might mean the worsening of the situation in Macedonia, where only a few weeks before war between Bulgaria and Greece had only been averted by the quick action of the Council of the League of Nations.

The King's interest in the implications of the settled Greek-Bulgarian border dispute seemed to me much more lively than that of his ministers, whose attitude was correctly cordial in the formal and official way. For the King it was evidently a personal problem which was so much on his mind that he spoke rapidly and without any apparent reserve, turning from English to French, in which he was more proficient. He impressed me as a young man who was not sure of himself, but especially well inclined toward the United States because of the contribution of Robert College to the education of the young men of Bulgaria. Had we been in the League of Nations at the time this influence would have been stronger.

The interview with the King was only the beginning of the day's work. The afternoon was given up to conferences with professors, of economics and politics, each of them of the conservative type which made him *persona grata* with his colleagues in the government. Then at six o'clock we were called for by the rector of the university to go over to their largest public hall, which, it should be noted, was that of the *Alliance française,* the great French propaganda agency. There we found a packed house to listen to my lecture before the Academy of Science. There is no need to pause

231

over this last public address of the journey, which dealt mostly with the work of the Carnegie Endowment and the War History. I was surprised, however, to find the next morning that the Sofia papers had reported the event in great detail, as though it were a matter of national importance. Evidently the word had got around that the King had been interested.

Next morning, November 9, keeping to our schedule we left Sofia for Constantinople on the Oriental Express.

My visit to Turkey was on a wholly different plan from that to the other Balkan countries. Its purpose was to draw the lesson for the Western countries of the effect of militarism upon the militarists themselves. Throughout the other countries of the Balkans there had been ample evidence of its effect upon the subject peoples, but here at last we were to come to grips with the central theme of militarism itself—a theme standing out more clearly here than in any other country.

The effects of German militarism were hard to disentangle from the effects of Germany's prodigious industrial output. The effects of Russian militarism were still harder to trace in the Bolshevik revolutionary movements. But in Turkey the lessons of history were clear, as clear, at least, as they ever are. For the Ottoman Turkish monarchy was, above all things, the rule of the soldier, the combination of two great militarisms—that of Rome through Byzantium, on the one hand, and of the warlike monarchies of Asia on the other. Concentrating upon the army, the Turks left civilian affairs to a bureaucracy very largely composed of Armenians and Greeks, as long as they were competent and willing to serve their Turkish masters. Religion played little part in this organization of government, chief interest of which was conquest and exploitation of the conquered.

As in the case of every great military system, the initial stages were those of power and magnificence. Nowhere else in the modern world is this law of history more evident than in the splendor of the creations of the Turkish sultans in the long line of massive domes and slender minarets that crown the hills of Constantinople.

In spite of its magnificence, however, the Ottoman Empire, like all monarchies that ruled by the sword, had in it from the very first

232

the elements of decay. Already by the eighteenth century its age of greatness was over. While this was partly due to the rise of sea power and the ocean route which cut in upon the Oriental trade, it was a decline inherent in the nature of the Turkish state. The economics of conquest are those of ultimate exhaustion, for the exploitation of the conquered calls for no co-operation on his part and lessens the interest of even the ruling class in the fundamental principles of its own welfare. This is a law of history which admits of no exception, but its operation is often slow because of many other factors in the evolution of politics. Had there been strong neighbors at hand or had the European powers been able to agree among themselves as to the fate of the Near East, the Ottoman Empire would have been broken up long before it was, for already by the middle of the nineteenth century the "Sick Man of Europe" was no idle phrase.

But the Empire lived on for a half century more, chiefly owing to the rivalries of the great powers. Hardly had Russia driven it from its hold on the Black Sea before the British, as a result of Napoleon's invasion of Egypt, began to take, for the first time, a lively interest in the Near East. These rivalries played into the hands of Bismarck when, at the Congress of Berlin in 1878, he made himself "the honest broker" of the bazaar of power politics.

All this was ended, however, when in 1912 the subject peoples of the Balkans took their fate in their own hands and showed to an astonished Europe the utter weakness of the caliphate whose sovereignty was still recognized throughout the Arab world. The World War, which for a time had seemed to check the threatened downfall of the Ottoman Empire, ended by registering its complete collapse, leaving to the Turks only the hinterland of Asia Minor.

Here was a theme which fitted perfectly into the scheme of the Carnegie Endowment History of the War, but it was one which could not be handled by any but a Turk who had both a clear understanding of the background of Turkish history and experience of the War itself. For in the postwar years the resurgence of Turkish nationalism had been an even greater surprise to the Western world than the eclipse of the Empire in the Balkan Wars. Judged on the surface of things, Turkish militarism had justified itself in the defeat

233

of the Greek invaders of Anatolia, who had succeeded, by the deft diplomacy of Venizelos, in securing the backing of Lloyd George. The support of the British for the Greek aggression was not backed up, however, by their allies or even by the British dominions, and it was as a successful military leader that Mustafa Kemal consolidated his power at Angora.

These recent events had made an analysis of Turkish militarism an extremely difficult task. Fortunately the qualifications for such a study were fully met by my friend and former student, Dr. Ahmed Emin.* Apart from my visits with him there is not much to record of the visit to Constantinople, and after visiting Robert College and the American College for Girls, we left by night boat for Greece.

It is strange that the country which first gave the world a science of politics should be one of the worst-governed in Europe, yet that has been the condition of Greece throughout most of its recent history. It was even true during part of the regime of Venizelos, whose brillant handling of foreign affairs was by no means matched by his domestic politics. A government of factions rather than of parties had suffered throughout the decade following the World War from the fact that King Constantine had been pro-German and that after his return to Athens in December, 1920, he had cherished for at least a short interval a dream of the restoration of the Greek Empire. But the war with the Turks ended not only in military disaster but in such intense partisan bitterness within Greece itself that six of the King's chief ministers were shot for treason.

In short, the impression I had when arriving in Greece, an impression not changed by my short stay there, was that with its economic poverty and its political feuds it had become the most backward of the Balkan countries.

This, however, did not hold true of the Greek intellectuals at the University of Athens, where a small but notable group of scholars were holding their own among the elite of European savants. Fortunately for me this was especially true in the field of economics

---

* Dr. Emin has added to his name the family surname Yalman. It was in 1935 that the introduction of family names was made obligatory and universal. Mustafa Kemal became Kemal Attaturk (Father of the Turks).

where Professor Andreades had made a place for himself that ranked with the leaders of economic thought in the universities of Western Europe. Before my arrival I had been in correspondence with him and had secured his consent to undertake the direction of a series of studies of the economic and social effects of the World War upon Greece. With his accustomed energy he had already drawn up his program of studies and secured collaboration from five of his colleagues so that within a few days we had completely worked out the plan for the War History of Greece.

I had made it a point to keep my visit to Greece purely unofficial, limiting my contacts to the academic world, having no desire to link up acquaintance with politicians in any country, but one afternoon I accepted what Professor Andreades said was an informal invitation to tea with the Foreign Minister, M. Roufos. To my surprise there was a formal ceremony in his apartment at which he told of my official reception in the other Balkan countries and ended by conferring upon me the Commandership of the Order of the Redeemer, a distinction which I would have appreciated much more if it had not come from the government of Pangalos.

After touring Greece for several days we took ship for Italy from the harbor in the Gulf of Corinth, to Brindisi, and from it by express train traveled straight to Paris and to Cherbourg for New York.

CHAPTER 14

Studies in Japan and China

While I was so deeply engaged in the effort to make real the organization of peace, without which the Briand-Kellogg pact would remain mere wishful thinking, a wholly new world— new to me—opened up in the problems of Japan and China. There were, first of all, the problems raised by the sudden modernization of Japan. Naturally, perhaps inevitably, it followed the path of the imperialist policies of European powers in their exploitation of China in the nineteenth century. But, while they applied pressure on the decadent Chinese empire from a distance, Japan waged war with it over the tributary kingdom of Korea (1894-1895), which by a humiliating defeat for China it took over, along with Formosa and the Pescadores islands. The supreme prize, however, Manchuria, was won by Russia, which held its railways and coastal regions until Japan defeated it in the war of 1904-1905. This defeat was so great a triumph for both army and navy that it still further militarized a militarist nation.

In China, meanwhile, a rising tide of discontent over the humiliations forced upon a proud, self-centered people was galvanized into a revolutionary force, and in 1911 the Manchu dynasty made way for a republic. But, instead of a unified nation, the new China suffered from civil wars, treachery of war lords and inexperience in government, of which Japan took full advantage, making demands which would have virtually put China in the place of a tributary nation. Then, in 1924, Sun Yat-sen, the father of the revolution, offered an inspiring program in his book of lectures, *The Three*

Principles (San Min Chu I)—Nationalism, Democracy and Welfare —which the Party of the Republic, the Kuomintang made into a national creed. The venerated leader died the next year, a national hero, but he left unsolved the final issue, whether China should go communist (he used communism as a revolutionary force but was not a communist himself) or follow the strong non-communist lead of the young military officer who now headed the Kuomintang, Chiang Kai-shek. By 1929, Chiang Kai-shek had not only established his ascendency in most of China, but had made surprising progress toward emancipation from the "unequal treaties" with the European Powers. The end of "extra-territoriality" was in sight, so far as the British were concerned. But, Japan, with its hold on Manchuria, still a Chinese province, took the opposite course by seizing the German-held province of Shantung and pushing on into Mongolia.

The door which opened upon this confused and dangerous prospect, The Institute of Pacific Relations, was planning its second (biennial) conference in Honolulu in the summer of 1927. The first conference in 1925 grew out of a discussion group initiated by two YMCA workers, Charles Loomis and Edward Carter, and reflected the unique position of Hawaii as a meeting place for East and West. With an amateur enthusiasm, which proved to be statesmanship, the discussion group, drawn from all the countries involved in the crisis in the Orient, laid bare the issues of war and peace in the clash of mounting nationalism in both Japan and China. So successful was this pioneering effort at mutual understanding, not necessarily at agreement, that the second conference, that of 1927, was almost like an unofficial parliament, with a membership of some two hundred, among whom were such distinguished figures as Ray Lyman Wilbur, President of Stanford University (later Secretary of the Interior under President Hoover), who had been one of the founders of the Institute, and General Sir Arthur Currie, Principal of McGill University (formerly Commander in Chief of the Canadian army in the World War). Sir Frederick Whyte, a specialist on China, headed the British delegation, along with Lionel Curtis, the political genius largely responsible for the creation of the British Commonwealth. From Japan came members of

237

the House of Peers and professors of history and law, Takaki and Takayanagi, from China, David Zy Yui and L. K. Chan.

To my surprise and concern I found myself nominated chairman of the Research Committee of the Institute. I felt strongly that this was absurd, as I had never had any contact with the Orient, but it was explained that the staff would look after the details and my job was to keep the engine on the rails. The situation was saved by the appointment of John B. Condliffe, a young economist from New Zealand as Executive Secretary, later head of the Department of Economics at the University of California, who was already showing the promise of his brilliant academic career. On the staff were keen young men like Kenneth Holland, who had been the Director of the IPR for many years.

In spite of the important personalities attending, the Honolulu Conference of 1927 was almost ignored by the newspapers. Their correspondents were limited to a hundred words a day, unless there were heated quarrels, in which case they were "to go the limit." But the issues raised by the Japanese and Chinese, if quietly presented, were vital to the peace in the Orient and here they could be discussed with a freedom impossible in official diplomacy. It was, therefore, a tribute to the conference idea that Japan offered to be the host for the next conference two years later. It was also a challenge to the conference method in international affairs.

To prepare for it I planned to spend three months in the Orient, studying the situation on the spot. The Carnegie Endowment for International Peace made this possible by a generous grant so that I could take Mrs. Shotwell and our two daughters, Margaret Grace and Helen, along. To keep within our resources, we motored across the continent, more than half of the way, from Omaha on, over unpaved roads of gravel, sand or clay. As I did not drive, it was not to be wondered at that the exploit of my wife and daughter evoked admiration from the Japanese ladies in Tokyo.

We sailed from San Francisco on the *Shinyo Maru* on August 14, 1929. The voyage was uneventful until we approached Japan. I do not know whether the Japanese Pacific liners plan it on purpose or not, but we came to Japan in the early dawn, almost as though we were following the track of the Sun Goddess, with the

238

Japanese passengers eagerly peering over the gray sea into a lavender sky for the first glimpse of the sacred mountain Fujiyama.

We were met at the boat by the Japanese delegation to the Kyoto Conference, who accompanied us to the Imperial Hotel, where we had lunch together.

It was not easy for us to find our land legs in the Imperial Hotel, for though it had withstood the earthquake of 1923, some of the floors had not settled to an even level, and fresh off the ship, we could not be certain if the tilting floors were due to imagined waves or to frozen undulations left behind by the tremor.

The Tokyo we had come to was a city still recovering from the effects of the earthquake and fire just six years before. Raw scars of leveled buildings were everywhere, but on all sides fine new fire and earthquake-proof structures were being erected. It was a city of tremendous activity, swarming with blue-jacketed coolies wearing white towels twisted around their heads to keep the sweat out of their eyes, of crowds of people each feverishly intent on his business and hurrying on his job.

I soon had a long conference with Baron Shidehara, the Foreign Minister whose liberal and enlightened policy with reference to China was in strong contrast with that of Tanaka whom he had just replaced. He was deeply interested in the definition of aggression of the Locarno treaties and the possible application of it in Asia. Then an even longer session with Mr. Saburi, who had been at the Peace Conference and had spent five years at Washington. He had just been appointed Japanese Minister to China and a new career was opening to him. But I was shocked to have a telephone message a few hours later that he had committed suicide. No one had any explanation for it.

There were so many visitors that I had no time to prepare a broadcast under the auspices of the *Nichi Nichi* newspaper and the League of Nations Association of Japan, but I had a clear field—the new international world of science, in which Japan was so fully launched, and the meditative mood symbolized by the great Buddha at Kamakura. The translation must have been good, for it got a rousing reception. In the audience was Prince Tokoghwa, who would have been ruling Japan if the Meiji restoration of the Emperor had not ousted the feudal Shoguns who had ruled Japan for three centuries.

The next morning we had the unique experience of a visit with Viscount Shibusawa, the "Grand Old Man" of Japan, and the only living statesman left from the era of the Meiji Restoration. The meeting had been arranged as a quiet conference between gentlemen only, to spare the old Viscount's strength: he was then in his ninetieth year. The ladies, therefore, would not be expected to meet him but would be privileged to wander in his beautiful gardens. But, to the consternation of the secretaries who hovered protectively around him, the Viscount greeted the whole party and invited everyone to his library, where we sat around a long table and listened to him.

Despite his age he was quick and vigorous in his movements and his voice was gentle but strong with only a suggestion of the cracked timbre of age. Through an interpreter, he spoke at length about Townsend Harris, the first American representative in Japan who came to Japan six years after Perry had sailed into Japanese waters in 1853. He recalled the remarkable effect that Harris had had in creating good understanding between Japan and the United States. By his personal courage, when he alone of all the foreign diplomats remained at his post during the threatened disorders directed against the foreigners, Harris had won the respect and admiration of all the young Liberals, including Viscount Shibusawa himself. It was as if Harris had modeled his conduct on the noblest interpretation of Bushido. It was not until later, at the Conference of which he was honorary chairman, that we understood the special emphasis we sensed in the Viscount's voice. For at that time he caused a statement to be read:

The controversy arising from American immigration legislation (The Exclusion Act of 1924) is not closed. The wound so needlessly inflicted on our national honor is still open and will remain open until the matter has been rightly settled.

I think it necessary to make this plain statement because there seems to be an impression in America that the incident is as good as forgotten in Japan. This erroneous impression is doubtless due to our courtesy and reticence on this subject in conversing with American visitors.

That same evening (September 4) we said au revoir to the friends who had come to see us off on the next lap of our journey. The train trip to Shimonoseki takes twenty-four hours and goes through some of the most beautiful scenery in Japan after passing the great shipping and industrial centers of Osaka and Kobe. The Inland Sea lay on our left for the greater part of the way, and we could see little fishing villages of thatched houses along the shore, resembling, from a distance, a collection of mushrooms. Occasionally there would be some ancient daymio's castle whose white walls were surmounted by uptilted roofs that looked like a white birch stump with a cluster of fungus. The sharp ridges of the hills were like sleeping dragons protecting the bays and harbors dotted with square-sailed fishing boats. Each view was reminiscent of some Japanese print by Hiroshige and a never-ending delight.

After an overnight trip across the turbulent Shimonoseki Straits, the ship slipped quietly into Fuscan Bay—better known in 1950 as Pusan—past some rocky islands at the entrance of the harbor. We could see the city crowded down to the water's edge by a semicircle of hills so steep no houses could be built on the upper slopes.

We were met by Mr. Oda, the English-speaking secretary of Count Kodama, the Governor of Korea, who was to accompany us to Seoul. From Pusan to Seoul takes twelve hours; from Seoul to the Manchurian border, another twelve hours. At one station we sampled food that was very familiar. We bought a straw basket of lovely red apples from one of the women who offered a variety of fruits for sale. Mr. Oda read the label and told us they were Jonathans, and we had the satisfaction of telling him that the Jonathan apple had originated on a ridge in our own Woodstock over a hundred years before and that a stone monument marks the spot.

The day spent in Seoul was divided between interviews with Korean delegates to the Conference and with the colonial officials of the Japanese Empire, and it involved a certain amount of delicacy not to offend one side or the other. The antagonism between the Koreans and the Japanese was of long standing and had deepened instead of lessened with Japan's annexation of Korea in 1910 after a protectorate acquired by the wars with China and

241

Russia. We had invited Miss Kim, a teacher of Bible at the only women's college in Korea, Ehwa College, and some other IPR delegates to lunch, but when it became evident that the Governor's secretary, the ubiquitous Mr. Oda, would be present, a distinguished elderly gentleman in Korean dress politely declined the invitation and departed much agitated. Diplomatically the situation was saved by having Mr. Oda seated at the far end of the table, hidden behind a large table decoration, ensuring a certain amount of privacy for our discussion of Korean participation at the Kyoto Conference. The Koreans were tactfully urged to avoid the controversial subject of independence which would not only be embarrassing to the Japanese hosts but to the other delegations and which, in the end, would do little to advance their cause. By stating their case in terms of facts rather than of emotions, they could make a valid contribution to the Conference.

Much the same line of approach was equally tactfully suggested to the Japanese at the business end of a banquet given by the Governor that night after the ladies had left the gentlemen to cigars and coffee. If they were to present the economic aspects of the Japanese administration of the occupation, it would help to avoid possible emotional outbursts.

The banquet itself was a lavish affair, graced with the presence of Countess Kodama and several other ladies all wearing rich kimonos with beautiful contrasting obis. Perhaps because they were so removed from the metropolitan centers of Japan, and the Western influences there they seemed to us to be even more like dolls than the ladies we had met in Tokyo. They were powdered a dead white, and the polite little giggles with which they greeted any remark addressed to them made communication with them, especially as everything had to be translated, somewhat difficult and limited. When one lady ventured the wish that she could learn to drive a car like her American guests, she was overcome by her own audacity and subsided into silence only broken by a nervous titter. As we left, the Countess presented each foreign lady with a small wooden box containing a family of tiny clay dolls.

Not long after leaving Seoul, we crossed the 38th parallel, although at the time it had no special significance for us. Between

Sinuiju and Antung, on the Manchurian side of the Yalu River, we crossed the border into Manchuria and boarded a train of the South Manchurian Railroad for Mukden, which we reached at 6:30 the next morning. Just outside Antung the sky was lighted up by the glow of the great iron works of the South Manchurian Railway, developed by the Japanese.

All the cities where Japanese influence had been superimposed on an older culture had a restlessness and a half-assimilated rawness associated with the frontier. It was evident in Seoul, Mukden, Dairen, and Port Arthur, where, in every case, new buildings in various stages of construction rose from the rubble of recently leveled native quarters and wide, dusty boulevards radiated from the administration buildings leaving pie-shaped wedges of the old town.

From Dairen we boarded the coastal ship *Tencho Maru* for the twenty-four-hour sail to Tientsin, across the Gulf of Chihli. It was not a comfortable trip, for we ran into the tail end of a typhoon, and the high seas drove all but the best sailors to their bunks. Besides, the forward hold and all the decks were crowded with homeward-bound Chinese, the cargo hold contained raw sugar, and the smell gave point to the nickname given the ship by old China travelers: the "Stencho Maru."

Early in the morning we passed the Taku fort at the entrance of the Hai River and began to make our way up the muddy sluggish stream, until we reached Tientsin forty miles up-river. There we were met by Dr. Franklin Ho and Mrs. Ho, who accompanied us to Nankai University, an institution built and supported solely by Chinese funds. Under its distinguished president, Chang Po-ling, and with professors trained in America or England, it played an important role in the modernization of China. Professor and Mrs. Ho accompanied us to Peking.

Peking remains in my memory, unique as a symbol of imperial splendor, with palaces and temples crowned with glittering tiles within its double walls, and the squalor of its slums. We explored it from the Temple of Heaven to the bazaars, from the Dragon Screen to the theater, where several times we saw China's greatest actor Mei lan Fang, from the Lama temple, filled with chanting

243

priests, to the Summer Palace, and even by ricksha and sedan chair out to the Western hills.

Our special guide to the intricacies of Chinese culture, especially its drama, was P. C. Chang, younger brother of Chang Po-ling, whose love of the theater and exquisite sense of the beautiful was a revelation in itself. But we were most indebted to Mr. and Mrs. Grover Clark, long residents in Peking. He was editor and publisher of the *Peking Leader* and Mrs. Clark taught English to the young Empress, after the days of the notorius Dowager Empress. Years later both of them worked with me in New York at the Carnegie Endowment. But Peking was not China, and I eagerly accepted the invitation of Y. C. James Yen, the founder of the Mass Education Movement, to visit his headquarters in the little country seat of Ting Hsien, a hundred and fifty miles southwest of Peking, in the very heart of China.

Here a dedicated group of young scholars had been brought together by James Yen to work with the people and teach them not only to read and write but to raise the level of agriculture and health. This pioneering experiment, completely divorced from politics, grew out of the experience of James Yen as a welfare officer in the front in World War I. Stirred by discovering the intelligence of the coolies, he devised a simplified—thousand-character—alphabet which they were able to use. Returning to China, he enlisted a small group of colleagues to live and work with the peasants. They had had to overcome the universal distrust of farmers to any outsider, and then step by step introduce new ideas and new methods.

The agricultural expert, Dr. Feng, had shared the perils and hardships of the inhabitants during the fighting of rival war lords two years before, and having won their confidence was now showing them how to double the efficiency of their harrows and how to turn a furrow by putting a flange on the old-fashioned plow that only scratched the surface of the soil, how to increase the yield by seed selection and animal husbandry. On several occasions, proud farmers showed us ears of Indian corn they themselves had developed that were twice the size of unimproved corn. In each of the villages we passed through, we saw evidences of the campaign

244

against illiteracy in the school rooms where young and old, men and women, were studying the thousand characters. And wherever we went, through crowds that pressed too close for comfort, we could see the urgent need for the health campaign that was just beginning. Much work had to be done to educate the people in the need for public and personal hygiene, and much skepticism had to be overcome. When a model of the common fly was exhibited to show how it carried disease, the reaction generally was, that if foreign flies were that big, no wonder the outsiders were afraid of them.

That we were able to see so much of the countryside was due to the co-operation of the military Governor of the district, General Yen Shih San, who supplied cavalry mounts (no larger than Shetland ponies) and an escort of soldiers. Because there were no roads, the party was strung out single file between the narrow fields of peanuts, cotton, kaoliang, and sweet potatoes. It was a very hilarious outing, for we joked and sang the whole dozen or so miles to the Agricultural Center.

The return to Peking was by a train overflowing with troops. We were wedged in a compartment with soldiers, most of whom looked hardly older than twelve or thirteen years old. They were friendly and to pass the time played cat's cradle with Margaret Grace. They knew endless variations of the game.

There were a few busy days left in Peking, long discussions with members of the Chinese delegation to the Kyoto Conference and addresses at the National University and at Yenching University, opening its new buildings on the outskirts of the city. Then, to make the journey to north China complete, we paid a visit to the Great Wall, the only experience that outranked Peking itself, in its incredible witness to the might of ancient China.

Toward the end of our stay in Peking more delegates to the Kyoto Conference joined us on the same kind of preliminary survey of the situation, and we were all guests at a formal banquet in the old Foreign Office building, disused since the government had moved to Nanking. There were at least a dozen tables seating ten or twelve, but they were lost in the vast expanse of the hall. It was October and, as the room was unheated, the cold was bone-chilling, so that the ladies kept their wraps on over their evening dresses. The meal was the most sumptuous Chinese fare; endless dishes in the center of the table from which the gentlemen picked the choicest tidbits with silver chopsticks to place in their partners' rice bowls. All through the meal scores of rats scurried from table to table. Polite conversation never faltered, and, though everyone kept tucking his feet up off the floor, neither hosts nor guests made the slightest suggestion that anything was wrong.

Finally, on October 9, I took a train for Tientsin, where I addressed the Nankai University faculty and students, then continued on the way to Nanking through the mountainous province of Shantung, with its sacred mountain, Tai Shan, still visited by the devotees of Confucius, then to the alluvial plain of the Yellow River, from the dry loess to rice paddies cultivated by water buffaloes. Even if we had not already been aware of the disturbed state of China, the concentration of soldiers at Pukow, across the Yang Tse Kiang from Nanking, and in Nanking itself, would have made it obvious. In fact the railway we had just traveled was cut by fighting shortly after we went over it.

Nanking still showed the marks of the capture and sack of the city two years before, but the government of the Kuomintang was now firmly established in it. It was also being rapidly modernized. Like Mukden, many of the old parts of the city had been leveled to make way for new government offices. It all looked raw and unfinished. But a touch of imperial China still lingered in the splendor of the newly built tomb of Sun Yat-sen on the Purple Mountain to the west.

The problems confronting the new China were tremendous. It seemed to be almost a state of anarchy (in Japan I was told that it was already in the process of breaking up), but I found complete confidence in Kuomintang success when I called on the Foreign Minister, C. T. Wang. He had been a student of mine and we had two whole days together, discussing China's chief grievance with the Western Powers—extraterritoriality, the regime under which foreigners have lived in China since the empire was opened to the outside world. This had meant a two-fold application, political and juristic. Politically it was territorial penetration, a territorial

246

invasion, which once seemed to menace a partition of the country, but which was now being brought to an end by all the other nations except Japan. But the juristic frontier remained; the foreigners insisted on using their own courts and their own laws in dealings with the Chinese. The reason for this was that there was a profound difference between Western law administered in consular courts; and Chinese justice, which lacked the impersonal, formal character of Western law. The Chinese people did not ordinarily take their cases to court, partly because of a lack of confidence in the administration of the law and partly because they could settle their affairs better by themselves, in the temples in the case of country folk or in the guilds or chambers of commerce in the cities. In this respect, their system of government was even in monarchical China a sort of government "of the people, by the people, and for the people," as was pointed out by the translator of the Supreme Court Decisions.

That this system worked in China is proved by the fact that it was maintained for so many centuries; but it did not furnish the framework for the kind of modern law which is necessary for the conduct of modern business. Nevertheless, this is what China understood the West to demand and what it undertook to comply with by the preparation of a whole system of codes, the last of which, the Civil Code, was to be complete just in time to permit the denunciation of extraterritorial privilege at the end of 1929.

To expect about one-quarter of the human race to change its idea of obligations overnight and repose its guaranty of good conduct in new and inexperienced institutions in place of the tried disciplines of family and guild control was at the least unrealistic. The system of the West, even if adapted by the most eminent of jurists, could not in the nature of things blot out four thousand years of Chinese customs and substitute for living forces the abstract impersonality of foreign law. Moreover, the foreign residents in China had no share in this great past and little understanding of the way it still operated in Chinese minds. Extraterritoriality was in essence the recognition of a divergence of methods for securing what both Chinese and foreigners wanted—or at least needed— namely, fair dealing between citizens as well as governments.

As I talked on this problem with Dr. Wang I suggested a compromise solution, that China, as an extension of its legal reform, should set up a limited number of special courts in a half-dozen places where foreign business was mostly carried on, such as Canton, Shanghai, Hankow, Tientsin, and Mukden, in which Chinese litigants would have recourse to principles already familiar to them and so enable the Chinese code to be widened out "from precedent to precedent" to cover conflicting national usages which by their very nature contain so much of the elements of international misunderstanding. I reminded Dr. Wang that this was the way the Roman law had grown to meet a new world situation. But the hardest part of the problem still remained. It was necessary that China should have the right to appoint the judges or jurisconsults, but the choice of China should be limited to a panel satisfactory to the West. I suggested using the World Court at the Hague as a final authority; but we left that unfinished item with the suggestion that "the details of any definite proposal should be left in the hands of a commission of jurists on the one hand and the established organs of diplomacy on the other."

We sailed from Shanghai to Kobe, arriving at Kyoto just in time for the conference of the Institute of Pacific Relations. Delegations from the different countries were already arriving, two hundred in all, forty from the United States. It was something wholly new in the Orient, a public discussion of the foreign policy of Japan on the soil of Japan, in which foreigners participated. Although its members kept insisting that it was wholly unofficial, the Japanese Premier Hamaguchi sent greetings to the opening session as did President Hoover and the Premier of New Zealand. The chairman of the Japanese delegation was Dr. Nitobe, formerly Japan's representative on the League of Nations. The chairman of the British group, Lord Hailsham, formerly Chancellor of the Exchequer, was accompanied by Malcolm MacDonald, son of the Prime Minister. From China came a large delegation, headed by David Uiu, distinguished scholars like Hu Hsu-shi and Chang Po-lin, administrators who had worked with Sun Yat-sen, like Dr. Wu, governor of the Bank of China, and W. W. Yen.

Kyoto was a perfect setting for the conference, a city of the past,

248

removed from all that busy world centered at Tokyo. For over a thousand years the emperors of Japan had held court in its palaces, and the traces of their medieval splendor still survive in the quaint houses on the river front and in the dress and habits of its citizens. We saw pageants staged in the open streets, when for a few brief hours gaily dressed actors marched in procession or gave exhibitions of stately dance and ceremonial that had come down from beyond the days of Charlemagne. If the Golden Pavilion by the lake of the imperial garden looks drab and weather-worn, farther up against the hillside lies an enchantment of terraced lawns and the ever-changing color of flower and tree, a landscape which scheming statesmen planned to make so beautiful that the emperor would choose its beauty rather than the exercise of power. Then, at the base of the encircling hills were the temples, set in their groves of giant cryptomeria—the redwood of Japan—temples to which pilgrims come from all parts of Japan, pilgrims no less picturesque than the temples they frequent. There were those dressed all in white, who walk from shrine to shrine, temple to temple, the country over, with a little food in a knapsack on their backs and with great umbrella-like hats on which the priests record the names of each shrine visited. And there were others simply dressed in the picturesque kimono, going in groups to chant in unison before some altar gleaming in the flickering light of candles from its recess behind the great, timber pillars, where the Buddhist clergy chants its ritual.

This was a strange, but enchanting, setting for an international conference on the problems of the present and future, such as we held in the rooms of the rambling old Miyako Hotel. But there was no romance, only an atmosphere of the utmost frankness when the conference members faced one another and expressed their utterly divergent views.

To take one major problm. When I arrived in the East I found no one anywhere, either in Japan or China, who regarded the Japanese occupation of Manchuria in any terms other than of ultimate war with China. Concerning this, I remember a letter which I wrote to President Butler on the conclusion of the conference, in which I said that it seemed impossible that the Chinese and Japanese could ever get together on a question that so deeply involved the vital interests of both countries. For instance, the first evening that I met with the Chinese members of the Institute in Peking, the common talk was that the only hope for China was to plan ahead for the inevitable war. This feeling was just as strong on the Yangtze as in the North, and the fact that China was not yet ready to meet Japan on the battlefield added an emotional intensity to Chinese feeling concerning Manchuria, for there was a sense of impotence added to that of national humiliation. I have seldom, if ever, found myself in a more embittered atmosphere than that. The Japanese were fully aware of the Chinese feelings and were, therefore, very apprehensive concerning the holding of the Conference on Japanese soil. They were afraid of an outbreak from the Japanese Nationalists, not only in the press but by way of mob violence, and especially there were plans on foot for bands from patriotic organizations to come down to Kyoto and, attacking the Chinese, force the Conference to close its doors. Fortunately these plans were never entertained in serious quarters, but the rumors of them made the atmosphere tense. Some of the Chinese delegates on their parts, getting wind of these possibilities, were apprehensive from the moment they landed on Japanese soil for fear they would be personally attacked or perhaps imprisoned for the things they had done and said concerning the Japanese in Manchuria.

It is against this background that one must judge the work of the Conference, and the chief and outstanding fact which it left in my mind was admiration for the superb statesmanship of Japan. From first to last, the Japanese played the game with generous courage. Even most of their Chinese opponents went away with a tribute to Japanese generosity and fair-mindedness. It was proved by the Kyoto Conference that the Manchurian question and any other similar question between China and Japan could be settled by pacific means instead of by the resort to force.

I left Kyoto on the morning of Armistice Day and stopped off at the city of Nagoya to give an address that evening in a public meeting held under the auspices of the League of Nations Association in that city of over a million inhabitants. The hall, a fairly large one, was packed to suffocation—people standing up in the

250

back of the aisles and squatting on the floor in front of the orchestra seats. It was a very different audience from that which I addressed in Tokyo in September, for in Nagoya there were many working-men and shopkeepers in the audience, and it was clear that only a very small percentage understood any English, so I had to have the speech translated section by section and almost phrase by phrase. It was a most disconcerting method of speaking. Neverthe-less, the audience stood it very well and they had been listening to other speakers for an hour before I began.

After my arrival in Tokyo the first two days were largely taken up with official and social functions rounding off the work of the Institute. Some of the social functions I omitted in order to have the final conferences with the delegates, of whom a fairly large number were leaving by the weekend. There was, however, a beau-tiful garden party given by the Emperor who, himself, appeared at it. The Imperial Gardens in which it was held were very much unlike the typical Japanese gardens familiar to us, for, instead of small and compressed scenery with doll-like houses along a mina-ture stream, the park was more like Hyde Park or any great Eng-lish estate than anything I have ever seen in America—great stretches of lawn with old oaks scattered here and there and a long sloping stretch down to the lake and stream. There were chrysan-themum displays along the main gravel walk that wound down the hillside to the valley below for about a quarter of a mile, and I had a very good glimpse of the Emperor, himself, and his party as they came along to greet the guests and view the chrysanthemums.

Next day, the Minister of Finance, Dr. Inouye, who had been Chairman of the Institute of Pacific Relations prior to his entering the Cabinet, gave a luncheon party to the Institute and this was followed by a garden party given by Foreign Minister Shidehara in the magnificent grounds that belong to a branch of his family. I had not realized before that Shidehara belongs to the great nobility of Japan.

The last function of all was reserved for Viscount Shibusawa, who gave a farewell dinner to some of the American Delegation in the famous "Maple Club," the most exclusive and ancient club of Tokyo. The Viscount was not permitted by his physician to attend evening functions so Baron Sakatani presided in his place. The performance which accompanied the dinner was drawn from the classical drama and performed in a most convincing way by what we had thought were geisha waitresses but who turned out to be some of the best-known actresses of the Tokyo stage. I, however, had to leave the dinner in the midst of things to address a public meeting in the Municipal Auditorium.

Fortunately, I was the last of a whole list of speakers drawn from the various delegations of the Kyoto Conference. The audience—there were about four thousand people in the huge hall—had been listening to speeches from about six o'clock in the evening, and when I began to speak it was almost nine. The audience seemed to be capable of unlimited endurance; by the time my translator finished it was considerably after ten, and yet I had the most perfect attention. I had expected to talk about the Pact of Paris but just before my turn came I was informed that the principal newspaper which was sponsoring the occasion wanted me to talk instead about American foreign policy. It was a difficult adjustment but when it was all over I was glad the change had been made, for I always find it possible to deal with a controversial question, however tense it may be, if the exposition can be kept in terms of history.

In Tokyo we had a very interesting evening as the guests of the Prime Minister, Mr. Hamaguchi. The dinner was simply *en famille* with Mrs. Hamaguchi and their two daughters, the Prime Minister's secretary and the Secretary of the Cabinet, and Mr. Taguchi and another, whose name I forget, to serve as interpreters. The Prime Minister is known as the most taciturn man in Japan, which is, I suppose, the acme of taciturnity. It was said that he had never been known to laugh and hardly to smile in public. Nevertheless, at his own table we found him quietly amused and even capable of cracking jokes and then watching with amusement the effort to translate them into English. After dinner came the photograph which is inevitable on all such occasions in Japan, and then a woman artist, who is said to have entertained at the Imperial Court several times, produced some squares of silk and India ink and brushes and set about showing us how to sketch Fujiyama or Japanese pine trees with hurried brush strokes.

The last day before sailing was in some ways the most interesting, for it was the day of my lecture at the Imperial University of Tokyo. The faculty gave me a luncheon prior to the lecture, and after it I was shown the splendid new library building and other buildings which have replaced those destroyed by the earthquake. The library was the gift of Mr. Rockefeller. Some two million dollars or so had gone into magnificent equipment. Some of the other buildings are gifts of wealthy Japanese, and the university made a great impression upon the eye. It had some eight thousand students or more and those who came to my lecture did not need a translator or interpreter. I must have had three or four hundred present in the lecture hall, and I found this experience quite as interesting as that of the similar occasion in Peking when I lectured at the National University there.

The youth of Japan was sadly at sea at this time, drifting toward radicalism but uncertain of itself. The old loyalties were slipping away, and the questioning that was going on went frankly to the heart of matters. Russian literature was the most widely read, and so I chose as the theme of my lecture the thesis that the full development of capitalism called for and ultimately was bound to produce that co-operative society which would adjust itself in terms of national as well as international justice. As I spoke I had in mind the fact that when Albert Thomas addressed these students some six months earlier he was literally booed out of the hall by the radical student body because they regarded him as a mere tool of capitalism. However, I got off without any such untoward results and from all outward signs got a pretty fair measure of agreement from the audience.

I had tried to get a sailing on an earlier ship but, although I learned in Shanghai that there was room on the *Korea Maru* which had sailed the week before, the shipping office in Tokyo was of a different opinion, and our party found itself on the *Siberia Maru,* the only first-class passengers who were not members of the Japanese Delegation to the Disarmament Conference. The arrangement was not of my own making.

I had met only two of the more important members of the Japanese Delegation, Mr. Saito, the head of the Information Section of the Foreign Office and formerly Consul General in New York, and Mr. Yamakawa, technical adviser to Baron Wakatsuki, the former Prime Minister who was the head of the Delegation. Mr. Yamakawa, President of the League of Nations Association in Japan and the expert on international law for the delegation, had presided along with Prince Tokagawa over the meeting which I addressed in Tokyo in September under the auspices of the Tokyo *Nichi Nichi*. (The *Nichi Nichi* sent me a very cordial wireless wishing me "bon voyage for a future return to Japan.")

Naturally I had long talks with Mr. Wakatsuki and Admirals Takarabe and Abo. One day Mr. Wakatsuki handed me a Japanese poem written in old Chinese. It would be like an Oxford don writing Greek verse. It was beautifully written on a gilt cardboard and the translation made for me read:

> The angry waves are lashing the heavens where the
>   slanting twilight trails its lingering shafts;
> And where the monsters of the deep gambol, the northern
>   blasts are cold
> But the men of America and Britain are lovers of goodness and
>   right
> And gods forbid that I be compared unto the Premier of Chow
>   bound for the kingdom of Shin!

(Explanatory note: the State of Shin had swindled the State of Chow into giving up the greatest treasure of the country—the jewel—under the false promise that it would surrender its fifteen castles; but on obtaining the coveted treasure, refused to carry out its promise; whereupon the State of Chow sent its famous premier, Rin, to the state of Shin to take back the jewel, which mission the Premier Rin successfully fulfilled.)

Being on the Pacific Ocean en route for the London Conference and happening to write the above verses, I have pleasure in submitting them to Professor Shotwell for his amusement.

RENIRO WAKATSUKI

The subtle reference to good faith in naval agreements was deftly implied. I had to reply without seeming to take up the challenge and sent him a mere congratulatory quatrain.

> Two ships there are upon the ocean: One
> Battles the waves beneath a stormy sun;
> The other, neither winds nor waves delay,
> Dai Nippon guides it safely on its way.

254

In my talks I carefully avoided the exact questions under negotiation between the United States and Japan. I did, however, suggest to Dr. Yamakawa, the technical expert at the Foreign Office, that the London Conference had a chance to rise above arithmetical ratios to a political settlement of the Pacific like that of the European Locarno. This appealed to him very much, and he prepared a careful analysis of the proposal, but I doubt if it ever got farther. Certainly it did not come up at the London Conference.

The year 1929 had another meaning for America than the record here recorded. While in Japan I got word that the bank in which my savings were deposited had gone bankrupt, along with so many others.

CHAPTER 15

Eastern Europe

In 1930, under the auspices of the Carnegie Endowment for International Peace, I undertook a study of questions of the Near East, planned along the same lines as the Institute of Pacific Relations. But when I reached Geneva in September, I found no serious support for the idea except in the Hungarian delegation. It happened that the Prime Minister of Hungary, Count Stephan Bethlen, was at that time a guest of the Permanent Hungarian Representative at the League, John Pelényi, and along with Professor Francis Deak I was invited to discuss the whole proposal in detail. Interesting and encouraging as this was, it was not until the following March that I received a letter from Count Bethlen inviting me to come to Hungary with a group of my colleagues from Columbia to study the situation which was developing in that unhappy country.

President Butler quickly arranged to have the Carnegie Endowment for International Peace support an investigation of the problems of Hungary and Southeast Europe during the summer of 1931, and at the end of June, Mrs. Shotwell and I sailed from New York on the *Carmania* to study once more the intricate problems of the organization of peace.

About halfway across the Atlantic there came a wireless from London inviting me to attend the British-American Historical Conference and move the vote of thanks for the Prime Minister's speech at the opening session. This is always a formal part of a British program, and I wirelessed acceptance. The conference was held in the Institute for Historical Research of the University of London, which, with Professor Pollard, I had helped to found in 1904, and I was glad to find myself among old friends.

The Prime Minister, Ramsay MacDonald, gave a charming informal speech, touching on the need for the historian to judge the politician with more sympathy. With a quiet humor he discussed the joys of the historian's life, his leisure for browsing in whatever interested him most and referred to his days as a reporter and hack writer for the *Dictionary of National Biography*. He also spoke of the importance of the revision of colonial history by an American historian to correct the unfair picture given from the British Whig point of view. This was a different personality from that which had so impressed the Assembly of the League in the great debate on the Protocol, when the clipped Scottish accent gave added force to his speech. Here he spoke not of history in the making, but of a history already made a century ago. I replied in the same tone, discussing the value of the Prime Minister's references to the "methodology" of history, and his philosophy reminiscent of Ranke and Foustel de Coulanges. I spoke of Professor Pollard's work in founding the Institute of Historical Research, and of George Louis Beer's, in connection with the true interpretation of British Colonial history. The Prime Minister stayed just long enough to hear what I had to say but then left before Sir Richard Lodge had a chance to get up and second it with a vote of thanks.

My reason for coming to London was not wholly academic, however. It gave me a chance to get my bearings for the journey through Central and Eastern Europe and my most important talks were with Arthur Henderson, Foreign Secretary, and Sir Josiah Stamp of the Bank of England; the one fearful of political unrest on the Continent and the other fearful that the Bank of England would, any day, go off gold.

To my surprise I found that Mr. Henderson had remembered every detail of my previous conversation with him in Geneva on the problems of disarmament, and stated his memory of that conversation with which I agreed. Then he said, "Now let's start from there," and he went over with me the origins and structure of the

International Labor Organization and then shifted to the problem which was to be his chief concern, the negotiation with Germany on a visit to Berlin, which he was planning for the following week.

He was much disturbed at the way in which President Hoover's offer of a moratorium on war debts had misfired. Whatever chance there might have been for France to have reacted generously under the impact of President Hoover's effort to liquidate war debts, the Germans spoiled it by subsidies for new battleships instead of attempting to meet the financial situation at home or abroad. The mere mention of new German submarines gave the British a real cause for concern over the apparent revival of German militarism. It was also known that the German youths were being given military training much in the way Prussia prepared for the war of liberation after its conquest by Napoleon. Mr. Henderson, as President of the Geneva Disarmament Conference, was more concerned over the revival of militarism in Germany than over the firm stand which the French Government had taken to the possibility of a German menace by its alliance with Czechoslovakia, Yugoslavia and Romania, members of the Little Entente.

It was under these conditions that Hitler's brand of militant nationalism was gaining ground in the German middle class, while Mussolini was trying to outrival Hitler's emotional appeals against the *status quo*.

It was clearly time for the British to look the dangerous situation in the face. But, instead, the policy of disarmament had the support of the whole nation. On July 11, I attended the great national rally for disarmament at Albert Hall, presided over by Field Marshal Robertson, Prime Minister MacDonald, Stanley Baldwin, leader of the Conservatives, and Lloyd George. They were followed by Lord Cecil, speaking for the League of Nations. There were gigantic demonstrations in Hyde Park and in sixty cities. Baldwin referred to the fact that there was no guarantee that the United States might not be on the side of the aggressors if, as a neutral, it was supplying munitions and other supplies to both sides. He said that war could be stopped by the mere application of the economic sanction of the Covenant, but that the United States would not give any guarantee in that direction. MacDonald was more impassioned, but said less. Lloyd George was distinctly disappointing. Everyone gave Britain full credit for being the one nation that was living up to its obligations under the Versailles Treaty. All other nations were increasing armaments; Great Britain was the only one to reduce them.

Incidentally, I was told later at the Foreign Office that the program of the disarmament rally had been carefully planned beforehand. MacDonald spoke directly to Great Britain, Lloyd George to France, and Baldwin to the United States. This was the natural outcome of the fact that the three heads of parties sit together on the Committee of Imperial Defense, and so they planned anything that had to do with armaments, not as opposition and government, but as equally responsible heads of various branches of government. I should add that while the British were holding to their disarmament program, they were not confident of the success of the Disarmament Conference called by the League to meet six months later.

There were elections to take place in France and in the United States, and the British did not expect that the United States would take any step prior to the elections which could be used as slogans in the election campaign. But the chief problem was that France, as the strongest financial power on the Continent, was not yet in any mood to make concessions, if Germany continued to show its unwillingness to stop building its war cruisers under pressure from the Hitlerites. I surmised that it was this situation that Henderson proposed to deal with in Germany. There was also the newly formed Tariff Union with Austria which the French regarded as a first step toward political union—the Anschluss, distinctly forbidden in the Treaty of St. Germain.

There was every reason for the French to be concerned over these signs of the growth of militant nationalism in Germany, which the British were discounting as the inevitable outcome of defeat in war. The time was ripe for Hitler to turn to the German middle class and make national socialism the dominant party in the Reich. I had not come to Europe to study the politics of the great Powers, however, but to pioneer in political research in the countries which had little or no experience in the social sciences.

Mrs. Shotwell and I left London on July 15 for Paris. Coming from Calais to Amiens, and again from Amiens to Compiègne, my mind kept going back to the battles that were now history, but which, only so short a time ago, were being fought just over the brow of the eastern hills. Year after year I went back to see the slow recovery of northern France. By 1931 it was all restored, and more than restored; it is hardly too much to say that these towns were better off than if there had been no war. They had been rebuilt in modern style, with up-to-date streets and houses and public works which would have been almost impossible otherwise. It was a strange paradox that the ravaged areas of the north were now the most modern part of France. This was part of the reason for the financial crisis in Europe. The post-war restoration shared in the extravagance of the post-war years, which in turn added to the financial ruin.

With the immediate destruction of the war so completely obliterated, it was hard to realize that the impact of the economic displacement of 1914-1918 was only now fully showing itself. The day's papers told of the meeting in Paris of the Foreign Ministers of England, France, and the United States to discuss the plans for preventing the complete collapse of Germany, and in a day or two the Chancellor and the Foreign Minister of Germany were to go to Paris to find what measure of hope there was for a nation whose credit had been almost destroyed both by the war and by the post-war policies, its own and those of the rest of the world. No such meeting had been held since the Peace Conference itself, and so far as the economic life of Europe was concerned, this second catastrophe seemed likely to be even more far-reaching in its effects that the first. The English papers were already talking of armies of unemployed greater than the armies that fought the war, while, beyond this economic chaos, Russia pursued relentlessly its program of a Five-Year Plan.

Somehow Paris failed to exert its old-time charm. Perhaps it was partly the cloudy sky and the dull drabness of the city, but I imagine the real explanation was that all of us were affected by the psychological crisis of Europe, and the relative values were not normal. There was something that resembled the wartime pressure of one's thinking, although perhaps not enough for one to be fully conscious of the disturbance.

At Geneva I at once telephoned Gilbert Murray. He was off for the day, and so I went up to the Secretariat and found it practically deserted. Murray later told me that one of his friends had characterized the situation in Geneva at this crisis of Europe when the Foreign Ministers were meeting in Paris to settle the fate of Germany as follows: "The British Secretary-General is away on his holidays; the French Secretary-General is away on his holidays; the Italian Secretary-General is away on his holidays; the German Secretary-General is at the League listening to a lecture on poetry by Masefield."

Nothing much could be done in Geneva to prepare for the visit to Hungary, but after the invitation from Count Bethlen I talked over the problems with Mr. Pelényi, whose judgment I had learned to respect the year before, and who proved throughout reliable in every way and most helpful.

Francis Deak offered to accompany us on our journey. Professor Deak still retained his contacts with his native Hungary, although he had already been, for some years, Professor of Law at Columbia University. It was very fortunate for us that his auto was waiting in Geneva for his own return to Budapest. Our journey through Switzerland and Austria opened up for us the magnificent scenery of the Tyrolean Alps, which otherwise I might never have seen.

I took along with me as secretary, Miss Carol Riegelman (now Mrs. Isadore Lubin), and profited from her quick appreciation of the problems confronting us. The first of these began at Vienna. I went to a session of the Socialist Conference, which began with an impressive tribute to the memory of Jean Jaurès, as it was the anniversary of the day that he had been murdered in 1914.

The first speaker of the morning was Léon Blum, leader of the French Socialist Party.* His power over his followers must have been largely intellectual, as he had none of the qualities of the orator which had so impressed me in Jaurès, when I had listened to him years before holding a vast audience of working men spellbound for over an hour, while he argued the case of socialism against the French bourgeoise. Léon Blum spoke at great length about the need for the wholehearted support of German workers by

* In 1936, Léon Blum became the first Socialist Prime Minister of France and also the first Jew to hold that office.

the workers of other countries, but did not seem to have any very definite proposal to make. He was followed by Rudolph Breitschnied, the leader of the German Socialists. Here was the Internationale in full operation, but impotent to change either the economics or politics of Central Europe.

During the translations of the speeches, I had a long talk with Philip Noel-Baker, whom I had known intimately in Geneva when he was working closely with Lord Cecil. He had become a member of Parliament, and although none of us knew it at the time, he was on his way to cabinet office. He said that he would gladly open up all his documents for the publication of the history of the Peace Conference, and later sent them to me.

We spent only one morning at the Socialist Conference and then we were once more in Francis Deak's car on the road to Budapest.

An early telephone call from the *New York Times* correspondent in Vienna asked verification of a statement received from New York that a committee of five Columbia professors were arriving that day to take over the financial control of Hungary, "with wide powers." Four of my colleagues at Columbia had joined with me in my survey of the political and economic situation of Eastern Europe. They were Professor Joseph Chamberlain, professor of international law and an authority on the history of European waterways; Professor Robert Haig, a specialist in public finance; Professor Lindsay Rogers, professor of public law; Professor Francis Deak from the law faculty, and me.

Warned by the journalists' exaggeration, we made the point quite clear that while we were beginning our survey in Hungary, we were also planning to go to Poland and other Eastern European countries to try to clarify the fundamentals of the new international situation created by the break-up of the Hapsburg Monarchy. But, although we had no such official mission as the *Times* correspondent stated, the fact that I had been invited by Count Bethlen to make the study, gave our group a semi-official standing. Although Admiral Horthy was titular head of the State, acting as Regent for exiled Hapsburgs, it was Bethlen who, in 1921, had restored order after both the communist uprising and the reprisals of the "White" reactionaries. For the next ten years he was the

262

virtual dictator of Hungary, reducing parliament by a restricted franchise and creating an upper house, dominated by the great nobles. They had been years of hardship for the Magyars, however, and Bethlen appealed to the League of Nations for financial relief, submitting to the oversight of a League Commissioner, Jeremiah Smith, Jr., of Boston, whose financial success and attractive personality made him popular in Hungary. Undoubtedly, Count Bethlen had this experience in mind when he invited our group to study the situation in 1931.

My first talk was with Count Teleki, who had been Foreign Minister during the Paris Peace Conference, then Prime Minister. He described the Hungarian peace negotiations at Versailles for which he with the aid of a group of experts, had very carefully prepared the Hungarian case, in many volumes and with maps showing the divisions of the population throughout Hungary and the outlying districts. He was quite certain that no one would have time to look at this material, but for purposes of future record it was made as full as possible and prepared with scientific accuracy. Then before the negotiations began he went to Switzerland to try to get in touch with members of the Allied powers but was unable to reach anyone of importance. Although he had a large group of "liaison people," none except one woman was ever able to get through to any of the Allied people. When they came to Neuilly, where they were housed, they had absolutely no idea of the state of negotiations or of the attitude of any of the different commissions, and they were unable to find it out. They were carefully guarded in Neuilly, although Count Teleki was occasionally allowed to go in to Paris alone to see some French geographers. The draft of the peace terms was handed to the delegations, and they were asked to take it home to study and return with a statement in twenty-four hours. The delegation then divided it up, each member taking a section or so and working out his comments.

On Count Teleki's advice we decided to postpone work in Budapest until we could see the conditions of Hungary at firsthand by an auto trip to its new frontiers. We set off in four cars across the Central Plain of Hungary—hot, dry, and dusty, except where irrigated. This was the very reverse of the impression which I had

263

had of Hungary as a rich farm country. Even the fruit was poor and second rate. Count Teleki was most anxious that we should see the way the frontier line had cut across farms and villages so that sometimes a house was in Hungary and the largest part of the farm land was in Yugoslavia. There were guards posted along the frontier to prevent any crossing except at designated points. The same was true of the frontier with Romania and also that with Czechoslovakia. No wonder Count Teleki was listing the grievances of Hungary in the hope of redress through international action, a hope which, in the nature of the case, could never be realized.

Those few days of motoring were filled with incidents unlike any other in my journeys through Europe. I recall, especially when we stopped at the town of Lillafüred. The music was supplied by a gypsy band which greeted us with Liszt's "Hungarian Rhapsody," played with all of the fire and romance of gypsy music. Then, from Count Teleki's whistling of a few notes of some old Hungarian ballad they played with either light-hearted abandon or a tragic quality that needed no interpreting. From Lillafüred, we traveled to the northern tip of the Great Plain of Hungary, motoring over the pasture lands of great estates in a country which reminded me of the ranges along Eastern Montana. The Carpathian Mountains in the northern distance were not snow-capped, but the meadows were for all the world like those of the Western ranges. Then just over the hills a few miles north of our road, was the border of Czechoslovakia and we were headed for the market town in the pass that leads from Hungary northeastward into the Ruthenian end of Czechoslovakia, a country where all races meet.

Our Hungarian guides showed us the Czechoslovakian boundary which ran along the little stream just at the east of the town. According to them, this stream had been described by the Czechs as a navigable river, and they took great delight in showing us a boy wading across a little brook less than two feet deep. The only navigation in evidence was a peasant's buggy having its wheels swollen to the tires in the water. As a matter of fact, the boundary did not seem to me so utterly absurd, for just across the creek, a few rods away, ran the railroad line that connects Czechoslovakia with Romania, and what the frontier commissioners apparently tried to do was to give Hungary all the land up to that railroad and so chose that little stream as the easiest natural marker for the boundary.

It was while we were motoring along this pleasant countryside that a chance remark of Count Teleki's suddenly revealed him to me in a new light. It showed me that in spite of all our relationships, I had been dealing with only one side of a man who, like the country itself, has a mind that is a frontier between the East and the West. Years ago Professor Wieser in Vienna told me that the Hungarian magnates had a dual personality; the one Westernized in ideals and outlook, highly cultured and strictly under control; the other Oriental in its passionate swiftness in act and feeling.

This came to my mind when, in a very casual way, Mrs. Shotwell turned the conversation to a point which she had raised at luncheon in discussion with Count Teleki, and to which he had made no reply on that occasion. She asked why it was that if so many people within the Hapsburg Monarchy expected that it would break up on the death of Franz Joseph, the statesmen had not planned to meet the coming event, but had been simply trying to hold together the old Dual Monarchy in the old-fashioned way. Would it not have been a prudent thing to have anticipated the national movements by readjusting the Empire itself so as to keep these autonomous movements within it instead of having Central and Southeastern Europe break into pieces?

Count Teleki's reply was that if any of his friends or colleagues among the leaders of the Hungarian nation had attempted anything like that, or begun to plan for it, he himself would have shot him without waiting for others. It was all said very quietly and simply and pleasantly. It threw a light, however, on more things than this single incident. There was more in Hungary to discover than lay before our eyes as we motored along the valley of the Tisza, and it gave a deeper meaning to the signs which we saw posted along the way to remind Hungarians of their ancient kingdom. The words *NEM, NEM, SOHA,* (NO, NO, NEVER) was the expression not merely of a resolve to undo the Treaty of Trianon, but of the age-long history of a frontier people on the border of the Turk and the Slav.

265

In the days that followed, there were other journeys to other parts of Hungary, so that before the week was over we had visited practically the whole country. But, there were also meetings with the members of the Cabinet in Budapest and a dinner given us by the Prime Minister and Countess Bethlen. This was extremely formal; with two house guards at the door and red and gold liveried footmen on the stairs. However, Countess Bethlen received her guests without announcement from the liveried majordomos. She was most attractive and charming in her informality in contrast with the setting of the reception. During the dinner Count Bethlen complained to Mrs. Shotwell about the long hours that he was forced to work as Prime Minister, and she suggested that Prime Ministers should be better unionized so that they could strike for a shorter day. She suggested an eight-hour day, but Count Bethlen said that he would be quite satisfied with a ten-hour day.

After dinner we withdrew into the reception room for coffee, as it was raining too hard to go on the terrace, from which there was a magnificent view out across the city, and the surrounding countryside. The room was hung with beautiful Gobelins tapestries, and furnished in severe Empire style. The house is part of the royal palace and used to belong to Maria Theresa. There was time for a further half hour talk with Count Bethlen in his study but not of any serious importance.

The only item of historical interest was his answer in reply to a question from me that Count Tisza, the Prime Minister of Hungary in July, 1914, had never explained to his associates why, after having opposed the Austrian demand for war on Serbia, he changed his vote to agree with Berchtold, although he knew it would bring a general European war. Count Bethlen said that Tisza was such a silent man that he did not share these matters with any of his friends. It made no difference to him if all Hungary mistakenly thought, as did the rest of the world, that he had been one of the chief instigators of the policy of aggression which launched the Hapsburg Monarchy into the war. It was evident that Tisza's strength of character had left a lasting impression in Hungary, and Count Bethlen told me that they still kept vacant the seat which he had occupied in the Hungarian Parliament. This conversation, it

266

should be recalled, was taking place in Tisza's own office, under the magnificent oil painting which looks down upon the desk of the Prime Minister of Hungary.

It was clear that history was still leaving its marks on the minds of the Hungarian statesmen, but the event which brought this most clearly before us was the ceremony of St. Stephan's Day, dedicated to the saintly King under whom the Magyars had been converted to Christianity over nine hundred years ago. It was our one glimpse of medieval splendor in old Buda. For hours throughout the morning groups of peasants in costume, walked behind their local priests and banners, through the square to the cathedral, while the palace guards mounted on marvelous horsese kept order, holding back the thousands of people crowding in the square.

Promptly at nine the band came out of the Regent's palace playing a magnificent old hymn, and followed by a group of nuns and priests who marched in perfect order in front of the officiating priests, bishops, and the cardinal. Then came the Regent in all his splendor, and Count Bethlen and the other magnates and dignitaries crowded up behind. Last of all came the relic, the arm of St. Stephan, escorted by the brilliantly robed palace guards marching from the palace to the Cathedral. The spectacle was overwhelming in its brilliance. It was also a reminder of the feudal past of a nation, which had gone forever.

Before leaving Hungary for Poland I went over to the Prime Minister's house for a two hour interview. It was a full and very frank discussion of all the possibilities which Count Bethlen saw in our visit and also of outstanding problems both economic and political in Hungary's foreign relations. I told him of the evidence which our preliminary studies had revealed of the fact that Hungary economically was not a going concern. Practically every enterprise of any importance and every branch of its economic life was dependent upon an open or disguised subsidy from the government. Until then foreign loans had averted the catastrophe which was inevitable unless a fundamental change was made, and that fundamental change depended upon Hungary's relations with its neighbors. The solution set forth in the Porto Rosa Conference—a radical lessening of trade barriers—had been reinforced by the Dan-

267

ubian Inquiry, which the Carnegie Endowment had been financing; but national antagonisms were too great for freedom of trade among the Succession States. This was the heart of the problem for Hungary as it had been for Austria.

The Prime Minister agreed with me as to the conclusions and expressed appreciation of our caution. He was rather of the opinion, however, that as soon as the present crisis was over, a frank statement of the exact situation would be necessary as a basis for future policies. Then he laid a map on the table and pointed out that if Hungary would recover the resources of that section of Slovakia which lies between Poland and Ruthenia, it would largely change the whole economic balance of Hungary. The ore for the iron works lies just up in the hills and over the frontier, and the timber which was so needed in the treeless Hungarian plains ought to be floated down the tributaries of the Tisza River, and the headwaters of that river ought to be controlled so as to permit irrigation in the dry plain south and southeast of Budapest.

I suggested that perhaps he was a bit optimistic as to the possibilities of recovery of both the mines that lie west of Misckolz and the forest region which lies to the East. But he seemed to think that there might be a return some day. I then raised the question as to what kind of government he was thinking of for any area which might be brought back under a treaty revision and stated that in my opinion there would be little chance of these regions ever being allowed to return into a unitary system of control from Budapest. The temptation of the Hungarian nationalists returned to these restored areas to avenge themselves on those who had remained under Czech or other foreign rule would be too great to be kept in check by a nationalist parliament in Budapest, largely in sympathy with the emigrant. The Prime Minister agreed absolutely with this and said that he would not propose a complete reintegration of any such territories into the Hungarian state, but would propose autonomy with the widest possible degree of local self-government.

This brought up the whole question of minority areas, and he emphatically endorsed the idea of Count Teleki that in every case there was a local nationality with a quite different outlook from

268

that which the minority leaders had given expression. He maintained that most people in these areas were first of all Transylvanian, or Moravian, or people of the Banat, before they were Hungarian, Romanian, Czech, or Slovak. For a thousand years they had been living together without the political consciousness which the nineteenth century and the post-war period had been educating into them. The proper settlement of these questions was a recognition of the fact that the nineteenth century had gone too far in its nationalism and that the extravagances of the post-war period represented the last phase of this system rather than the pattern of things to come. I had a suspicion at this point that perhaps I was inducing a little too much agreement with the liberal point of view, but he gave unhesitating agreement to these ideas.

Then I took up the question of the methods by which these changes could be brought about. I outlined what seemed to me to be the complete case against Hungary's use of force. There were just three alternatives in that line: one was to make use of a general European conflagration, another was to prepare to defend its own interests by its own arms, and the third was to profit by local disturbances when some one of Hungary's neighbors would be temporarily unable to defend itself. This last case had been provided against by the neighbors in their reinsurance policies not only through the Little Entente but by their relations with France.

It was, of course, possible that diplomacy might change this alignment, but more likely that the threat of force would keep the diplomacy on a hostile line than would be the case if the idea of military action were frankly ruled out. As for the use of Hungary's own unaided armed force, the second of the contingencies, that was utterly impossible, as the country has no raw materials for munitions and all the frontiers lie open to Hungary's neighbors. Every strategic point is in favor of the enemy. As to the other alternative of a general European war, there would be less chance still of Hungary's making anything out of it, as the military operations would be so largely conditioned by the economic capacity of the country for endurance. The Prime Minister agreed heartily with the whole line of reasoning and said, with evident conviction, that military action was ruled out. On the other hand, however, the

269

instruments of pacific settlement had hitherto worked poorly, and while he heartily believed in the general principles of the League of Nations and the World Court, he intimated that Hungary had not had the most encouraging experiences with them. He seemed to be looking more to bilateral diplomacy, getting a little here and a little there, making the most of it. He seemed to be cherishing hopes of a more reasonable mind on the part of the Romanians and Yugoslavs, but said that the hardest to deal with were those who had the most important things to offer, the Czechoslovaks. (The negotiations with Romania terminated favorably a day or two later and he undoubtedly had that in mind. The tariff war with Czechoslovakia was still on, but a few days later they started negotiations again, with the Czechs coming down to Lillafüred.)

We then turned to less contentious problems, like those in the history of culture which we were shaping up with Count Teleki, and I made clear the whole drift of our research. When I came out to the outer office where Francis Deak and the Prime Minister's secretary were waiting for me, the secretary said that Count Bethlen had given me a longer uninterrupted interview than anyone else in the last six months. However, the last words were an invitation from Count Bethlen to come back next day at the same time for another two hours with my colleagues.

Two days later I gave my formal dinner for Count Bethlen. After the dinner Bethlen drew me into a corner, and I was obliged to neglect my other guests for the whole of the evening, for it was a quarter to twelve when he looked at his watch as the Countess started to come over to him to break up the party. It was too intimate a conversation to record in my diary, for we got down to the closest, most friendly basis of discussion. He gave no indication that he had any idea at that time that he would resign a day later, for he talked about his plans for the future and the possibility of our keeping in touch. He had in mind finding some occasion when he could make a notable statement of policy which would place Hungary definitely in the new era of international relations, a sort of proclamation of liberal statesmanship such as Wilson used to make, and I was to be in close touch with him on this project.

We then discussed the ultimate possibilities of using research

270

for practical purposes without denaturing the research itself. My only regret was that I had no chance to talk things over with Count Karolyi, who was to succeed Bethlen two days later. However, my colleagues had had a good chance to profit by Karolyi's equally cordial attitude to our little Columbia delegation.

The survey of Hungary was over. Professor and Mrs. Haig left for New York, while Professor Chamberlain left for Berlin, where we planned, after a hurried visit to Poland, to hold a first meeting of the international research institute of Europe, which was the final object of my journey.

The visit to Poland in which we were joined by Professor and Mrs. Rogers was little more than an appendix to the survey of Hungary, but it opened up questions more menacing to peace than those we had just been studying. For Magyar nationalism, deep-seated as it was, was fully matched by the passionate nationalism of the Poles, but their success at the Peace Conference in isolating East Prussia, the homeland of the Hohenzollern and the Junkers, along with winning Upper Silesia, made Germany less a neighbor than a dangerous enemy. It was more than humiliating to have to travel to East Prussia through a Polish Corridor, a railroad with trains locked to prevent passengers landing on the intervening Polish territory. The old Hansa city of Danzig was left under a League of Nations Commissioner, although its population was almost 100 per cent German. But Poland had been offered its own access to the Baltic, and to realize this dream its engineers had dug out of the sandy shore a whole new basin for a new sea port, Gdynia—an exploit designed to show that Polish engineers could outdo even the Germans in creative achievement.

The problems of Poland have now so completely changed as to make those we studied seem almost unreal, and we need not linger over them. But political gossip travels fast in Eastern Europe. The Foreign Office in Warsaw was fully aware of our plan of study and had an official meet us on our arrival at Cracow. After an all-day railroad journey, we were tired and wanted above all to have a quiet restful evening, but a banquet was waiting for us, at which we met professors from the university and leading businessmen, as well as officials. The conversation was all in German and all about

271

Polish claims in Upper Silesia and Danzig; but the worst thing about the dinner was the utter lack of water. There was a moment of deep silence, however, when Professor Rogers poured vodka into his glass, thinking it was water and everyone awaited the result. Fortunately, he saw what was wrong in time. At least that left one bright spot in our memory of our first evening in Poland.

We took the midnight train for Warsaw, where we arrived in the early morning. After finding our quarters in the hotel, which had been arranged for us by the Foreign Office, I went to the university with Professor Handelsmann, who had been editing the first volume of the Polish series of the *Economic and Social History of the World War*. I found that he was also chairman of the Polish Society for the Scientific Study of International Affairs, as well as Dean of the University. He readily fell in with my suggestion that the luncheon which he had been planning for us out at his home in the country should be turned into a discussion group with reference to the possibility of developing a Polish committee of the proposed Institute of Europe.

Riding out through the country for something like ten miles, we followed the great trunk road from Warsaw to Brest-Litovsk, a countryside made famous to this generation of Poles for the battle which they had won there over the Bolshevists in 1920, the Polish "Battle of the Marne." It was a decisive victory, but General Nollet, the French military advisor who witnessed the battle, had told me in Paris that is was really little more than a skirmish, for the Bolshevists broke and ran on the first attack.

After lunch Professor Handelsmann arrived with the former Prime Minister and Minister of Finance, M. Grabski, and Professor Rogers and I went into a little conclave at which I expounded once more the whole theory of studying foreign affairs by autonomous correspondents in different countries. It was a long and arduous task, and it was about five when the session was over. General Stachiewicz, a military historian, was also present, a somewhat skeptical listener who interjected a few doubtful remarks from time to time. Grabski, however, was splendid and impressed me greatly. The correspondent from the *Times* later told me that everyone had great respect for Grabski's firmness in grappling with the most difficult problems. He did not impress me as a financial dictator. He was very quiet in manner with a soft, rather high-pitched voice. He showed a great understanding for our problem and was ready to cooperate.

The next day there was an official luncheon given by the Foreign Minister, Zaleski. There were about twenty people and although the government was giving its formal assent to the work of the Institute, I had a feeling that everyone, including the host and hostess, was really indifferent. After lunch we drove through the Jewish quarter and were surprised to find conditions less cramped than in Cracow. It seemed comparatively prosperous, and many in the streets had left aside the orthodox dress and manner. The type was quite different from the Galician Jew of Warsaw, and far less backward socially and physically. After a large dinner given in our honor by the American Ambassador, Mr. Willys (of Willys-Knight cars), we left on the midnight train.

In Berlin we had our first international conference. Count Teleki had come up from Budapest, Professor Handelsmann from Warsaw, and Dr. Lorwin, economist of the Ministry of Labor in Washington, joined with Professors Chamberlain, Rogers, and me. We had no German colleagues; we were dealing only with non-German problems. The discussion of the former work and the future program took a whole day. The work was challenging, but it was a challenge which we were never to meet as European conditions worsened in the coming year. The next day, however, I had a long interview with Von Bülow, the permanent head of the Foreign Office, who talked very freely with me about Germany's relative indifference to the League of Nations and its concern over its own immediate problems with Poland and France. No mention was made of the unrest in Germany itself, which was soon to bring the Nazis to power.

When we arrived at the quiet little station of St. Martin, we found no one on the platform to meet us except a railway porter with a wheelbarrow in which he took our goods to the village hotel. From there he telephoned to the President's secretary at Bystricka, who was much distrubed to learn that the chauffeur had missed us at the station farther down the line where they had expected us and that another car

273

would arrive in half an hour. So we ordered breakfast in the hotel dining room, but we had hardly reached the second cup of coffee when Jan Masaryk came hurrying into the room, in a most apologetic mood. He had driven over himself to correct matters and to tell us why plans had gone astray. Although no person had been informed of it, not even the heads of the government itself, his father had been thrown from a horse the day before and had been very badly shaken up. As the President was nearly eighty-two, they were terribly anxious for fear there had been some internal injury, and his private physician had come out on the train with us from Prague that night.

We motored up through the little village street across two or three miles of sloping farmlands to the hamlet at the edge of the valley and at the base of the mountains which the Masaryks spent their childhood in and where his daughter, Dr. Alice Masaryk, had just finished rebuilding the old home in a somewhat elaborate manner for a village house but a very unpretentious, simple dwelling house for the head of the state. It was a two-story building with apparently not more than about a dozen rooms, all told. It was freshly plastered stucco with no ornamentation and the plainest kind of doors and windows. The fence around it was no higher than an ordinary garden wall, and there were no guards in sight. There were one or two plainclothes men in the little hamlet, whom Jan Masaryk pointed out to us later on when we took a stroll to the foot of the hills. But there was no one with any visible weapons anywhere, either on the road leading to the hamlet or in the village itself. As Jan said later, his father was utterly without thought of any of these precautions and hated above all to have any symbol of militarism about him.

Shortly after ten President Masaryk sent word that he was ready, and I found him at his desk, apparently unchanged from my last visit to him. He was always thin, and I'd never known him other than as an old man with white beard and hair. He seemed to me to be just the same as ever.

He began by telling me that he had read my memorandum and the letters and other papers, and that he liked their general tone. I found, however, that as we proceeded with the discussion he had not got as much of this practical concreteness in his mind at the

274

time as his opening words had led me to hope, and I began to wonder if he had really given it any very serious attention. Before the interview was over, however—and it lasted steadily until half past one—it was clear that he had done a good deal of thinking on the matter, but equally clear that a personal interview and a leisurely discussion were absolutely necessary in the presentation of any new scheme like this. A typewritten text or a printed page is a very poor vehicle to stimulate new thinking on old subjects, compared with the give and take of conversation. This was another proof of the value of the Institute proposal for combining research with discussion.

There was nothing especially new in the subject matter as I presented it. It was the same story I had told to each group in each country, but I had a longer time to develop it and the President was as keen in his interest at the close as when I began. Before we finished he said that he would see to it that there would be erected a Social Science Council in Czechoslovakia and that he would himself provide the funds for starting it. He asked me, however, to send him back full memoranda and a complete statement of some definite problems to take up. He was especially keen on collaboration with Hungary and suggested that instead of thinking wholly in terms of multilateral cooperation there ought to be work done two by two. I assured him of a similar interest in the Hungarian group, and hoped that this could be developed in the future, whatever else happened.

Lunch was served in the simple dining room with absolutely no formality. The President held back to let his guests, not only Mrs. Shotwell but me as well, precede him into the room. He sat down at the end of the dining table with one of us at each side, then his daughter beside me and then the village pastor—a nice, quiet middle-aged man who spoke only Czech—and Jan beside Mrs. Shotwell, then the two grandchildren and their father at the other end of the table. The President was a quiet and reserved man, but he enjoyed the sallies across the table and joined in them from time to time. After lunch we all went out into the garden at the back of the house, where coffee was served under the apple trees. Apples fell from time to time, but no one paid any attention. It was almost four o'clock when we suddenly recalled that we had to catch a five-twenty-seven train about twenty-five miles away. It was also clear that the daughter was anxious to have her father go and rest, and as by that time we had covered everything it was possible to take up on this visit, we returned to the house, said good-bye, and in a few minutes Jan Masaryk was at the wheel of his eight-cylinder Packard, and we were whizzing down the country road through the valley of the Vah to Zilina.

Coming back to Vienna from our long journey over central and eastern Europe, we found the old capital of the Hapsburgs more like that hollow shell which President Hoover had described than when we lived there in the midst of the breakdown of the old monarchy, eleven years ago. Of that brilliant group of economists and statesmen who had worked with me on the War History, only one remained, Dr. Joseph Redlich, but there could be no one better qualified to pass judgment on my plans for institutes to study the organization of peace in the "succession states," as the new nations carved out of the Hapsburg empire and kingdom were called. The outstanding authority on English public law, he had written the most penetrating study in my War History on the breakdown of the Austrian bureaucracy, but, while critical of the system, he had come to the paradoxical conclusion that "thanks to the fact that in fifty years of racial strife the conflicting nationalities had gradually made their way into the machinery of state, a civil service capable of carrying on the new government stood ready to their hands, and so put at the service of the new states the traditions and experiences of the old. This in its turn meant that the political and military catastrophe instead of spreading social ruin was able to provide a constructive opportunity."

This tribute to the work of the civil service in keeping the new governments on an even keel is all the more remarkable in coming from a liberal who had been their chief critic. But, as we had found out in Hungary and Poland and even in Masaryk's democratic Czechoslovakia, rampant nationalism was holding sound policies in check and the result of the disruption of the Hapsburg monarchy was economic failure. In Austria itself, the result was disaster.

I found Dr. Redlich at his desk, snowed under with the crushing

276

burden of an appalling task, trying to keep Austrian credit from complete bankruptcy at a time when even England seemed ready to go under. An English loan had tided Austria over its worst hours, but it was made only from week to week and it was beginning to be called in. Dr. Redlich's intimate acquaintance with British statesmen helped to avert an immediate catastrophe, but the sword was hanging by a thin thread.

The Ministry of Finance, where I found Dr. Redlich, was just around the corner from our hotel, in the famous palace of Prince Eugene, the savior of Europe from the Turk. It was a magnificent edifice of the Baroque style. The stairways were enormous, with straining Atlas columns holding up the stone above. The galleries were decorated with stucco figures and designs, some of them gilded with so much ornamentation as to be really overpowering. It was a weird office for that utmost prose of statecraft, the struggle with debt.

At dinner that evening in the old hotel of Archduke Charles, which had traditions from Kossuth and the Vienna of the early nineteenth century, Dr. Redlich had brought along Professor Pribram, the outstanding historian of the Austrian monarchy and a sympathetic liberal; for it was agreed that the chief work of an Austrian institute, if one were set up, would be largely in the field of history. Professor Pribram insisted that even historical research was impossible without an American subsidy, and so that visit to Austria brought no results.

The discussion, however, was animated by historical anecdotes, one of which by Pribram, is worth recalling for the light it throws on the diplomacy of the old regime. In going over the records of the alliance of Austria with England and Russia in the French Revolutionary war of 1792, there was a letter from the Austrian Foreign Minister, Kaunitz, to his ambassador Stadion in London, giving him a letter to show to the British Prime Minister explaining the Austrian point of view. But, on the same day there was another letter from Kaunitz to Stadion to show to the Russian ambassador giving a different explanation of Austrian policy. Later on, Professor Pribram found a letter from Kaunitz to Count Mercy-Argenteau, a friend of Marie Antoinette, in which Kaunitz said:

277

"Stadion is a very clever man, but he is young and inexperienced. Will you go over to London as a private person and take up the question with the Prime Minister and give him my real opinion." The incident is all the more revealing when one recalls that Count Stadion was himself to be Foreign Minister, and indeed played a major role in the opening years of Metternich's regime.

Clearly, there was nothing more to do in Vienna. Both Redlich and Pribram were liberals of the kind that works best outside of institutes, and none of my other Viennese friends were left. So we stayed only a day or two and then left for Geneva.

Geneva was crowded for the 1931 meeting of the Assembly of the League of Nations, even more than it had been for the historic meeting of 1924, which had produced the Protocol. For one thing, there were about three hundred Americans eager to see what the League would do to meet the two dangers to peace and security in Europe, the economic crisis which was an aftermath of the Great Depression in the United States—a last liquidation of the bankruptcy of the World War—and the rise of militant nationalism in Italy and Germany, impatient with Geneva and contemptuous of its plans for disarmament. I had been led to hope that a commission of the League would take over the studies we had been making in the economics and politics of the new states; but, although the proposal was personally supported by Sir Eric Drummond, the Secretary General of the League and Ambassador Norman Davis, soon to be appointed the United States member of the Disarmament Conference, Mussolini opposed the whole project and that meant a veto in the eyes of France and Great Britain.

The other outstanding problem before the League, disarmament, was not to be got rid of by so brusque a gesture, although in the end it met the same fate at the hands of Mussolini and Hitler. In December, 1925, the Council of the League had set up a Preparatory commission for a Disarmament conference, of which Germany, the United States and the USSR were members. But progress was discouragingly slow, and it was not until five years later, December, 1930, that a draft convention was submitted to the Council of the League. In its deep-rooted fear of a revival of German militarism—a fear too tragically justified in 1939—France had

278

built up the alliance of the Little Entente, with Czechoslovakia, Yugoslavia and Romania, while insisting on German disarmament in the terms of the Treaty of Versailles.

It was natural, therefore, that the German Foreign Minister, Dr. Curtius, should lead off in the Assembly of 1931 by a sharp reminder of the things the League had not done in the years Germany was excluded from it and call for a more even-handed treatment of the armament question as set forth in the Treaty of Versailles. The speech, delivered in rasping German, had a bad reception except among the Germans and some English—for English liberals have been rather generally anti-French. But as I listened, I was reminded of the comment of Professor Wieser, when, speaking as an Austrian liberal, he said that the Prussians were their own worst enemies, because, unlike the South Germans, they were forthright, which meant that they were less devious in politics and diplomacy. I was not sorry, therefore, to have an invitation from Dr. Curtius for a frank talk on the whole European situation.

The interview took place in the Hotel Metropole, where I had visited with Stresemann and his Foreign Office staff. Dr. Curtius began by expressing regret that Germany had not been represented in our Berlin conference and said that he would do anything he could to further the plan for international research on the organization of peace which I had been developing throughout the summer. I was surprised to have him recall in detail our discussion of a year ago on the Danzig Corridor problem and the relations with Poland. The overlapping of the German and Polish frontier tended to block free transportation to the Baltic and he was much interested in the way in which such obstacles had been overcome between the United States and Canada. But the main point of our discussion was the project which had appealed so strongly to Norman Davis that there should be a new international conference—"a real peace conference"—to reopen all the problems in the peace treaties except territorial frontiers.

Our conference lasted until it was time for me to take the train from Geneva to Paris.

In spite of all the old familiar scenes—or perhaps because of them—Paris seemed strangely empty and lonely as I came back to it this time. The morning that I was in Bystricka, Jan Masaryk interrupted my talk with his father to hand me a telegram that told of the death of Arthur Fontaine, one of the best and truest friends I have ever had. I had first learned to know and admire his sterling character and liberal outlook during the trying days of the Peace Conference. For a quarter of a century before the First World War he had been the anonymous but efficient mover in all the social legislation of France. Yet, as modest as he was capable he left the credit to the politicians who came and went at the head of the administration. It was this work which prepared him for the part he played in the creation of the International Labor Office.

Somehow or other it seemed as though with the passing of this generation to which Fontaine belonged, France was definitely losing touch with the great liberal movements which had grown out of its Revolution. Arthur Fontaine was a liberal of the old school, not in the conservative sense of those who hold back from radical experiments, but in the assertion of individual liberty in both thought and action and the maintenance or creation of conditions which would give the individual life its fullest expression, even if those conditions should have a socialistic trend, which he deplored. He was an outspoken opponent of all that makes for reaction and nationalism. I recall his visit to my hotel that winter evening when Poincaré threw the French troops into the Ruhr. He was almost broken-hearted, for he, and not Briand nor Coudenhove-Kalergi, was the first exponent of the idea of the United States of Europe.

This memory of Arthur Fontaine's reaction to Poincaré's invasion of the Ruhr brings to mind another incident. On the evening of the day that the Senate voted Poincaré its consent to his action, Baron D'Estournelles de Constant, the Carnegie Endowment representative in France, came to my hotel room brokenhearted. He had been the only Senator to vote against Poincaré, and after the session he was cut and ignored by all his old friends and found himself ostracized in the Senate. But there were other liberals like him, and they were my friends in those dark days overshadowed by the threat of war.

Strangely, there was little appreciation of French liberal thought or politics in either England or America. I recall the surprise of

280

Judge Learned Hand on one occasion when he met with my friends Professor Rist and D'Estournelles de Constant at the Hotel des Saints Pères at which we were living, and found in them kindred spirits, like his old friends at the Century Club. I had a rare opportunity to see this open-minded attitude on the problems of Europe at conferences held by a group of intellectuals at the old Abbaye de Pontigny, down in the heart of France.

It was the monastery to which Thomas à Becket fled when he took refuge from the first Plantagenet. When, almost eight centuries later, the secular administration of the Third Republic dispossessed the monastery, a far-seeing professor of literature in the Lycée of Sèvres bought the remains of the Abbot's palace and formed a little corporation known as the Friends of the Abbaye de Pontigny. In this he interested some of the leading liberal spirits of France, and every summer they held a little gathering of a score or so of personally-invited guests from the various countries of Europe. Mornings and evenings they gathered either in the old monastic library or out under the shade of the lime trees to discuss, in genuine Socratic fashion, the problems of Europe. One week it would be literature, another week, politics or social welfare or philosophy. It was the maintenance of the best traditions of the philosophic enlightenment of the eighteenth century. There I have seen Poles and Germans, Italians and French, Hungarians and British, thresh out their different points of view with even a passionate ardor but at the same time with that mutual respect and generous appreciation of the limitations of the other side which characterizes academic discussion.

Between the morning and evening sessions we rambled over the hillside to the vineyards of Chablis or to the cathedral of Auxerre, in old Burgundy. It was a perfect preparation for an evening on literature or politics.

There were still a few days before the *Aquitania* sailed, and I took the night passage to London to be sure of my bearings for the next months at home. By telephone from Oxford, Professor Gilbert Murray gave strong support to the plan for appointing political scientists and economists to the Committee on Intellectual Cooperation. Then, after a visit to the Foreign Office, lunch with

281

my Peace Conference colleague, the Rt. Hon. George Barnes, who offered full access to all his War Cabinet documents for the History of the I.L.O., and dinner with Sir Malcolm Delevingne who also placed all his documents at my disposal, we discussed more general topics in a reminiscent vein and also the problems England was facing.

The next day, September 19, the Japanese army struck in Manchuria, occupied the city of Mukden and strategic points in South Manchuria, the Chinese troops having previously withdrawn. It was a coup by army officers, which surprised not only foreign governments but the government of Japan itself. The liberals supporting the policy of Shidehara, who had welcomed the Tokyo conference, were not only guiltless of complicity, but the victims of murderous assaults in Tokyo by the reactionaries, who thought in terms of Japan's past military glory, and who organized a reign of terror, assassinating liberal statesmen and their supporters. Among the victims during the years 1930-1932 were the Finance Minister Inouge, Premier Hamaguchi (who had entertained us in his official residence) and Baron Dan, a financier, whose son was our guide in Japanese art. Dr. Nitobe, the saintly political philosopher in whose home we lived, was for months in mortal terror. It was a priview of what the Nazis were to do only a few years later.

CHAPTER 16

The End of an Era

The Council of the League was in session on that fateful September of 1931, but in the absence of the United States and Russia, the other foreign power most deeply interested, Great Britain, could do no more at Geneva than propose that the League send a commission of inquiry to investigate the situation in Manchuria itself. After all, this is what the League had done in the past when wars had threatened. The United States Government gave an official approval of this initial action of the League by appointing General Frank McCoy a member of the commission under the chairmanship of Lord Lytton.

I was especially happy about this, because General McCoy and I had been closely associated when he served on a commission to try to end the Chaco war between Paraguay and Bolivia, working alongside the League of Nations. As we talked over his appointment on the Lytton Commission, I was struck by the breadth of his scholarship and his capacity for applying it. He knew all about Lord Milner's work in Egypt and the differences between that and the problem of Manchuria.

The co-operation of the United States with the League was perhaps as good as might be expected from any non-member state, for its aims were identical with those of the League. But there still remained two centers of policy, two general staffs of the peace forces, and the result was misunderstanding in the most critical hours. Uncertainty of plan and shifts of front can be as fatal in politics as in battle; both were evident in the strategy of Geneva and Washington.

283

The first step taken by the League was to appeal to the governments of China and Japan "to refrain from any action which might aggravate the situation or prejudice the peaceful settlement of the problem" and to withdraw their troops immediately. This appeal communicated to Washington brought forth a cordial endorsement and the statement that it was working along the same lines. But two days later (September 23), when the Council began to consider favorably the appointment of a commission of inquiry to report on conditions in Manchuria, the Japanese Delegation in Geneva had word from Washington that Mr. Stimson would not join in formulating any action envisaged under the Covenant, but would only give moral support to bring public opinion to bear on the prevention of war. This was surely the voice of Senator Borah, whose influence in Washington was catastrophic.

It was at this critical time that I had a telephone talk with Ambassador Norman Davis urging me to see Secretary Stimson, for it was now clear that the Government of the United States would have to put something more tangible behind the Pact of Paris if it was to have any influence on Japan. I found Secretary Stimson friendly but reserved, somewhat in the manner of Elihu Root. The reserve was lessened, however, and then cast aside as we discussed the situation in Geneva. I knew, of course, as all Washington did, that his declared policy to co-operate with the League was at variance with what President Hoover wanted, which was isolationist concentration on the domestic economic problems of the great depression. As the Japanese aggression grew, however, it was clear that the United States could not remain indifferent to the fact that it was, as Secretary Stimson put it, "in flagrant violation of the spirit and probably the letter of all war treaties with it." Therefore, on January 7, 1932, he sent identical notes to the governments of Japan and China, setting forth the principle which became popularly known as the "Stimson Doctrine" but was in reality the application of a principle accepted by the American states from the days of Secretary Blaine in 1890. The notes stated that the United States:

> does not intend to recognize any situation, treaty or agreement which may be brought about by means contrary to the covenants and agreements of the Pact of Paris of August 27, 1928, to which treaty both China and Japan, as well as the United States are parties.

284

This statement of the policy of non-recognition was taken up by the League of Nations with a slight rewording so as to make it apply to a violation of the Covenant, as well as of the Pact of Paris. In this form it passed the Assembly on March 11, 1932, and stands almost without change in the final action taken by the Assembly on the Sino-Japanese dispute a year later.

When I returned to Geneva I found Secretary General Drummond keenly interested in the Stimson Doctrine as it applied to the crisis in Asia, but he said that it was a strange and sad fact that just when the United States was taking parallel action with the League, the League's credit in Europe was going down. Under the circumstances my friends in Geneva, especially Philip Noel-Baker and William Martin, the editor of the *Journal de Génève,* were strongly set against tampering with the Covenant, especially in view of the reluctance of the British Government to apply even the economic sanctions envisaged in the Covenant.

While I shared in the anxiety over the crisis in Geneva, I argued that nerveless inaction meant sure death to the League, that it should be ready to shoulder whatever responsibility would be involved when the Lytton Commission reported, which it must do a few months later. Fortunately, the French election of May, 1932, had brought Herriot back to power. Norman Davis, who had visited him in Lyons, found him in the same courageous spirit as when he had led the movement for the Protocol in 1924. At Mr. Davis' suggestion I went to see him again at Lyons, taking along my friend Wickham Steed, the editor of the *Times,* an enthusiastic supporter of my ideas.

My diary is full of Herriot's cautious then full acceptance of the plan for France to lead in strengthening the League. Back in Geneva, I had the co-operation of M. Vigier, the French legal adviser of the Secretary General, but as we worked at it, a wholly new idea dawned. While the Lytton Commission was still at work on the Oriental crisis, why not concentrate on the Disarmament Conference, then in complete stalemate. Its President, Arthur Henderson, lacked his old-time fire and vigor to prevent the sabotage of the conference by the military and naval experts attached to it.

I had a frank talk about this with Herr Nadolny, the representative of the new German Government—mostly military heads—

which filled in the interval between Bruning's resignation and Hitler's advent to power. I found him a typical Prussian junker, but not actively working with the militarists. Nazi Germany was not yet ready to strike at Geneva, though the threat already lay in the background. But when I saw Arthur Henderson, I was shocked to see how weak, ill, and haggard he was. Herr Nadolny was at least right in insisting that so vital a post should be held by one strong enough to hold his own against the delaying tactics of his opponents.

The drafting of the text for M. Herriot to offer as the contribution of France to disarmament was no task for an American citizen; but when I talked it over with my old friend Professor René Cassin, Vice President of the Conseil d'Etat, the supreme court of France (the President of the Republic is ex-officio president of the Conseil), I readily agreed to sit with him in his study on the Boulevard Michel in Paris, and work on the section in which France proposed to realize its program of security by strengthening collective security through the League, which would in turn strengthen the basis for disarmament. I have a vivid memory of the hours we spent on this text. Later, I was happy to see it in the French disarmament proposals—substantially as we wrote it.

Meanwhile the Lytton Commission was finishing its work. It reported on September 24, 1932, clearly establishing the aggression of Japan in violation of the Covenant. It was adopted by the Assembly on February 24, 1933, on which occasion the Japanese delegates dramatically left the Assembly. A month later, on March 27, the Japanese Government formally gave notice of its withdrawal from the League.

It was the twilight of the long day which had begun with the Paris Peace Conference. It was also the ominous foreshadowing of World War II. Seven months later, in October, with Hitler in power, Germany withdrew from both the Disarmament Conference and the League of Nations preparatory to a massive rearmament program, not to be outdone in militarism by Mussolini's Italy, openly moving toward war with Ethiopia. The saddest spectacle in the history of the League of Nations was the eloquent and moving appeal by the Emperor of Ethiopia, Haile Selassie, to an Assembly in which the British Government refused to withhold supplies from Italy for fear of reprisal.

I was not present at Geneva during these last ominous and tragic events, but while the political crisis was taking shape the Committee for International Intellectual Cooperation kept at work and called two conferences, one in Milan and the other in Madrid, both of which I attended. Even in these purely academic discussions the rising tide of nationalism showed itself, however, and finally in Spain we witnessed the actual on-coming of civil war.

The first night we were in Madrid a bomb was exploded in the entrance of our hotel, utterly wrecking it. But, to our surprise my wife and I seemed to be the only ones alarmed by it. The hotel porter calmly explained that it was only one branch of anarchists in the working class making reprisals against another.

Then we got our bearings from Professor Castellejo, former exchange professor at Columbia University, whose delightful home we visited on the eastern outskirts of Madrid, on the plateau rimmed on the north by the snow-capped Guadarrama Mountains. He explained that the government of the republic, which had replaced the monarchy in 1931, was composed of nineteenth century, laissez-faire liberals and was losing control of the country, which was turning more and more to direct action, inflammatory Falangists and workers groups fighting each other. Government by compromise meant, among other things, protecting the church, a bulwark of reaction, against attacks by the peasantry or the leftists in the cities.

Everywhere we went we found that the walls of cathedrals and churches were smeared with anti-clerical slogans, and to deal with threatened sabotage the government quartered troops in church-yards or adjacent public squares. These tented encampments lent a sinister aspect to otherwise quiet cities, but the show of force was all that was needed in this police measure. Compromise was no settlement however. The peasants struck for increases from 2 pesetas a day (26 cents) to 15 pesetas, and city workers made similar demands. Professor Castellejo assured us, however, that this uneasy situation was typical of Spain, that there were only a few communists, less than 4 per cent of the voters, and that we need not cut short our journey throughout the country.

We might have been more concerned if we had known that the reactionaries were in touch with German Nazis and Italian Facists, and that the army was preparing for action under the leadership of former Chief of the General Staff, Francisco Franco, then in retirement in Spanish Morocco. But we had left Spain before he returned to lead the rebellion.

If the problems of the present and future of Spain seemed elusive, the country as a whole, with the exception of busy Barcelona, seemed more like a museum of history, from the bleak high-lands of Castile to the sunny groves of Andalusia. No other country, not even Italy, makes so strong an impression of a richly varied past. But of all the impressions which we treasure from that journey, strangely enough the one that lingers most is the memory of the songs of the nightingales in the groves of the gardens of the Alhambra. Neither of us had ever heard them before. There they sang in chorus, as they must have sung when the Moors ruled southern Spain.

History has its own way of molding the problems of the present into the romance of the past.

The journey to Spain was, so far as we were concerned, a strange interlude. In the year 1937 there was another one. My friend Thomas J. Watson, the creator of International Business Machines, was appointed American Commissioner at the Paris World's Fair. He turned to me to work out an exposition of American industries by way of motion pictures. I had used films in education in recent years and I was now given the chance to go the limit with films contributed by the great industries, costing over a quarter of a million dollars. We had a gallery in the American pavilion and our films proved to be the one great attraction. Our hall was always crowded while the rest of the American display was given only casual inspection. It was really the first great test of commercial films. The steel industry, for example, showed the showers of glittering sparks against the dark outlines of a Bessemer converter. As the pictures themselves were silent, I arranged sound effects to synchronize with the action, using a symphony of Beethoven, music by Virgil Thompson or a march by Sousa. No wonder our hall kept full.

I had at my right hand my daughter Margaret Grace and a young electronics engineer who later became her husband, Llewlyn Summers, son of a colleague of mine at the Paris Peace Conference

288

who was a close friend of Bernard Baruch. My only compensation from the government was a medal, but the experience was an education in itself.

From this exposition of the arts of peace I went to Germany to study the new militant state that owed allegiance to Hitler. On the invitation of the German members of the International Chamber of Commerce Malcolm Davis, President Butler's representative at the Carnegie Endowment in Paris, and I went to Frankfurt to a national conference of jurists, called to establish a Nazi-controlled system of law—a Deutsches Recht—free from any taint of those high principles of the rights of man which had been worked out in the jurisprudence of the Empire. It was a shocking spectacle to see the men in brown shirt uniforms, with army boots and spurs presiding over the assembly of the new nationalist system of law.

But the scene in Frankfurt was nothing compared with what I found in Berlin, listening to Hitler and watching a Nazi celebration. Hitler spoke to a mass meeting from the second-story gallery of the Foreign Office. His rasping thin-toned voice carried over the whole square, packed with a crowd which, as I mingled with it, showed every sign of high tension as the Führer played on its emotions. Unimpressive in personal appearance, he made himself the embodiment of a cause as he denounced the enemies of the Fatherland, both foreign and domestic. The gospel of hatred was never more passionately proclaimed.

Although the Nazis were in power, it is doubtful that their creed would have wholly dominated Germany, as it did before long, if it had not been for Prussian militarism, reacting against defeat and, especially, the wonderful showmanship of the Nazi leaders. I saw only two of their great spectacles, but they left a lasting memory. The first was a monster demonstration in the Sport Palast, the Madison Square Garden of Berlin. The announced purpose of the meeting was to collect funds for Nazi charities, but the great hall was filled with banners which were kept flickering in the light by fans along the walls, while the stage was a blaze of color. Hitler had, apparently by design, stayed away, so that when Goering and Goebels made their appeal for contributions they made it in Hitler's name. I still recall the shock I felt when, almost as if he were in-

289

toning a liturgy, Goebels said, "Hitler 'suffered for you, he has borne your burdens.' Can't you do a little for him?" Then, from the crowded hall I went over to Unter den Linden, Berlin's proudest street, to see a torchlight procession of the Hitler youth. It was fantastic and splendid. From the height of the Brandenburger Tor down toward the old palace of the Hohenzollerns, a river of fire from the torches, under the murk of their smoke, filled the central pavement as far as the eye could see. This, of course, was but a prelude to the magnificence of the annual meetings of the Nazis at Nuremburg, but this was the only glimpse I had of the new, ominous power which was to blot out the Germany of kindliness—*Gemüthlichkeit*—and freedom of thought, of Lessing, Kant and Goethe.

CHAPTER 17

Canadian-American Relations

For fourteen years after the Paris Peace Conference I had been working under the auspices of the Carnegie Endowment for International Peace, first on the history of World War I, then on a series of seven volumes on the Paris Peace Conference, of which my own diary *(At the Paris Peace Conference)* was one. But, as the above record shows, my chief interest lay in the organization of peace, mostly in Europe.

Then, in 1934, with the financial support of the Carnegie Corporation, the Endowment authorized me to undertake a study of Canadian-American relations. At first sight it might seem strange that those relations, in which there was not the slightest possibility of war ever arising, should have been chosen as a promising field for work on the interlocking problems of war and peace. I pointed out that it would be a narrow conception of the processes of peace to deal with them only in terms of the police measures of governments on guard against dangerous neighbors. Peace at its best has as much to offer as peace not yet emancipated from the haunting fear of recurring war. To put it more definitely, the relations of the United States and Canada are certainly as significant as those between Balkan States or between immature nations which lack the traditions of responsible government.

As a matter of fact, the world-wide peace movement has suffered as much through misunderstanding between nations who should be allies in a common cause as through the opposition of militaristic

291

governments. Nowhere is this sort of misunderstanding more absurd than between the United States and Canada, the sharers of a common heritage, the embodiment of similar social and political ideals. Yet, as our studies on those relations progressed, we were repeatedly reminded that the "unarmed frontier" had not been unarmed during trying periods of history and that for generations after the war of 1812, the searing memory of invasion left its mark on Canadian history and literature, a scar rubbed raw again in the mid-nineteenth century over the Northwest frontier, "fifty-four forty or fight," and again over the Alaska frontier and the cod fisheries dispute in the Atlantic.

The first thing, therefore, was to review the whole field of history and public relations. This was done in a series of twenty-five comprehensive volumes, *The Relations of Canada and the United States**, which recast the whole perspective and made possible for the first time university courses on Canadian-American relations, a possibility immediately exploited not only in Canada but in the universities of the northern states as well.

The theme was nothing short of the great American epic, a theme which had never yet been fully developed. Most histories of the United States began with the epic of New England and the trek west from the seaboard, the story of the United States and of it alone. The real epic of America has a larger and richer content. It deals with those who took possession of the whole continent north of the Rio Grande, and who have developed two great systems singularly alike, yet treasuring their differences as part of the heritage of freedom. Parkman, years ago, wrote the poetic prelude to this great theme but not the real story of pioneering and settlement.

The history of Canada is almost from first to last a protest against the economic theory of history; no people has ever grappled with a harder problem and achieved a greater result. Thousands of miles of rock and forest lay in the pathway of the Canadian pioneer. The natural markets for the most of the provinces were just across the

---

* *The Relations of Canada and the United States*, ed. James T. Shotwell (25 vols., New Haven: Yale University Press, Toronto: The Ryerson Press, London: Humphrey Milford: Oxford University Press, for the Carnegie Endowment for International Peace, 1936-1945).

southern border, and yet with pride and splendid persistence they linked the watercourses and crossed the mountains, paralleling, under more rigorous conditions, the great theme of United States history, which was the conquest of the West.

After these efforts and with a sense of achievement keenly nourished from generation to generation, the two national economies faced new problems in their interplay of investment and trade. The volumes of the Endowment series, therefore, dealt with current problems as well as those of continental history. My editing of this series proved to be an easy task, for my collaborators were highly qualified economists and political scientists. The series remains a monument of their scholarship and that of my chief collaborator, Professor John Bartlet Berbner, whose final volume in the series, *The North American Triangle,* was a brilliant and illuminating survey of the interplay of Great Britain, Canada, and the United States.

The making of books was not enough, however. A series of conferences was held from 1935 to 1939 under the auspices of the Carnegie Endowment. St. Lawrence University, Canton, New York and Queens University, Kingston, Ontario, acted as hosts to the conference in alternate years. These were unique occasions. There was nothing new in the holding of Canadian-American conferences by lawyers, bankers, labor unions, professional, or businessmen. But those were relatively limited to special professionals or technicians. This was the first time in the history of Canada and the United States that representative citizens of both countries met together to take stock of the fundamentals in their inter-relationship in all the varied fields of intellectual, economic, social and political activity.

The shadows of approaching war were already stretching out over the field of international relations when the conference of 1940 met for the last time, and the danger of war abroad accentuated the common interests of the two countries. But now that Canada was involved as a belligerent in World War II, international affairs were no longer a distant and detached element of our lives. I was much interested to see that as we turned from a consideration of the economics of peace to the ominous danger of war, we lost sight of the economic character of the domestic situation. We were, of course, conscious of the fact that the larger problems of the adjustment of peace-loving nations to a world set upon the accumulation of the means of war could not be solved by this Conference or the next, or the next after that. At the conclusion of the Conference I summed up our aims and methods:

> The processes of democracy are slow and, to the impatient, seem stupid. They register the last drag of reluctant peoples upon the wheel of thought and not the swift-moving, impetuous action that you get under dictatorships. So we shall likely blunder and make mistakes, as we have in the past. We shall likely continue to think of disarmament as a thing of arithmetic instead of a counterplay to force, following the lines we have followed in the sad history of that futility. We shall likely continue to ignore the substitutes for war, while demanding that war be given up. We shall likely continue to turn to every promising slogan that moves across the darkness and symbolizes the heavens above us. But while we may continue to do this, we are, nevertheless, on the sure path to ultimate success. For this process of trial and error, this slow thing that at times invites disaster, is the embodiment of intelligence itself; because it is the nature of intelligence that it should be free to make these blunders, that it should find its way by experiment, unguided by dictatorships, untrammeled and unhampered by that narrowing concept of efficiency which reaches for the immediate advantage and forgets the fact that the one lasting, permanent asset of a nation is intelligence itself.

The conclusions which I had drawn from my study of World War I applied here. The bureaucratic, militaristic nations began with an initial advantage, and their military machine registered that advantage in victories on the field. Nevertheless, when the democracies really became aware of the full measure of the crisis with which they had to deal, they discovered in themselves a resiliency which the bureaucratic nations were denied, a resiliency which continued and stood the storm and stress of the years of war. Then, when the stimulus was gone, when war effort was over, we slumped back to old, traditional methods; the Ice Age recovered its control. Static in thought, in emotion, in action, we were unwilling to experiment with the greatest challenge that has ever been thrown upon the stage of history, that of Woodrow Wilson. Yet I stated that

294

it was my belief that, out of that present crisis, or the next, or the next, would ultimately come a recourse to those methods of intelligent constructive statesmanship which stirred us in the great days of 1918.

This reaffirmation of faith evidently moved the conference deeply, for they were wholly with me at its conclusion.

The success of these conferences gave me a special satisfaction. It was the technique of the Institute of Pacific Relations, which had a temporary success in the Orient, but which I had been unable to set going in Europe. Here was the ideal situation for it, showing clearly, at last, that the organization of peace could become a reality if supported by an enlightened public opinion. The experimen begun in 1935 is still going on. The series of conferences which the Carnegie Endowment initiated has been continued in Canada under the auspices of the Canadian Institute of International Affairs and at Rochester University.

CHAPTER 18

Mexican Studies

The success of the Canadian-American collaboration naturally suggested similar studies on the far more difficult problems of the other neighboring country, Mexico. The Carnegie Endowment had limited its interest in Latin American affairs to its Division of International Law, to avoid interfering in politics. But after the long regime of Porfirio Díaz (1884-1910), one revolution followed another in Mexico, anarchy in the eyes of foreigners but freedom in the eyes of the natives. War feeling mounted in the United States when the American flag was torn down at Tampico in 1914. When Villa, with a troop of bandits invaded New Mexico in 1916, President Wilson sent a punitive expedition into northern Mexico, under the command of General Pershing. War seemed inevitable.

In alarm, a group of which I was a member decided to intervene in a way which could not be open to the charge of violating the Logan act against unofficial interference in international disputes. In hundreds of telegrams to newspapers we simply quoted the text of the treaty of Guadalupe Hidalgo of 1848 after the war with Mexico, which provided that neither country would resort to war in the settlement of future troubles between them. This forgotten text became first-page news, and the belligerency in Washington came to a sudden end.

The revolution in Mexico continued, culminating in the confiscation of the great estates and the American-owned oil industry, but so completely had the policy of the United States changed that by 1923 it sent weapons to the socialist government of Obregón to help maintain law and order, and accepted a settlement of the oil dispute. But resentment continued on both sides until it was dispelled by the patient and wist diplomacy of Dwight Morrow, a partner of the banking firm of J. P. Morgan, who proved to be a messenger of good will, balancing American just claims with Mexican basic needs and ending in 1928 the sixteen-year-old feud between the two nations.

It was a troubled peace, however. The Mexicans continued to take foreign-owned estates and oil refineries without paying for them. This policy of confiscation reached a peak during the administration of President Cardenas (1934-1940), under whom over fifty million acres were distributed to the natives, while railways, oil and sugar mills were turned over to labor unions to manage. Naturally there were angry outbursts in the United States, but again, as in 1928, the crisis was eased by the American ambassador to Mexico—this time not a financial expert like Dwight Morrow but a journalist politician, Josephus Daniels. Secretary Cordell Hull ordered Daniels to stand stiffly for American rights, but President Franklin Roosevelt, with his instinctive sense of political realities, backed Mr. Daniels' effort at arbitration and conciliation as the only way to ensure a friendly neighbor on the south.

This much of the history must be recalled to explain why in 1940 President Butler and the Trustees of the Carnegie Endowment for International Peace asked me to make a survey of the Mexican problems as a basis for a program of future work. At the University of Texas, in Austin, I made the unexpected discovery that the most dangerous source of quarrel with Mexico still remained unsettled, the disputes over the Rio Grande. That boundary river kept shifting its course and a final line had never been drawn between the two countries. Then, although most of its water came from the United States, there were Mexican tributaries as well, and Mexico objected that the Texans took more than their share in irrigation. I found that Professor Timm, Professor of Government at the University, had made this his special field, even motoring all over the hundreds of miles of boundary country and mapping the disputed areas. So my first recommendation to President Butler was that Professor Timm be given the chance to go to Washington and take up the whole matter with the State Department. A grant-in-aid was made by the Carnegie Endowment, sufficient to provide for travel over the entire drainage basin of the Rio Grande, to study not only the physical aspects of the country but also to make personal acquaintance with the people.

Then I got in touch with the State Department, and the result was the appointment of Professor Timm as special adviser to the Division of Mexican Affairs, so that he could carry on his work within the Department. The final result was that, on February 14, 1944, the President transmitted to the Senate, which promptly ratified it, a treaty which settled the utilization of the waters of the Rio Grande and its tributaries and prescribed the powers and functions of the International Boundary and Water Commission, one of the best achievements of the Good Neighbor policy of President Roosevelt and Secretary Cordell Hull.

Arriving in Mexico City, we found the hotels crowded with tourists and our guide took us to a newly built apartment hotel, the Departamentos Washington on the Plaza Dinamarca, a thoroughly good but simple arrangement which we found was being used by those American travelers who seek quiet. It was only two blocks away from the Embassy, and I was soon in touch with Ambassador Josephus Daniels, one of the most lovable of men, who by his simplicity and friendliness had become a trusted friend of the leaders of Mexican policy. He and his equally lovable wife welcomed us almost as members of their family. It happened, however, that the Counsellor of the Embassy, Mr. Pierre Boal, had an exact knowledge of the kind of work the Endowment had been doing because he had been Counsellor at Ottawa when we started the Canadian-American Conferences and had followed our work closely; in fact, he attended the first St. Lawrence Conference and was very helpful. He at once set about securing for me the same kind of co-operation, as far as possible, as in the Canadian-American studies.

I began semi-official work by a call on the Minister of Education. The new Minister appointed by President Camacho was Sr. San-

298

chez Ponton. He had been chairman of the Mexican Committee on Intellectual Cooperation and his successor there, Sr. Pruneda, arranged for a joint conference which lasted for over an hour. He was faced with an extremely difficult situation because of the fact that in the Constitution of Mexico of 1917 there was a famous clause, Article Three, which stated that "education shall be socialistic." Fortunately, that term was defined in vague and somewhat contrary phrases later on, so that it did not necessarily mean education in Marxian socialism, but one of the first points of attack upon President Camacho by the clerical party was to have the Constitution revised so as not only to strike out this article but to enable them to bring back the old clerical form of education. There seemed to be a fairly strong movement of modern liberals who were anxious to go halfway with this reform, but they were aware of the fact that any step taken would be certain to be used by the clericals for still further demands.

I took up with Sr. Ponton the more immediate problems of the Endowment's collaboration with Latin America in the various social sciences, especially history, and also discussed with him the problem of translation. Special mention was made of the use of Spanish refugee scholars. I was glad to learn that there were some who have very high standing and who were regarded by their Mexican colleagues as an asset to the intellectual life of Mexico.

Mr. Boal took me to call on the rector of the university, Lic. Mario de la Cueva. He was a man of about forty-five. Like so many Mexican intellectuals, he was a jurist as well as an historian and educator. He had specialized somewhat in labor legislation, naturally a field of major interest in Mexico. I found that he knew the history and achievements of the International Labor Organization and seemed well disposed toward its activities in the Americas.

He was going to give some lectures at Tulane University that July but had not yet been invited to visit the North, and upon judicious inquiry I had found that he would be delighted, if the opportunity were open to him, to see more of the United States. The State Department apparently had no money available to make this arrangement and it seemed to me to be a real opportunity for us.

After a survey of the National University an entirely different world was opened up, that of the Colegio de Mexico. Sr. Alfonso Reyes, the rector of this newly founded institution, a distinguished philosopher and scholar, spoke English quite well. The college which, as he said, resembled the College de France in name only, was founded by ex-President Cardenas to serve as a coordinating center for higher education. There was little indication, however, that it was succeeding in this mission, for if there was one thing that was lacking in higher education in Mexico, it was coordination.

I was quite taken by surprise to find that it was Sr. Reyes who was responsible for the choice of my volume, *The History of History,* as the first in the series of publications of the academic body which was affiliated with the Colegio, the Fondo de Cultura Economica. This subsidiary institution might be described as a kind of faculty composed of refugee and European scholars, chiefly Spaniards. The activity of the Fondo, however, was less that of instruction than of the translation and distribution of literature throughout Latin America.

Cuernavaca is a center for country residences (although some of them are right in the little provincial city) of the diplomats and government officials in Mexico. It is only five thousand feet up and Mr. Boal made it a point to spend long week ends there in order to be able to stand the high altitude of Mexico. That, at least, was a valid excuse for spending as much time as possible in one of the most beautiful and delightful places in the world. It is a land of flowers set against the mountain range that culminates in Iztaccihautl and Popocatepetl—Mont Blanc and Fujiyama side by side. Cuernavaca was the city of Cortes and the residence of Maximilian and Carlotta. The walls of the great arcade in the Palace that Cortes built had been filled with frescoes by Diego de Rivera, for which the funds were furnished by Dwight Morrow, the ambassador to Mexico who did so much to overcome anti-United States feeling in Mexico. Although highly regarded by ultra-modern criteria, it seemed to me that they were of questionable taste, even if they do carry the story of Mexico from the conquest to the uprising of Zapata. Everywhere I saw Rivera's frescoes, for they cover many walls in Mexico; but I have a feeling that instead of interpreting the genuine spirit of the people, he tried to create a revolutionary

300

pamphlet in such crude form that it would not be forgotten by the peasants. And yet, I do not see how they can accept this grotesque caricature of themselves.

After several days' conference with education authorities in the government, we left again on one of the most interesting journeys that I ever made, the motor trip to Guadalajara over the mountains and along river valleys for some four hundred fifty miles or more, with additional side trips—a total journey of about a thousand miles before we reached home again. Apart from the towns and cities, the experience of crossing the mountains was absolutely unforgettable. At one point we looked out over a range of mountains cut by canyons almost as colorful as the Grand Canyon of Colorado. They call it *Mil Cumbres* (The Thousand Peaks). The guidebook says that some of these mountains are so remote and inaccessible that they have never been explored. Nevertheless, the Mexican engineers have built a marvelous road through the mountain passes, where one can travel with perfect safety and no discomfort.

The University of Guadalajara was closed when I was there, but I visited two other provincial universities, those of Puebla and Morelia. The University of Morelia—which, by the way was founded in 1540, and claims to be the oldest university on the continent—cherishes a proud tradition as the historic center of Mexican liberty and democracy. Its greatest figure was, and still is, Hidalgo the inspirer of Morelos, and it claims to have influenced the whole line of political reformers ever since, including Juarez. The cathedral and university buildings of Morelia have a perfect setting in a city of old colonial, that is to say Spanish, architecture, which is without a rival anywhere, even in Mexico City itself. There are courtyards which immediately carry one to Madrid or Seville. The deep arcades are cool and restful, where one looks out on a colorful square not too much disturbed by business and not spoiled by tourist travel. Above this scene rises the massive pile of the cathedral, with its fortress-like façade surmounted by towers in which the architect exhausted his fancy in richness of design. No American college has such an old world environment.

Sunday in Mexico—especially in Lent and at Easter—offered scenes of historical and religious interest that can hardly be paralleled anywhere else in the world. We heard Mass in the basilica of the Virgin of Guadalupe, that supreme shrine of all Indian Latin America. It was filled with so great a crowd of Indians (mostly city folk) that there was hardly room to move, and they followed the liturgy with every evidence of intense devotion. The shrine is a center of pilgrimage, like Mecca, for it is the supreme desire of every Indian to visit it at least once.

There are other memories left by this journey to Mexico, but with this reminder of its great past and challenging present the narrative must close.

CHAPTER 19

Franklin D. Roosevelt, Cordell Hull, and the Birth of the United Nations

By a happy chance I came to know Cordell Hull rather intimately, and have always treasured the memory of our friendship. I first met him at the 1932 Democratic Party National Convention in Chicago, which nominated Franklin Delano Roosevelt for the presidency. It was the only party convention I ever attended, and I went there for only one reason, to try to get a clause in the platform supporting United States entry into the World Court. The chairman of the Resolutions Committee was the senator from Tennessee, Cordell Hull, whom I found accessible and friendly, and we worked at the draft together, though the final text reflected his senatorial caution more than my eagerness for a full and frank commitment.

Shortly after the elections which had swept Roosevelt into power, I was in Washington and called on Senator Hull in the senatorial office building to discuss the outlook. I said that I supposed Norman Davis would be Secretary of State as he had held high office under Wilson. Senator Hull heartily agreed but said that for some reason which he couldn't make out, Roosevelt had been inaccessible to him, although he had been his strongest supporter in the South. He was much put out about it and said that evidently his services had been forgotten. Only a week or so later it was announced that he himself was to be Secretary of State. Instead of sending him a letter of congratulations, which would have been hard to write in view of our conversation, I called on him at his senate office. As the door was opened he got up from his desk at the back of the room and came over to me with a winning smile, and before I could say a word, said: "I still think Norman would have been a better choice!" It was all so disarming, so intuitive. He kept me on to talk of the problems ahead, the first of many such talks in the months and years which followed.

It was this intuition, this sense of what people were thinking that was the key to his success in both domestic politics and diplomacy. It was also the key to his cautious, almost conservative policy in foreign affairs. Once, in my campaign for the League of Nations I got the United States Chamber of Commerce to poll their local chambers on the question whether they would support an international sanction against an aggressor—the old issue of the League—and the response was over 60 per cent in the affirmative. But, when I took this vote to Secretary Hull, he refused to take it seriously, for he said that it couldn't be relied upon when challenged, and in any case Congress wouldn't act on it. The memory of Wilson's defeat was still too strong. The one point on which we wholly agreed was the need for lowering the tariff barriers, which had been raised to unprecedented heights by the Smoot-Hawley Tariff, passed after the crash of 1929 to make the nation "self-contained and self-containing," and signed with special gold pens by President Hoover, in spite of the fact that it had been denounced by a statement signed by a thousand members of the American Economic Association. Against this economic nationalism Hull had fought in the Senate, the low tariff traditions of the South strengthened by a study of Adam Smith. But he was too experienced in politics to be a doctrinaire freetrader and as Secretary of State proposed only reciprocal tariff reductions in treaties with nations meeting our terms, and with the possibility of extending their scope by the most favored nation clause. This proved to be a lasting contribution in statesmanship, for the reciprocal trade treaties are still the avenue for American tariff policy.

Fortunately I was in a position to do something in support of a lessening of trade barriers through my connection with the International Chamber of Commerce. In November 1935 this organization joined with the Carnegie Endowment for International Peace in holding an important conference of distinguished business leaders from all the European countries and the United States, among them a young monetary expert from Sweden, Dag Hammarskjold. It was my task to organize this conference, although I must confess that I got lost in the highly technical arguments of specialists on science and commerce. The keynote of the conference in the words of the American President of the International Chamber of Commerce, Thomas J. Watson, "World peace through world trade," was almost immediately seized upon by Hitler's two lieutenants Goering and Schacht to turn the conference into pro-German channels.

Mr. Watson was not the kind of man to let this falsification of his formula for international peace stand without rebuttal, and, securing funds from the Carnegie Endowment, he created an Advisory Economic Committee of the American Committee of the International Chamber of Commerce, of which I was Chairman and Professor John B. Condliffe of the University of California (an economist of high standing with whom I had worked in the Institute of Pacific Relations) was editor. We made an exhaustive study of the whole problem and published some twelve studies. Mr. Watson was not satisfied with academic monographs and he prepared a moving picture film for use both in Chambers of Commerce and in schools. The argument for freer international trade reached a wide audience, especially through women's organizations, and at least one state, Iowa, was won over from isolationist protection.

It is fitting that I should pause a moment here to pay tribute to Mr. Watson, for he was a most remarkable man—a statesman in the busiest world of affairs. We were close friends for over fifteen years, a friendship which remained unbroken until his death in 1956. I came to know him first in the League of Nations Association, of which I was president and he a generous and deeply interested member. At that time, in the early twenties, his International Business Machines—the name was more a challenge than a reality—had only one factory in Endicott, New York, and a modest office on Broadway opposite City Hall. But he inspired in his staff a conviction of success and a loyalty both to him and to the company which his creative genius changed from a minor manufacturing concern into one of the greatest of business organizations.

President Roosevelt had made it clear from the beginning that he intended to be his own foreign minister. That may have been one of his reasons for choosing Cordell Hull as Secretary of State; for, unlike Norman Davis, who was intimately acquainted with European statesmen, Mr. Hull had visited Europe only once, in 1925; but in the first great test he came out ahead of the President, so far ahead indeed that his position was assured from then on. This was the World Economic and Financial Conference, held in London in the summer of 1933 at the call of the League of Nations. Although the Secretary of State was the head of the limited States delegation, the President did not consult him on the choice of the other members, and as an added slight sent Raymond Moley, of his "brain trust" entourage, to London as his personal representative, to whom the European statesmen turned as though he were another Colonel House. But that situation did not last long. The Conference had not been prepared by experts before hand, and such conferences almost always fail. I was in Geneva at the time, and found that its economic experts were much distressed over President Roosevelt's failure to understand the point of view of the Europeans. They were chiefly concerned with the problem of worthless or unstable currencies—Great Britain had been finally forced off gold in 1931—and wanted, above all, to get back to the gold standard which had worked so well in the nineteenth century.

Tariff problems seemed secondary to them. But Roosevelt, who had once lowered the gold in the dollar, took this as directed against American freedom of action in the future and wrote a bitter and abusive letter to the Conference, accusing them of having lost sight of their purpose which was "to agree on permanent solutions of world economics and not to discuss the economic policy of one nation out of the sixty-six present." It was an insulting letter, and the conference would have broken up but for the courage and persistence of Secretary Hull, who rescued it from immediate collapse. Moley having been discredited, and the monetary problem out of the way, the old champion of free trade made an eloquent appeal to the Conference to turn to what to him was still the fundamental problem. It was only a wreck of a conference, and nothing came of it, but it was a personal triumph for the man whom Roosevelt now hailed in a final cable: "Before you sail I want you to know once more of my affectionate regard and confidence in you."

The contradiction between Roosevelt's action in wrecking the Economic Conference and his kindly words to Hull can only be explained—and only in part—by the fact, now generally forgotten, that the President was as ardent a nationalist as Hoover had been. His "first hundred days" in which he fought the battle for recovery from the near bankruptcy of the nation, were based on the principle that international trade was secondary to recovery at home; and he shared a popular suspicion that international bankers in Europe were undermining the dollar. As for the war debts, on which economists urged an international settlement, he refused to allow the delegates in London to discuss them. His mind was wholly set upon the domestic scene. Here he wrote one of the finest chapters in the history of the United States, but history will also have to place over against it the fact that he wrecked the last effort at international economic action in Europe, where the aftermath of the American crash had brought new financial disaster in countries already bled white by the war. The ominous rise of militant nationalism, symbolized by Hitler's advent to power in January, 1933, was still not fully understood. But if F.D.R. had seen the demonstrations which I watched in Berlin, he might have paused before disrupting the forces of liberalism in Europe.

I came back from Europe with Secretary Hull on the small, slow liner, *President Harding* (of all ships!) and for over a week, with our deck chairs side by side, we spent many hours together, reviewing the situation, both at home and abroad. As he had never specialized in finance, leaving that for the Treasury, he was less critical of the President's "bomb shell" than of the refusal of the European governments to give more than polite attention to his appeal for lessening the barriers to international trade. He was especially disappointed in the British, to whom imperial preference had become as much a fetish as protectionism in the United States. But if Secretary Hull was reluctant to blame the President for his letter, he had no kind words for Raymond Moley, whom he blamed—apparently in error—for having got himself appointed as a special envoy of F.D.R. to oversee the conference. Moley was certainly not to blame for the President's letter, which really hit him more than it did the Secretary; nor could he be blamed if the European governments treated him like another Colonel House. But the Secretary needed his Tennessee mountain vernacular to describe the incident with sufficient strength and color.

I have gone into the history of this conference in detail, not only because of its importance but also because it is now almost forgotten. My interest, however, was less in it than in the plans which I discussed with Secretary Hull on the voyage home. I had thought up what I hoped might offer him a new way for lessening international trade barriers, by the use of the International Labor Office, and I drafted a memorandum on it, which at least took our minds off the London Conference for several days. The main idea was simple—nations which raised the wages and standard of living in the production of goods should have favored tariff treatment in the country to which they were exported. The plan was directed against the argument for high tariffs because of low wage costs in other countries. It also aimed to increase the total volume of foreign trade by the increased prosperity of the workers, who make up the great body of consumers. I admitted that the problem of comparable wages would be difficult and sometimes impossible. But the International Labor Office, the scientific secretariat of the I.L.O. could at least furnish basic standards for nations to negotiate on.

Neither Mr. Hull nor his economic assistants liked the scheme, because of its lack of a fundamental free trade principle. I said it was the Trojan horse to get inside the protectionist walls. But I had to admit that it was at least premature, as we were not yet (until 1939) members of the International Labor Organization. This gave me a rare opportunity to explain the I.L.O.'s origin and method of working. The result was that, in 1934, at his request I drafted the document for Senator Pittman, chairman of the Senate Committee on Foreign Affairs, which, with the strong support of the Secretary of Labor, Frances Perkins, made the United States a member of the I.L.O.

The London Economic Conference has now passed into the limbo of forgotten things, but its failure was a blow to the League of Nations which had sponsored it, at a time when the League's prestige had already been shattered by Japan's conquest of Manchuria. That first chapter of World War II had been timed by the Japanese militarists to fit the calendar of economic disaster in Europe, the aftermath of the American economic collapse of 1929, when in 1931, one of the largest banking houses of the Continent, the Kreditanstalt of Austria, failed and the Bank of England had to go off gold. The tragic consequences of the abstention of the United States from the League of Nations were clearly revealed on that occasion. The British were unwilling to apply the League sanction against Japan unless supported by the United States and, as we have seen, all that Secretary of State Stimson could offer was "the Stimson Doctrine," that the United States would not recognize a change of status brought about by force.

By telephone to Norman Davis in Geneva, Secretary Stimson proposed an international conference called by the League of Nations, but the Japanese militarists would have none of it, and the League ceased to function in Asia. Now in the economic field its effort to build a European community was torpedoed by F.D.R. It had only a slight chance of success at best, in view of the rise of Fascism and Nazism, but the best economists of Europe were working for it, and liberal opinion was bitterly critical of Roosevelt.

The second chapter of World War II began in 1935 when Mussolini attacked Ethiopia. Again the Secretary of State was unable to work within the League of Nations, but he was willing to work alongside it. When the British Foreign Secretary, Sir Samuel Hoare, speaking at Geneva, made a veiled reference to the shipment of American oil to the Italian navy, he either did not know or preferred not to know that Secretary Hull was doing his best to get the United States oil companies to stop their increasing shipments in the interests of peace. The Secretary told me that he had got assurances from the great oil companies that they would comply with his request. But he said that by some failure in diplomacy the British Foreign Office seemed not to know of this and the Foreign Ministers of Great Britain and France, Sir Samuel Hoare and M. Laval, refused to take similar action for the League of Nations, on the pretext that United States oil would be available to Italy anyway.

As I was going to England at that time, Mr. Hull asked me to make clear to the Foreign Office what he had tried to do. It was a difficult and delicate mission, and all I could do was to talk informally with my friends in the Foreign Office. It was also too late, too vague, and unofficial, and both Sir Samuel Hoare and Laval were on Mussolini's side. The League of Nations never recovered from this blow, as both Hitler and Japan soon acted in utter disregard of it in their aggressions.

It was in this connection that at Secretary Hull's request I served on a joint committee of State Department and Pentagon. I mention this only because its secretary was a young officer, Major Dwight D. Eisenhower. We had only a few meetings and nothing much came of it. But years later when the General was President of Columbia University, I called on him at the request of General Telford Taylor to ask him to use his influence in cataloguing the German war documents which had been gathered up in baskets or crates, and remained unpacked in the Pentagon or in the Archive Building. He readily agreed and a month or so later the archival work was under way—to the great advantage of historians of World War II. But in the middle of my talk with General Eisenhower he looked over at me with a genial smile and said, "You don't seem to remember that we've met before." I said that I couldn't recall our meeting. Then, with that winning frankness, now so well known, he said "When you were sent over by the State Department on that security problem, I was the young major sitting across the table taking down what you said!" Only a great man is capable of that kind of self-effacement after he has reached the heights.

To return to Secretary Hull—I realize that these reminiscences are slight, and give no adequate picture of Cordell Hull as Secretary of State, of the quiet dignity of the man in his meditative mood or the flash of anger in the eye when confronted with what seemed deception or lack of good faith in those with whom he was dealing. But, I recall one little incident which reveals the inner tenderness of this old Tennessee mountaineer. One afternoon I was sitting with him and, Robert Walton Moore, formerly Congressman from Virginia, Counselor to the Department, and the Secretary's closest friend, when a little mouse put its nose out of a hole in the wainscot just beside Secretary Hull's chair. He kept still and asked us not to move either. Then, after a reconnaisance the mouse came over beside Mr. Hull's shoes and curled up on one of them. It was the most incredible sight I have ever seen in Washington! Everyone kept absolutely still. Then as the mouse slipped back into its hole, the Secretary of State turned back to the affairs of the nation, with the casual remark, "I've been making a friend of it." I forget what we were talking about, but shall never forget the way everything stopped for Cordell Hull's mouse.

Throughout the years immediately preceding the outbreak of World War II as the ominous shadow of Japanese and Nazi aggression began to threaten international peace, there was a strong movement toward neutrality, especially in the Middle West. This resulted in a strengthening of the neutrality laws to prevent the involvement of the United States in foreign wars. Convinced that for the United States to remain neutral in a resort to war by an aggressor in violation of its pledge to settle its disputes by peaceful means would make it *particeps criminis* in the crime of such a war, I accepted the honorary presidency of a nation-wide organization for the revision of the neutrality laws to enable the United States to discriminate between aggressor and victim. With the actual outbreak of World War II this more or less academic body was merged into the Committee to Defend America by Aiding the Allies, under the leadership of the Kansas publicist William Allen White, which, according to the Secretary of State was largely influential in securing the passage of the Lend-Lease Act by the Congress. But more important than our work was the impact on the mind and conscience of the nation by the bombing of London, the heroic defense of its outnumbered air force, the ringing challenge of Churchill and the radio description of "England's greatest hour" by Edward Murrow, in the nightly message "This is London," reflecting courage by sharing in it.

World War II left nothing of the structure of peace, nothing but the faith in its ultimate restoration with all the lessons learned by catastrophe. So we began over again, in a Commission to Study the

Organization of Peace, which I founded in 1939. Once a month a hundred of us would spend Sunday, generally all day long, in the frankest of discussions, the result of which were set forth in a report, the first of an annual series, beginning with an analysis of war. These reports covered the problems of politics, economics, and international law. This work was naturally, well known in the State Department. When it set up a small committee with Sumner Welles, the Under-Secretary of State, as chairman to draft a post-war policy, both Clark Eichelberger of the League of Nations Association and I were invited to serve on it. At first it was to be kept ultra-secret, for it would not do to give either our allies or our enemies the idea that we were thinking of peace terms in the very crisis of the fighting. But it was in this committee that the first blueprint was made of a charter for the United Nations.

After some months of work, Secretary Hull held several sessions under his own chairmanship, to which he invited the members of the Foreign Relations Committees of the Senate and the House. In these open sessions there was free discussion, and I found myself in the awkward position of having to oppose the proposition backed by Mr. Welles and Dr. Bowman, the eminent geographer, that Germany should be dismembered in order to ensure a lasting peace. I held, to the contrary, that it would make a lasting peace impossible.

More embarrassing, however, was the fact that Mr. Welles was in close touch with the President and it was evident that Secretary Hull was not. Still more important was the fact that every time Mr. Welles came back from the White House he warned us against planning anything like a revival of the League of Nations. FDR was determined not to repeat the failure of Woodrow Wilson and had been much disturbed over the isolationist uproar at his suggestion that an aggressor should be "quarantined." So, all he had in mind when we began work, was an international Farm Bureau, perhaps at Des Moines, Iowa; a banking center, perhaps at London; a health center, perhaps at Paris; and other non-political bodies working on their own.

Mr. Welles asked the members of his committee on post-war planning not to refresh their memories of the League or even look at the Covenant, but to try to get something different. However, after a few months work we found that our blueprint for an internaional organization was almost the same as the Covenant. It was simply a statement of fundamental realities. This document, revised at the Conference of Dumbarton Oaks, was then worked over into the Charter of the United Nations at San Francisco.

Looking back over our blueprinting, I am inclined to think that the major blunder was the proposal to limit the Council to problems of security. The Council of the League was a general executive, ready to deal with all kinds of disputes, such as the government of the Saar. It did not meet as potential enemies on the one issue of war and peace, but as an agent of constructive politics, using conciliation as its major technique. The lack of such a body in the United Nations is increasingly felt as the Assembly becomes so great in size as to be ineffective in action.

The work of the planning committee of the State Department was kept secret, until finally, at a conference of foreign ministers in Moscow in November, 1943, Secretary Hull secured the consent of Stalin to "establish a general organization, based on the principle of the sovereign equality of all peace-loving States . . . for the maintenance of international peace and security." The result was the San Francisco Conference in April, 1945, to draft a charter for the United Nations.

Recognizing the great popular interest in the success of this conference, the State Department invited "Consultants" to its delegation, consisting of representatives of business, labor, agriculture, education, law, and religion. This semi-official body met daily during the conference, and it is not too much to say that it was chiefly responsible for the economic and social provisions of the Charter, including the problem of human rights. The State Department was opposed to this extension of the work of the United Nations to cover such vast fields of an uncharted future. The Secretary of State, Edward R. Stettinius, Jr., showed obvious indifference to our proposals when they were laid before him at the session of the Consultants. But when my colleague Judge Joseph M. Proskauer, reminded Stettinius that the members of the Consultants represented bodies that controlled four million votes, Mr. Stettinius suddenly woke to the political significance of this remark, and we had no further trouble with the State Department.

I was chairman of the Consultants for six weeks, until laid up by an attack of pneumonia which forced me to return home. I have never had a more inspiring experience than that of helping, at last, to weld the aspirations for peace into a world-wide organization. It seemed as if the long road which I had been traveling for years was at last reaching its goal. Yet such hopes were soon overcast.

Even during the conferences the attitude of the USSR was disquieting, as President Truman made clear to the dour Molotov in an outspoken demand that the Kremlin live up to its engagements. The way in which this divergence sharpened into a cold war lies outside the limits of this story, but it would be wholly wrong to end it there.

The Charter of the United Nations, drafted at San Francisco, provides an inspiring program for the organization of peace, which both sides of the great communist controversy invoke to justify their policies. This is not mere political hypocrisy; it marks the growth of new, if divergent, ideals coexistent in a world in which war had always been held to be the final and legitimate instrument of national policy. The full and adequate implementation of the revolutionary concept in the Charter may be long delayed. It took the English over four centuries to perfect representative government and the rule of law, and that was within a homogeneous nation. The United States is the most heterogeneous body in history, yet the forces of modern science are creating an interplay of interests, which is the way people will be living from now to the end of time. We are still only pioneering, but as Bergson, the philosopher, pointed out half a century ago, scientific invention and discovery hold promise of ever-increasing betterment and of man's release from unremitting toil, as well as from want and poverty. These, as well as the renunciation of war, are now the concern of the United Nations. The success or failure of that organization is, therefore, a measure of civilization itself. There can be no surer guarantee of its ultimate success.

314

CHAPTER 20

The Control of Atomic Energy and the Recovery of Western Europe

In February, 1945, the League of Nations Association was transformed into the American Association for the United Nations, with Mr. Sumner Welles, former Under Secretary of State, and I as the two honorary presidents, and Clark Eichelberger continuing his splendid service as Director. My own work for the United Nations continued through the Commission to Study the Organization of Peace, now under the chairmanship of Professor Arthur Holcombe.

But more pressing than these continuing problems were the two problems directly due to the war, the control of atomic energy and the recovery of Western Europe under the Marshall Plan.

The first, and most obdurate of problems was the control of atomic energy. In August, 1945, at Hiroshima and Nagasaki, the conclusion which I had drawn in 1927 of the revolution in warfare due to science* was tragically fulfilled, and a new and terrible chapter in history was opened, that of thermonuclear warfare. Appalled at the prospect, public opinion insisted that steps be taken to check such a development, and in January, 1946, the United Nations Commission on Atomic Energy was created. At its first meeting, in June, 1946, the United States delegation, headed by Mr. Bernard M. Baruch, called for an International Atomic Development Authority, exercising direct control of all atomic activities in all

* See Chapter XII.

countries, a supra-national body, free from the veto of the Security Council of the United Nations, in short, an irresponsible body with the greatest power in the world.

While fully recognizing the sincerity of purpose which prompted Mr. Baruch and his associates, I could not accept their conclusion. The proposal to set up a world government primarily as a defense mechanism against the danger of atomic war would threaten the structure of democratic life throughout the world, in view of the fact that atomic power was also an ultimate power for peace-time economy. Therefore, in line with the discussions in such bodies as the Council on Foreign Relations and the Foreign Policy Association, in 1946 I organized a Committee on Atomic Energy under the auspices of the Carnegie Endowment for International Peace, composed of some fifty of the leading physical and political scientists and organizers of industry.

The report of our Committee differed from the official American proposal in that it did not provide for the ownership of all uranium and thorium in the world by an international commission which would also operate all atomic power plants. Instead, our report left such ownership in the hands of national bodies in each country, while an International Atomic Energy Commission vested with wide powers of control would be charged with the positive function of promoting the utilization of atomic energy for peaceful purposes. Each of the five states' permanent members of the Security Council would select one member of the International Commission, and the General Assembly would select four other members so that it would not be a mere organ of the Security Council, and its decisions would be taken by a simple majority vote. Thus, the veto of the Security Council would be at least partially overcome. The International Commission would have power in the course of its routine activities to take preventive measures against a nation shown by inspection to be planning atomic war. In the case of actual resort to atomic war, the Security Council would act under the Charter. The International Commission would have its own staff and maintain offices, laboratories and plants for its work. It would be assisted by an advisory board of scientific and technical experts, and monthly reports would be made to it by each national commission. It is perhaps

316

unnecessary to add that neither the Baruch plan nor that of the Carnegie Endowment was ever realized, although the Endowment's subcommittee report on the *Feasibility of International Inspection of Raw Materials* was the first document which the Scientific and Technical Committee of the United Nations Commission was able to agree upon after their long stalemate in the summer of 1946.

The pioneering work of the United Nations Commission has not been sufficiently recognized. On July 5, almost six months after its creation, Mr. Baruch, as the American representative on it, offered a plan which would have brought the proposed Atomic Energy Authority within the Charter of the United Nations, by the provision that all serious offenses, constituting a threat to the peace, should fall within the jurisdiction of the Security Council. However, the opposition of the USSR to effective inspection left the whole problem unsolved.

The Baruch plan for the control of atomic energy was matched in political daring by the proposal of Secretary of State Marshall that the United States should ensure the recovery of Western Europe from the disastrous effects of the war, by sharing the cost of that incredibly difficult task. So great an innovation in international affairs called for a campaign of education in American public opinion, and I worked on it long days and nights, until the early morning hours, alongside the new president of the Carnegie Endowment, Alger Hiss, concentrating on anti-communist strategy because Moscow had turned violently against the Marshall Plan.

This brings me to the strangest chapter in the story of my life. On the retirement of Dr. Nicholas Murray Butler from the presidency of the Carnegie Endowment, John Foster Dulles, chairman of the Board of Trustees, nominated Mr. Hiss for the position. He had a brilliant record in Washington, secretary and law clerk to Supreme Court Justice Holmes (1929-1930), Assistant General Counsel to the Agricultural Adjustment Administration (1933-1935), and other legal offices. Then as Assistant Secretary of State he was assigned the important task of organizing the San Francisco Conference for the creation of the United Nations. His nomination to the presidency of the Endowment was unanimously accepted by the Trustees and everything done by him as President justified that

317

choice. Whatever Mr. Hiss may or may not have done before he came to the Endowment—and John W. Davis, Vice President of the Endowment, agreed with me that we do not yet have the full story—the fact remains that while I knew him, Mr. Hiss worked strongly and persistently against the policies of the USSR. I testified to this effect at his trial.

CHAPTER 21

The Last Journey to Europe

In the summer of 1955, at the age of eighty-one, I paid my last visit to Europe. Fateful years had passed since I had left it on the eve of World War II, when the structure of peace on which I had been working for the twenty years of the life of the League of Nations crashed under the blows of the Axis Powers. To restore that structure or erect one like it, in the United Nations, had been my chief interest during those trying years. But again the magnificence of the world organization—and it was magnificent in conception—was menaced by the rift between the Communist and the free nations; and the center of this conflict shifted from the United Nations to Western Europe, with the North Atlantic Treaty Organization (NATO) as the military shield for the free nations against Soviet aggression, and the Organization for European Economic Cooperation (OEEC), the creation of the Marshall Plan, as the expression of common economic interest. A new chapter was opening in the history of that part of Europe which had been the nursery of war in the past. It was to study this problem at first hand that I sailed for Europe the first week of June.

The European Movement, the term used to cover the whole effort to unify Western Europe, began with the pioneering work of Count Coudenhove-Kalergi, whose book *Pan Europe,* published in Vienna in 1923, proposed a political federation like that of the United States. It was a bold challenge to the national state system and, indeed, to the whole history of Europe, but with courage and eloquence he held meetings in various countries and won support for the idea from statesmen as well as publicists. I always remained skeptical of it, however, for I did not believe that the parallel with the history of the United States was valid. Even there full sovereignty of the federal system was only won by a desperate civil war. The federation of the European nations would involve a much greater strain on ancient ties. I was, therefore, doubtful about the reality of this first phase of the European Movement, in spite of the fact that at first it had the backing of Briand and Churchill. My judgment was justified by Briand's vague generalities when he presented the idea to the League of Nations and by Churchill's subsequent withdrawal from support for the Movement, of which he had been the most eloquent advocate. In his speech at Zurich University in 1946 Churchill proposed as a "sovereign remedy" for the tragedy of European wars, a United States of Europe, which would "provide a structure under which it could dwell in peace, in safety and freedom. . . ." But this was one time when Churchill spoke irresponsibly, for he never followed up this dream of a federated Europe. My doubt as to the reality of a political union seemed justified.

Then the incredible happened when six western nations—France, West Germany, Italy, Belgium, the Netherlands, and Luxembourg —created a supra-national body, the Coal and Steel Community, to deal, independent of any governmental interference, with the heavy industries—coal, steel, and transportation—which are the indispensable munition industries of modern war. The purely businesslike name of the Community was misleading, for it had a government of its own—legislature, court, and executive offices. The Movement for European Union was being realized not by working from the top, but from the practical needs of an interdependent economy.

It was, however, the implied guarantee of peace which the French Foreign Minister Robert Schuman emphasized when he presented the plan to the French Chamber of Deputies. But, once launched on its career, the success of the Coal and Steel Community led its brilliant founder, Jean Monnet, to mobilize popular support for an attack on the whole war system by a proposal to create a European Defense Community (EDC), which would in-

320

ternationalize the armies themselves. The rejection of this plan by the Chamber of Deputies showed that the old nationalism was by no means dead. But if internationalizing the armies was going too far—and to the distress of some of my friends I said that I thought it was—there still remained the question which interested me most: what were the possibilities of the Western European Union (WEU), the political body which had begun as a consultative body at Strasbourg, composed of members of parliaments and governments?

Stirred by new hope, but sobered by past experiences, I sailed for Europe to study this new chapter in the history of freedom. Happily my daughter Helen went along with me. She was already an established painter, with canvases in museums, and while I spent my time in interviews, she set up her easel in London, Paris, Chartres, Strasbourg, or Luxembourg; and while my memory of our journey grows dim, I have only to look at her canvases, glowing with light and color, to recall those scenes of my last visit to Europe. Happily, too, the European offices of International Business Machines, following instructions from New York, looked after us in London and drove us from city to city in luxurious cars, so I was able to study the problem, not only from foreign offices but on the spot. To get my bearings, I went first to London. Somehow it seemed the natural place to start, but I soon found from intimate talks with officials at the Foreign Office and members of parliament that there was little to be gained from this second-hand way of studying the problem of continental politics. The British still remained isolationist at heart, almost as distrustful of the French as of the Germans. In diplomatic circles there was complete skepticism, except for a few "back benchers" in Parliament who had attended sessions of the European Assembly at Strasbourg.

Fortunately, just as I arrived in Europe a conference of Foreign Ministers held at Messina had greatly cleared the situation by recognizing the Strasbourg meeting as the Council of Europe, and by setting up a working office in London. But the British, who had never joined the Steel and Coal Community, still held back. Foreign Secretary Eden had been only an observer at Messina, and when I tried to find out more about the London office of the Council, I found that it had been set up in an ordinary house at 2 Eaton Place, a purely residential section. The Belgian in charge of it told me I was the first visitor who had ever found his way to it. My friends at the Foreign Office seemed even a little taken aback by my having discovered it.

However, on June 8 the *Times* spilled the beans by a news item from Paris from which I quote, because it stated the program for European union with the clarity of French diplomacy at its best. In a press conference at the quai d'Orsay, M. Pinet, the Foreign Minister, summarizing the results of the Messina conference, stated that:

> It had been decided to set up a new organization which would finance and direct atomic research in all six countries of the European Coal and Steel Community. Cooperation in the fields of transport, gas and electricity would also be developed, by giving wider powers to organizations already existing.
>
> A European common market was still the aim of all six governments, but this could only be brought about progressively. At Messina France had secured the recognition by her partners of the prior need for: (1) a common tariff policy; (2) the equalization of social and wage rates; (3) a fund for the reconversion of local industries affected by international competition; (4) general agreement between all members before the adoption of convertibility by any one of them.

There were no comments in the *Times*. Evidently it was time to leave London for Paris and the countries of the Coal and Steel communities.

Before leaving, however, I had the chance to state my point of view in an address at the Royal Institute of International Affairs. I made two points which seemed to me vital for the future of the free world. First of all, European union would not develop into a federation like the United States, as some idealists seemed to think. It would develop functionally, where common interest impelled unity of action and policy, rather than by the acceptance of a new federal state system. The European Coal and Steel Community had been the first to realize this unity of interest in its own field. Now it was proposing to take over the vast potentialities of atomic energy. No one could tell how far this movement would go, but it was no longer merely a dream.

I ended my address with a prophecy which has now been fulfilled, five years later. I pointed out that the control of atomic energy would become the major problem of all nations when the process for making the A bomb was cheapened, and I said that the history of applied science showed that such a cheapening was inevitable, because it was a problem of engineering. The progress of steam power had depended not on the power in the steam, but on the invention of Bessemer steel, which made the engines safe. The same dependence on engineering was true of electricity as Edison had shown.

I pointed out that the cheapening of the thermonuclear process would be a political fact of the first importance because it would mean that the smaller nations would have a different place in the power structure of nations. From this point of view little Belgium, I implied, with its access to African uranium, could rank as a great power. It would not need to accumulate the vast supply of atomic weapons that the great powers could bring together. It would need only half a dozen bombs to acquire a new influence on the political decisions of its neighbors. Half a dozen such bombs as were then available would be enough. This possibility of the small nations acquiring new power can make it either a nuisance on the pathway of progress or an aid to progress itself; but it raises international problems of an entirely new nature and recasts the old ones in a completely different setting from that of the national state system of history. This is an entirely different situation from what has existed until now. We have not sufficiently awakened to the problem which this revolutionary fact implies.

A few weeks later I had the chance to state my theory before one of the leading atomic scientists, then visiting Europe, and found him convinced that nothing like that could happen. The thermonuclear process would always be the monopoly of the great powers. He and his colleagues on the Atomic Energy Commission were wrong, for all the time, a cheaper process had been known and had been discarded for the gaseous diffusion plants such as those on which the United States had spent over three billion dollars.

It was not until October 11, 1960, that the *New York Times* published an account of a cheaper process and pointed out that this

323

was creating an entirely new problem in the control of atomic energy. My address at the Royal Institute of International Affairs, five years before, was finally and fully justified. Today, in fact, the possibilities have become even more extraordinary, for the new, undeveloped nation of the Congo, for example, with the world's largest known supply of uranium could soon become a major power, given time to utilize the capital and skill offered from abroad. The cheaper thermonuclear process will, of course, cut the time required to a minimum.

My two weeks in London had been sobering in more ways than one. The city itself still bore the wounds of war. Although the wreckage of the blitz had been removed everywhere, there were hundreds of acres of gaunt cellar walls, mute reminders of the hours when England remained the one last hope of freedom in Europe. But Britain's "greatest hour" was for the defense of its heritage, not for the untried experiment of the structure of peace, which was taking new shape on the Continent.

On my arrival in Paris there was a telephone call from the Director General of policy at the Ministry of Foreign Affairs, M. Danridan, inviting me to come to the Quai d'Orsay. It was almost thirty years since I had been there, in the days of the Briand peace offer, and I was puzzled at the interest in my visit to Europe. Evidently the young men at the Foreign Office were concerned that I should give a good report on the French attitude on European union. I was told that arrangements would be made for me to keep closely in touch with the French delegation at Strasbourg, and I was taken over to see the specialist working on disarmament. He had no new ideas, but the incident recalled my work on Herriot's plans for a disarmament conference on which I had worked with M. Cassin in the last days of the League of Nations. I always found it somewhat strange that I could work more closely with the French Foreign Office than with the British, but I left the Quai d'Orsay convinced that it was more forward looking than at least the British Civil Service, whose chief service was to keep the machinery of empire—or commonwealth—going.

More important than these contacts with the Quai d'Orsay was my visit with M. Robert Schuman, who, as Minister of Foreign

324

Affairs, had piloted the Coal and Steel Community—known then as the Schuman Plan—through the Chamber of Deputies. I had long talks with him at his new office in the Ministry of Justice. He had not lost any of his optimism. He was particularly happy that M. Spaak was chairman of the committee to "study" the plans of the Messina Conference for European Union. To M. Schuman that, alone, was a guarantee that the program was real. He also paid a warm tribute to his colleagues in the cabinet for their continued support and co-operation.

This confidence in the sincerity of French policy was strongly insisted upon in the Ministry of Public Works, which was responsible for the detailed plans for enlarging the Coal and Steel Community to include transportation. On the invitation of the Chef de Cabinet of this ministry, M. René Servoise, I went over these plans with the minister, M. Corniglion Molinier. He said that the plan was nowhere near so revolutionary as people thought, for already 40 per cent of the railway rates were under the Coal and Steel Community. The Swiss and the British were the only opponents to the the plan, but it could be set in operation by a common fund for financing, modeled somewhat on the Bank and Fund in Washington.

This was the bright side of the picture. But I found that the friends of Jean Monnet, including my old friend M. Henri Bonnet, former ambassador at Washington, were still distrustful of the fine promises of the government. Evidently Paris was little better than London for studying the new Europe. So we left for Strasbourg, to be at the center of action.

The city of Strasbourg—a crossroads of the old and new—was an ideal site for the shadow parliament of Europe, reaching out from the old city with its timbered houses, along broad boulevards, to the new buildings of the Council of Europe.

The Consultative Assembly of the Council of Europe was in session when we arrived. At this meeting, composed of one hundred and thirty-five members from sixteen countries, it got a shot in the arm from the presence of practically all the Foreign Ministers of Western Europe, fifteen in all, including Harold Macmillan, later Prime Minister of Great Britain. The sessions which I attended lasted from 10 A.M. to 1 P.M. and from 3 P.M. to 7 P.M., I was frankly exhausted at the end of a week of listening to so many debates. Most of them were based on the steps which each government had taken or was planning to take in fulfillment of the Messina program. It was at once clear that the Council of Europe was facing up to realities, beginning to co-ordinate policies instead of merely talking in generalities. It dealt with all the phases of functional international action along the lines laid down by the Benelux Powers at Messina: international transport control, extension of postal and telegraph facilities, lessening of barriers to trade, and, finally, the control of atomic energy.

This was as much as could be done without a revolutionary change in the European state system. The Council of Europe was for consultation and agreement among sovereign powers. It was a convention, not a parliament with authority to act independently of its members. It was merely applying and extending, as far as it could, the revolution that had already taken place in the creation of the Coal and Steel Community. So, at the end of a week in Strasbourg, we left for Luxembourg, where I had engagements with the Prime Minister of the Duchy, M. Joseph Bech and M. René Mayer, former Prime Minister of France, who had succeeded M. Monnet as head of the Coal and Steel Community. They surprised me by telling me that they had read some of my books, and we talked at length about the impact of the Coal and Steel Community on the political problems of European unity. M. Mayer brought up the point which the Quai d'Orsay had made to me in Paris, that the agreement on atomic energy raw materials between the United States and Belgium was a real obstacle to Europeanizing atomic energy production. When I tried to tell him that the United States would not want to be "a dog in the manger," we found there was no parallel expression in French. Sir Cecil Weir, the "observer" of British industry at the Coal and Steel Community, felt sure that M. Spaak would find a way out.

M. Bech had been on the committee of three—himself, M. Spaak and M. Beyen from Holland—which had been meeting in Brussels to "study" the way to enlarge the Coal and Steel Community to include transportation, electricity and atomic energy. They had been surprised to have support of the German representative as well, although he had come merely as an observer.

From Luxembourg we went on to Brussels, which, as I had learned both in Paris and Strasbourg, was the power house which was transforming the European Movement—which Churchill had hailed and then left in the lurch—into a working organism.

I spent three busy days in Brussels, ending with the talk with M. Spaak. He was having conferences with Benelux statesmen until 6:30, but showed no sign of fatigue and kept me for an hour in which we went into the heart of things. In these complicated political situations, he said, personalities and personal relationships count. But when I suggested that what the European union needed most was forceful, eloquent, imaginative leadership, his reply showed his own very winning personality. He said that not long ago he was addressing a political meeting in a country town, and his theme, as always for the last twenty years, was the unity of Europe and the criminal folly of nationalism. After he finished, an old farmer came up to him and said that it was splendid, but why hadn't M. Spaak been saying it before? He laughed gaily over it.

Then I turned to the problem of atomic energy, especially the plans for the control and development through the Coal and Steel Community. He had not had time to follow the blueprints of Paris and Strasbourg, but the one time when I saw intense concentration in his eyes was when I opened up on the cheapening of the thermo-nuclear process and the revolutionary effect this would have on the power structure of the European States, offering a new place to smaller nations, not now but in the future. As we parted it was agreed that the interview would continue by letters and documents. But that was not to be.

There was one more capital to visit, Bonn. At Bonn the head of the IBM office met the train, and we arranged to visit the American Embassy in the morning. Dr. Conant, our ambassador, had had to go to Geneva, but he had left a message for me and instructions to his staff. I found that the first secretary of the embassy, Raymond Lisle, had been a student of mine, and he took pride in recalling to me portions of some of my Columbia lectures from as long ago as 1938. He brought in other members of the staff, and we spent over two hours going over the whole German situation.

I had known that there was no chance of meeting the one man I was most anxious to see, Dr. Hallstein, who had made a great impression on both Prime Minister Bech and M. Spaak by his firm adherence to their plans for extending the Messina program. He was back in Brussels, while Chancellor Adenauer was in Switzerland. The visit to Bonn was rescued from complete failure, however, by Mr. Lisle who got me in touch with the official of the Foreign Office who was actually in charge of the negotiations. This was Frau Putkammer, the only woman official with whom I had talked in my whole journey. She was thoroughly conversant with every phase of the movement for European unity, but was strongly in favor of solving the problems of the six nation group before dealing with the larger issue of the free trade national group led by London. It should be union, not merely co-operation. Her point of view was shared by Dr. Caspari, who was to represent West Germany at the United Nations in the fall. It was also strongly endorsed by the German ambassador in London, to which I returned by plane from Dusseldorf. Again, an IBM plane was waiting for me at the London airport.

There were a few days left for London before leaving for home. I at once got in touch with my friends at the Foreign Office. They were still skeptical of the six nation supra-national approach to Europe. This was becoming more than a difference of opinion; it was beginning to look like a fundamental split between the British and the Continental nations, the difference between a willingness to co-operate and a willingness to unite. To trained British civil servants—and to British opinion generally—international bodies were simply instruments for getting things done rather than the initial stage of a new undeveloped organ of international government. Here, in another setting, was the same kind of distrust of commitments for the future which had led the British to reject the Protocol of Geneva thirty years before. But this time, the Continental nations were going ahead in disregard of British failure to join.

The last journey to Europe had come to an end. What were the conclusions to be drawn from it? My answer to this question was set forth in the closing section of the diary which I had kept, and from which this narrative is drawn.

There is no doubt that Western Europe is undergoing a revolutionary change in which the old state system of absolute sovereignties is giving way to a new international complex; but it is equally clear that history determines the way the different nations look at it. Continental nations, inheritors of Roman tradition, built their political institutions like architects, mindful of form and structure; to the British, politics is more like engineering, the test being whether it works. Its motive power is adjustment to practical needs. As a matter of fact, this same pragmatic process is at work in the reshaping of the Continental nations. The supra-nationalism of Jean Monnet was, after all, a way to get things done—in other words the practical method which the British so strongly emphasize. The solution of their differences lies in opening the doors of the Union to wider avenues of trade, and inviting not only Great Britain, but America and all the free world to associate itself with the Union. Some such idea, as we have already seen, lay in the grand design of General De Gaulle, but obscured and falsified by his insistence on French nationalism. It was also the slogan of the movement Union Now, led in the United States by Clarence Streit. Fortunately that movement, which began as a movement for political federation, has now put the accent on co-operation in an economic Atlantic union.

Finally, on September 7, 1960, President Eisenhower signed a bill, passed by Congress, which offers a new approach to the whole question. It sets up a "United States Citizens Commission on NATO," comprised of twenty private citizens appointed by Vice-President Nixon and Speaker Rayburn to organize and take part in a convention composed of similar commissions from other NATO countries "to explore means by which greater co-operation and unity of purpose can be developed to the end that democratic freedom may be promoted by economic and political means." In the election campaign both candidates gave assurance of their interest in this participation by the United States in the movement for union of the free world. After the elections no time was lost to make good this promise. Vice President-Elect Lyndon B. Johnson, accompanied by Senator J. W. Fulbright, Chairman of the Foreign Affairs Committee of the Senate, and Senator John Sherman Cooper, Republican of Kentucky, attended a meeting of the parliamentary

329

conference of NATO, strongly urging the enlargement of its program to include international economic relations. To make good on this will mean action by the Congress, but Mr. Johnson sought to reassure his European listeners:

> Our recent elections have resulted in the choice of new leadership. In no sense is that a repudiation of President Eisenhower's support for the instruments of mutual strength in Western Europe.
>
> A new generation of Americans—who came to early maturity fighting for freedom on the fields of Europe and the islands of the Pacific—is coming to power in the leadership of our land.
>
> In their hearts is a determination to make the most vigorous use of America's resources and capacities to assure their children, your children, and the children of all nations a life without war—a future of peace.

The Vice President further pledged that the United States would do "everything in its power" to strengthen the North Atlantic Treaty Organization with the long term objective of "a true Atlantic community with common institutions." The pledge was also a challenge not only to American isolation but to the structure of sovereign national states, which had been the heritage of centuries of historical development. It was a recognition of the reality of a new international world.

CHAPTER 22

The Long Way to Freedom

The last visit to Europe was the last of my travels. It was also the last of that pioneering along the frontiers of the organization of peace which had been my chief work under the auspices of the Carnegie Endowment, of which I had become Acting President in 1948 and President in 1949. In 1950 at the age of seventy-six the time had come to retire and the presidency of the Endowment was taken over by Dr. Joseph E. Johnson, of Williams College, who had been a member of the State Department during the war and had left golden memories there. I was happy to find in him a kindred spirit, generous but critical in his judgment on international affairs. The Trustees of the Endowment still kept an office for me and on my eightieth birthday, in a meeting presided over by President Grayson Kirk, dedicated a plaque to the James Thomson Shotwell Library and celebrated the occasion with a dinner presided over by Edward Murrow, then a Trustee.

Except for continued membership in the Commission to Study the Organization of Peace and the Committee for a Sane Nuclear Policy, I took almost no part in the new, and more dangerous, cold war with which Khrushchev was challenging the free world.

But there was one service in which I continued active, the American Fund for Czechoslovak Refugees, of which I was chairman and Dr. Jan Papanek president. In this work Dr. Papanek and his associates kept alive the ideals of President Masaryk saving from Nazi and Communist tyranny thousands of Czechoslovaks and helping them to settle in the Americas and various other countries of the free world.

If held back from further active service, there was one service for the free world which I could do. Its history had never been written in terms of its greatest achievement, freedom itself. The confusion in the efforts to build a new unity for free nations of western Europe was due in large measure to the fact that freedom meant different things to different peoples; and this, in turn, was largely due to their variant histories. On the other hand the communist revolution so cut across the history of Russia and eastern Europe—and China—as to offer a solidity of strength and unity of purpose which the West, mindful of its heritage of freedom, could not match. With so little history behind it, it still presumed to present the West with the challenge, "history is on our side."

I decided to meet that challenge on the grounds which history itself presented, and trace the long process of civilization, from primitive life to our own time. First of all I concentrated on the history of the United States in a volume entitled *The United States in History*.* This grew out of a memorandum which I had prepared at the suggestion of Professor Gilbert Murray for the League of Nations Committee on Intellectual Cooperation, an effort to make clear to my European colleagues the real meaning of American history. Then in 1959 at the age of eighty-five I enlarged the horizon to cover the history of all mankind in a volume entitled *The Long Way to Freedom*.† The publication of this volume was celebrated at the Carnegie Endowment luncheon, presided over by my friend Albert Edelman. These works embody my philosophy of history and also touch upon the vital issues of the present and the future, and I have drawn upon the text of *The Long Way to Freedom* for the closing paragraphs of this long story of my own life and times.

More potent than all the armies of all the nations, thought is grappling with human destiny. As Marshal Jan Smuts has so eloquently put it, mankind has struck its tents and is on the march in a vast unending trek of pioneers into a new civilization, of which only the distant outlines lie

* *The United States in History*. New York: Simon & Schuster, 1956.
† *The Long Way to Freedom*. Indianapolis: The Bobbs-Merrill Co., 1959.

before us, indistinct but shining far away. But we cannot leave history behind us as we make it. It still stays with us, to warn and to inspire. "The past is prelude. . . ." That greatest line of the greatest English poet is inscribed on the National Archives Building in Washington; but it does more than remind us of a nation's achievement; it is a summary of the long story we have been telling here: for the story of freedom is the story of all mankind.

CHAPTER 23

The Road to the Hills

While I was still only an adjunct-professor, struggling to make ends meet on an inadequate salary, we learned from an artist in the art colony of Woodstock in the Catskills of a hundred-acre farm on the slope of Overlook Mountain which could be bought for $2,000. Margaret and I had paid an over-night visit to Woodstock the year before, when we went to visit Professor and Mrs. John Dewey. The purchase price might as well have been ten times that amount so far as we were concerned, but my friend and colleague Charles A. Beard had just received a large inheritance and offered to buy the farm if we wanted it and let me rebuy it from him when we got ready. I insisted on a business agreement at interest. The farm itself was security for the loan as I slowly paid it off, but Beard could easily have placed it on mortgages in his native Indiana, and I never ceased to be grateful to him for an act of friendship which was to make possible a wholly new chapter in our family life.

This is the community which is home to us, in the fullest sense of the word, more than the apartment in the city. A really hard blow came the first night we arrived in Woodstock to take possession. We were having some repairs made to the old farm house and went to a neighboring boardinghouse for the night. Just after midnight we were awakened by shouts that our house was on fire. By the time we reached it, it was a roaring furnace. I had forgotten to transfer the fire insurance when buying the place, and the former owner tried to collect it.

So we had no home to go to and had to build a new one. It had a studio for Margaret to paint in and later for Helen, who joined us about that time and early decided to make painting a career. I had a study to myself also. We put it on a high ridge with a view to the south over sixty miles of the Hudson Valley and a blue mountain gap on the west for the sunset.

But this new home had to be paid for. I taught an extra four summer months at the University of Chicago, gave additional lectures all the next year, wrote articles for magazines and edited history textbooks. I used to say that I could hear the scratching of my pen sawing wood and the lectures driving nails. It was not until 1910 that the house was completed enough to rent, and for the next two years we were in Europe. On our second long stay in Europe after World War I, our house was rented by George Bellows, and some of his most famous pictures were painted in its studio.

The years that followed were rich in art and music and in friendships both of neighbors and foreign guests. Painting still mirrored beauty in color and line, not yet having got lost in abstraction. Chamber music had—and still has—something like a shrine in a rough shed in the Maverick woods where such musicians as George Barère, the flutist, William Kroll, the violinist, and Horace Britt, the cellist, interpreted along with visiting pianists, the great works of Beethoven and Mozart under the baton of the aging Pierre Henrot and then—and still continuing—under that of the distinguished composer, Alexander Semmler. There were also basket picnics with our neighbors on our lawn and gay celebrations of birthdays, culminating in a surprise party on my eightieth birthday, when over two hundred neighbors marched up the hill to our house with banners and music. Mr. Thomas J. Watson—only a few months younger than I— drove all the way up with Mrs. Watson from New York, as did my friend Norman Cousins, the editor of the *Saturday Review,* who acted as master of ceremonies.

There were also keen discussions on politics and economics throughout the summers, for Woodstock had become a haven for intellectuals. Of these, one of our dearest friends was Walter Weyl, editor on *The New Republic,* the weekly oracle of The New Freedom, which traced its varied career under such diverse leaderships as those of Theodore Roosevelt and Woodrow Wilson. Walter Weyl's analysis was always touched with a sense of humor as in his book *The Tired Liberal,* with its frank recognition of the untiring work of the professional politician. Others of our friends, like John Kingsbury, were less patient of the slow processes of democracy, faced by the swifter decisions of communist Russia.

There were also visitors, mostly foreigners, with whom I had worked in their own countries. There were, among others, Count Sforza, formerly Foreign Minister of Italy, then a refugee from Mussolini—whose offer of high office he had indignantly refused; Huh Shi, distinguished philosopher and Ambassador of China to the United States; Dr. and Mrs. Nitobe of Japan, the Under Secretary of the League of Nations, with whom we stayed when in Tokyo; Dr. Walter Simons, Chief Justice of Germany, who had presided over my inaugural lecture in the Hochschule für Politik; Bishop Nicolai of Macedonia; Count Ignatiev and Prince Mirsky, liberal leaders in Czarist Russia; and Sir Paul Vinogradoff, Regius Professor of Jurisprudence at Oxford. Professor Mendelssohn-Bartholdy, also a jurist and my colleague in Germany, was greeted by the French and Belgian musicians of Woodstock as the grandson of the great Mendelssohn and was invited to play the piano at a special concert arranged for him. On the mountain road opposite our place he saw the name Engelbert Roentgen on a post box and discovered, to his excitement, that our near neighbor was the grandson of his grandfather's first violinist. Especially memorable were the days spent with us by both General Tasker Bliss, with whom I had worked at Paris and on the Geneva Protocol, and Professor Michael Pupin, the physicist, whose discoveries opened up new possibilities in radio communication.

Meanwhile a new era had swept into the mountain valley. We had been happy in our isolation when there were no telephone bells ringing, no automobiles chugging up the hills, only silence or bird song. There was time for living, and little to distract one from it, which made time all the longer and living all the pleasanter. Now Woodstock has grown to be a suburban town, but our home is in the middle of a hundred acres, and looking out to far horizons remains untouched by the quickening pace of those in the valley below. The problems of peace and freedom with which this narrative deals, tend to seem unreal in the silence and beauty of the hills.

I close this long and rambling story with a sonnet based on the immortal lines of François Villon, but changed from a minor to a major key:

THE SNOWS OF YESTERYEAR
(Où Sont les Neiges d'Antan)

Like a lone bird that climbs the sky at dawn
  And sees the darkling landscape slowly yield
  To form and color; village, road and field
Shaped in their shadowy outlines, etchings drawn
By hands unseen, high trees and level lawn;
  And all the quiet things in slumber sealed
  Wake to the day; so stands the past revealed
At memory's touch, the veil of years withdrawn.
Look! Here are English gardens, Chartres' spires
  And soaring vaults, and Nikko's wooded fane,
  Splendor of Peking, might of ancient Rome;
While, mingling faintly, as in distant choirs,
  Voices we loved, now silent, speak again,—
  And last year's snows are on the hills of home.

Index

340

Novi Sad, 107

Ontario, 17
Organization for European Economic Cooperation (OEEC), 319
Oriel College, 64
Orlando, 115
Osborne, 102
Oulahan, 121
Overlook Mountain, 334
Oxford Union, 29
Oxford University, 31, 43, 64

"Palmer's Index of the Times," 63
Pan Europe, 319
Panteleoni, Pasquale, 144
Papanek, Jan, 331
Paris World's Fair, 288
Paris Peace Conference, 43, 76, 78, 80, 81, 83, 84, 94, 95, 96, 97, 99, 100, 101, 105, 108, 111, 113, 117, 119, 122, 127, 133, 134
Parkman, 292
Patek, 124
Pennsylvania, the, 86
Percy, Lord Eustace, 96, 111
Perkins, Frances, 308
Pershing, John Joseph, 90
Pétain, Henri, 81
Phelan, Edward, 96, 97
Pichon, French Minister of Foreign Affairs, 90, 114
Pinet, French Foreign Minister, 322
Pirenne, Henri, 139
Pittman, Senator, 308
Pittsburgh, Pa., 18, 59
Plassey, 36
Plowman, Piers, 28
Poincaré, 36, 92
Political Science Quarterly, 93

Pollard, A. F., 65
Ponton, Sanchez, 299
Pope Leo I, 54
Popovics, Alexander, 153
Princeton University, 45
Proskauer, Joseph M., 313
Prou, 66
Pruneda, 299
Pueblo University, 301
"Punic Peace," 84
Pupin, Michael, 336
Putkammer, Frau, 328

Quakers, 20, 21, 22
Quebec, 27
Queenston Heights, battle of, 27

Raditch, Stephen, 226
Rand School, 47
Rappard, William, 116
Rashdall, 52
Rasin, Alois, 142
Rathenau, Walter, 147
Rawlinson, 45
Rayburn, Sam, 329
Redlich, Joseph, 276
Reidl, 146
Relations of Canada and the United States, The, 292
Republican Party, 48
Reyes, Alfonso, 300
Riegelman, Carol, 261
Rist, Charles, 139, 281
Robinson, Henry, 116
Robinson, James Harvey, 41, 42, 44, 46, 50, 52, 53
Rochester University, 295
Roentgen, Engelbert, 336
Rome, 50, 51, 66, 69, 72
Roosevelt Franklin D., 306, 307
Roosevelt, Theodore, 48, 71
Root, Elihu, 109

345

University of Athens, 234
University of Bologna, 145
University of Chicago, 335
University of Guadalajara, 301
University of Ghent, 139
University of Illinois, 75
University of London, 65
University of Morelia, 301
University of Notre Dame, 93
University of Prague, 142
University of Texas, 297
Utah, 48

Vanderveldis, 124
Vatican, The, 66
Verdun, Battle of, 74
Versailles Treaty, 111
Vermont, 48
Vigier, 285
Villa, Pancho, 296
Villon, François, 337
Vinogradoff, Sir Paul, 64, 336
Viollet, 54, 65
Vardar, 107
Vogelweide, Walter von der, 53
Von Kuhlmann, 99, 100
Vosnjak, Bogumil, 105

Wakatsuki, Reniro, 254
Walpole Island, 18
Walter, John, 62
Walters, 98
Walton, Izaak, 24
Wang, C. T., 105

Wanger, Walter, 90, 102
War of 1812, 27
Ward, 64
Warrin, Frank, 90
Watson, Thomas J., 288, 305, 335
Watson, Mrs. Thomas J., 335
Weir, Sir Cecil, 326
Welles, Sumner, 315
Westermann, 102, 114
Western European Union (WEU), 321
Weyl, Walter, 123, 335
White, Henry, 106
White, William Allen, 311
Wieser, 140
Wilberforce, Robert, 65
William II, 99
Williams College, 331
Wilson, William B., 131
Wilson, Woodrow, 48, 72, 77, 81, 82, 83, 84, 85, 86, 88, 89, 90, 91, 105, 114, 115, 122, 125, 128, 131, 133
Wilson, Mrs. Woodrow, 87, 88, 92
Wisconsin, 73
Woodbridge, Dean, 56
World Economic and Financial Conference, 306
Wyoming, Ontario, 24, 58

Yen, General Shih San, 245
Young, 98

Zurich University, 320